Spiritual Calculations

Spiritual Calculations

*Number and Numeracy in Late
Medieval English Sermons*

CHRISTINE COOPER-ROMPATO

The Pennsylvania State University Press
University Park, Pennsylvania

Library of Congress Cataloging-in-Publication Data

Names: Cooper-Rompato, Christine F., 1970– author.
Title: Spiritual calculations : number and numeracy
    in late medieval English sermons / Christine
    Cooper-Rompato.
Description: University Park, Pennsylvania : The
    Pennsylvania State University Press, [2022] |
    Includes bibliographical references and index.
Summary: "Explores discussions of numbers, arithmetic,
    and other mathematical operations in late
    medieval English sermons, revealing that popular
    English-speaking audiences were encouraged to
    engage in a wide range of numerate operations
    in their daily religious practices"—Provided by
    publisher.
Identifiers: LCCN 2021047968 | ISBN 9780271091624
    (cloth) | ISBN 9780271091631 (paper)
Subjects: LCSH: Sermons, English (Middle)—History
    and criticism. | Sermons, Medieval—England—
    History and criticism. | Mathematics—Religious
    aspects—Christianity. | Numeracy—Religious
    aspects—Christianity.
Classification: LCC BV4208.G7 C66 2022
LC record available at https://lccn.loc.gov/2021047968

Copyright © 2021 Christine Cooper-Rompato
All rights reserved
Printed in the United States of America
Published by The Pennsylvania State University Press,
University Park, PA 16802–1003

The Pennsylvania State University Press is a member of
the Association of University Presses.

It is the policy of The Pennsylvania State University Press
to use acid-free paper. Publications on uncoated stock
satisfy the minimum requirements of American National
Standard for Information Sciences—Permanence of
Paper for Printed Library Material, ANSI Z39.48–1992.

TO MY FORMER STUDENTS WHO ARE SORELY MISSED
ROBERT, BEN, AND DEVIN

CONTENTS

ix | *Acknowledgments*

1 | Introduction: Spiritual Calculations

11 | 1. Encountering the Divine Through Number in Middle English Sermons: An Overview

38 | 2. Numbers in *Dives and Pauper* and the Sermons of Warminster, Longleat House MS 4: Models for Spiritual Understanding and Practice

63 | 3. "Knowing Thyself" and God Through Number in *Jacob's Well*

95 | 4. Quantitative Reasoning in the Latin Sermons of Robert Rypon in London, British Library, MS Harley 4894

115 | Conclusion: Practical and Spiritual Numeracy in *The Book of Margery Kempe*

129 | *Appendix: Methods of Counting and Calculation in the Later Middle Ages*
137 | *Notes*
165 | *Bibliography*
183 | *Index*

ACKNOWLEDGMENTS

This book was almost a decade in the making, so I am pleased to have the opportunity to thank many people who have helped along the way.

First, I would like to thank the executive editor of Penn State University Press, Eleanor Goodman, for her encouragement on this project and for meeting me year after year at Kalamazoo to listen to updates on the project. I would also like to thank the Penn State University Press staff, including Laura Reed-Morrisson, Jennifer Norton, Brian Beer, Alex J. Ramos, and Maddie Caso, for their work on the book's design and production; I owe a debt of gratitude to my copyeditor, John Morris, for his many improvements on the prose. I also thank the anonymous manuscript reviewers, as well as one of my promotion dossier readers, who sent me anonymous revision suggestions. I am grateful for the attention and work of others who have helped to improve this project.

Second, I would like to thank my colleagues at Utah State and at other universities who have supported me in this project by reading drafts and listening to many conference papers—from my writing group that commented on early drafts (especially Keri Holt, Keith Grant-Davie, and Patricia Gantt) to those who read over my conference papers (Steve Shively, Keri Holt, and Alice Chapman), as well as Phebe Jensen and Terry Peak for their ongoing support. I owe huge thanks to the Utah State University English Department staff for their help, kindness, and friendship over the years, particularly Carol Nicholas. I also owe thanks to faculty and friends from other universities whom I sent drafts of the book to, most notably C. David Benson. David, my dissertation advisor, is always an immensely helpful reader, and I often keep his words in mind, when I would complain that writing a book was difficult: "If it were easy, everyone would do it." David will always be my academic role model. Other faculty both at USU and at conferences who have been particularly encouraging to me and to whom I am grateful include William G. Marx, Naoë Kukita Yoshikawa, Elizabeth Benson, Rebecca Krug, Nicholas Watson, Lisa Gabbert, Jeannie Thomas, Nicole Rice, Alexa Sand, Thomas Liszka, Barbara Zimbalist, and Holly Johnson; many thanks to Holly for welcoming me warmly to the International Medieval Sermon Studies Society as well as for sharing her works in progress on Robert Rypon. I would also like to express gratitude to my former two coeditors from the *Journal of Medieval Religious Cultures*, Bob Hasenfratz and Sherri Olson, for their friendship, encouragement, and good advice.

Third, I would like to thank the math faculty at Utah State University who allowed me to sit in on their classes so that I could get a little more up to speed with my math, and encouraged me to ask as many questions as I wanted about the history of mathematics, numeracy, and ethnomathematics. I would like to give a special shout out to Jim Cangelosi for his history of mathematics course, and to Brynja Kohler for her work on mathematics education as well as for allowing me to consult with her about various math-related issues. Of course, all mistakes are my own in this book.

Fourth, I would like to thank my family—both immediate and extended—for their support during this process. To my husband, Giovanni, who has listened to me talk about numeracy and sermons for the past decade; to my son, Luka, whose trips to Preston, Idaho, in the car at night helped me to refine the topic, and to my daughter, Chiara, who originally sent me on an exploration of numeracy. I would also like to thank my parents, Ruth and Ron Cooper, for their unfailing support—my father for his interest in mathematics and my mother for reading every chapter closely (and sending me extensive comments) at least twice; my brother, Alan, who is also interested in math, as well as to aunts and uncles in the United States, England, and Italy who have helped to support the project as well. I would also like to express my deepest gratitude to those who have helped guide Chiara through school and who have taught me so much about being a patient teacher, especially Heidi Baxter, Jaydin Harames, and Megan Naylor.

Fifth, I would like to thank the College of Humanities, Arts, and Social Sciences and the English Department at Utah State University for their support for this project, and for their ongoing investment in the Religious Studies Program and the Medieval and Early Modern Studies Area Studies Certificate Program. I owe a debt of gratitude to the Merrill-Cazier Library at USU, without which I could not have undertaken my project. As I have a child with profound special needs, I was not able to travel as easily and as often as a project like this might require; the library went above and beyond to acquire sources for me, and interlibrary loan worked overtime many a day to locate just about everything I asked them to. Thanks to the library for purchasing the *Repertorium of Middle English Prose Sermons* (which I have almost permanently checked out) as well as the *Acta Sanctorum* in database form.

Sixth, I would like to thank my current and former students who have supported my teaching and offered me friendship and encouragement through the years. Nothing has brought me more joy and fulfillment than watching the paths my students take in this world. I would like to give special thanks to Chris Avgerinos, Kirianna Florez, Erin Hepner, CJ Guadarrama, and Andrew Romriell. I would like to remember three of my medieval literature students who subsequently passed away—I dedicate this book to them. Robert Gordon II was an undergraduate at the University of Connecticut who took my medieval-themed literature and writing class; his interpretation of the *Lais* of Marie de France has profoundly affected how I teach the text. Benjamin Clarke was an undergraduate at Utah State University and went on to enroll in the PhD program in English at Boston College. Devin Hepner was an undergraduate at Utah State University and after graduation contemplated law school and computer science before entering the US Coast Guard. My teaching of the *Canterbury Tales* has been shaped in part by Ben's and Devin's essays and projects. Hundreds of students have studied these texts with me over the years, and I like to think that a little of Robert's, Ben's, and Devin's intellect and sensitivity lives on in the students who have come after them.

Introduction
Spiritual Calculations

But you have arranged all things by measure and number and weight.
—Wisdom 11:20

For he maad alle by myght and sleyght
In certeyne noumbre of mesure and weyght;
Bot sotyl may there no mon bee
That mesuryng to know bot hee.
—*Prik of Conscience* 7.157–60

For God made all by might and wisdom
In certain number of measure and weight
But of cunning there is no one
Who knows that measuring except for him.

If medieval people believed that God ordered everything in the world in a certain number and measure and weight, they also knew, according to the incredibly popular fourteenth-century penitential poem *Prik of Conscience*, that it was impossible to appreciate fully God's supreme measuring abilities. But this did not stop late medieval preachers from encouraging their audiences to measure, quantify, count, and perform quantitative acts to describe God as well as to venerate him. This book explores the use of numbers, arithmetic, and other mathematical operations in late medieval English sermons, both Middle English and Latin. It argues that these texts teem with examples of quantitative reasoning, from the arithmetical to the numerological, and that they engage with numerical concepts in ways that are largely underappreciated by today's scholars. These examples are significant because they demonstrate that mathematical concepts were promoted as a way for audiences to connect with the divine and to appreciate divine truth. However, many of the texts reveal a tension between the desire and ability to know the divine through number, while at the same time offering resistance to the divine's ultimate quantification. My thesis is that medieval sermons educated audiences in what I call a hybrid form of numerate practice—one that relied on the audiences' pragmatic quantitative reasoning combined with spiritual (i.e., numerological) interpretations of number provided by the preacher, which created a deep and rich sense in which number was the best way to approach and understand the divine mysteries of the world, as well as how one could best live as a Christian in that world.

Attention to numbers and mathematical operations can be found in a wide variety of medieval religious texts. Middle English treatises such as *Prik of Conscience* and Walter Hilton's *Scale of Perfection*, visionary texts including Catherine of Siena's *Orcherd of Syon* and Margery Kempe's *Book*, biblical cycle plays, the poetry of John Lydgate, Geoffrey Chaucer, and the Pearl Poet, metrical charms, and so forth all engage with discussions of number, measures, or quantitative reasoning in various forms, and many of these texts will be referred to during the course of this study. My book, however, focuses on sermons because discussions of quantitative reasoning in sermons are often more developed and more intense than those found in other genres. Moreover, sermons reveal a range of remarkable approaches to engaging with number. As a form of pastoral literature, sermons are rhetorically crafted for exhortation and instruction, as well as for enjoyment, and I have come to consider sermons to be some of the most intriguing and interesting texts of the Middle Ages. As Holly Johnson persuasively describes in her introduction to the sermons of the early fifteenth-century Benedictine Robert Rypon,

> Far from dry theological treatises or mere statements of official doctrine, many sermons were lively, rhetorical endeavors, artfully constructed and, presumably, energetically delivered. Attending a sermon by a good preacher was often an event, even a form of entertainment, as Chaucer's Wife of Bath implies when she includes sermons, along with vigils, processions, pilgrimages, plays, and weddings, as occasions on which she has "bettre leyser for to pleye / And for

to se, and eek for to be seye" ("better leisure to play / And to see and also to be seen").¹

Sermonists composed their texts with multiple purposes in mind: they were of course intended to educate audiences about Scripture and doctrine as well as to exhort audiences to repentance, but they also were intended to express God's love and to model practices of veneration.

I first became interested in what lay medieval people thought of numbers and mathematical operations when I was involved with a local adult literacy program in Logan, Utah. I remember a particular volunteer meeting when one of my fellow volunteers, a math teacher, argued that for adult learners, gaining skills in numeracy was just as important as (or even more important than) gaining literacy skills. That conversation, coupled with my interest in the history of mathematics and technology (which has been fostered by my teaching at a science- and technology-rich campus, Utah State University), led to this project. That same year, my older child was in preschool and struggling with some basic numerical concepts, which eventually led me to volunteer in a local public elementary school to help children with their math skills. A sabbatical spent attending university math classes such as the "History of Mathematics and Number Theory" by Carnegie award–winning professor Jim Cangelosi and a course on math pedagogy for elementary schoolteachers helped to awaken some of my long-dormant quantitative skills, as well as to familiarize myself with many concepts in math education. I began to notice evidence of numeracy and mathematical engagement in the medieval literature I was reading at the time, in particular *The Book of Margery Kempe*, which provides many examples of Kempe's quantitative thinking.

I recognize of course that there are many ways to approach the question of medieval quantitative reasoning and numeracy. One could look at merchant account books or churchwarden records to understand medieval methods of calculation; one could also look at building technologies to explore geometrical understanding, or even agricultural and farming practices to appreciate what calculations were involved, a suggestion made by Alexander Murray in 1978: "The primitive exigencies of land-division, sheep rearing, and the measurement of arable produce may have coaxed even peasants into elementary arithmetic earlier than records show."² Murray's study *Reason and Society in the Middle Ages* was the seminal text on medieval numeracy for many years, and it argued that the development of commerce created an "arithmetical mentality" by the end of the Middle Ages because "the spread of money through a society is a direct invitation to it to calculate with numbers."³ This idea of the "arithmetical mentality" of the late Middle Ages has proved greatly influential to several generations of scholars (me included),[4] and I will return to this question of the role of currency and spirituality in chapter 4. It seems only fitting to begin this book with a nod to Murray and his argument about the influence of the spread of money on late medieval cultures, and then to draw chapter 4 to a close with a discussion of counting money as a spiritual exercise in a sermon by Robert Rypon. In addition, the conclusion to *Spiritual Calculations* picks up on this question of how attention to money may have affected memory and text in *The Book of Margery Kempe*.

Although cultural artifacts and farming practices will be mentioned in my study, they are not the focus. As a scholar of literature, I approach the question of the role of quantitative reasoning in medieval popular religious culture by exploring the literature produced by that culture in order to uncover lay and clerical understandings of number. Because sermons reached a wide lay audience, an audience that is both reflected in and educated by those sermons, they are at the center of my study and form the base of my evidence. Hence, it is my belief that the sermons discussed in this book both reflect medieval audiences' understanding of numerate practice and helped to shape that understanding and practice.

In reviewing the scholarly literature on this topic of medieval number and numeracy, I have found several broad areas of study to be particularly useful. First and foremost is the scholarship on the history of mathematics in the Middle Ages. There are many such history texts, most notably Carl Boyer and Uta Merzback's *A History of Mathematics*, which cover the history of mathematics from the ancient world to the present, and their chapters on how ancient Greek and Roman mathematics passed to medieval Europe, often through the mediation and development of Arabic sources, have proved particularly useful.[5] Other specific studies focus on individual authors or texts, including, for instance, the work of Menso Folkerts, which traces the transmission of texts by Euclid through the centuries.[6] Other scholarly texts discuss the development of algebra, as well as the introduction of other concepts and arithmetical tools in the Middle Ages, including the abacus.[7] Much scholarship on the history of European mathematics looks at specific contributions by mathematicians such as Robert Grosseteste and Thomas Bradwardine and the "Oxford Calculators," as well as studies on Leonardo di Pisa (Fibonacci) or the development of accounting systems for banking in Italy in the thirteenth and fourteenth centuries. Although these studies are not directly discussed in my book, they are important to recognize as they do inform some of the background underlying the concepts that sermons explore. All in all, these many studies on the history of medieval mathematics demonstrate that medieval mathematical thinking was complex, ingenious, and productive.

Another branch of scholarship that has been particularly useful in shaping my project is those studies that examine how number was used symbolically or allegorically in medieval texts. Although there are many modern popular books on numerology and arithmology that I would recommend avoiding, there are some excellent studies of medieval numerological practices. The first place to turn is to the German encyclopedia on numbers by Heinz Meyer and Rudolf Suntrup, *Lexikon der mittelalterlichen Zahlenbedeutungen*, which describes twelve ways that numbers were assigned symbolic meanings in medieval religious commentaries and other writings.[8] Discussions of the symbolic value of numbers in medieval culture also appear in a wide variety of studies where one would not necessarily expect them; for instance, a particularly good source is Elizabeth Sears, *The Ages of Man: Medieval Interpretations of the Life Cycle*, which describes how writers developed symbolic meanings behind various numbered entities, such as the four seasons or the three ages of man.[9]

Equally useful in conceptualizing my project were those studies that focus on how quantitative reasoning was used in medieval religious practice. An excellent starting place is the essay collection by Teun Koetsier and Luc Bergmans titled *Mathematics and the Divine: A Historical Study*; this book contained the first essay I encountered by Faith Wallis, whose writings on what she terms "philosophical numerology" and "allegorical numerology" have been particularly influential on my thinking of what I refer to as "hybrid numerate practice."[10] Perhaps the most fascinating essay I have read on quantitative reasoning in religious practice is Thomas Lentes's "Counting Piety in the Late Middle Ages," in which Lentes explores what he terms the "arithmetic of salvation" that "appeared as an essential component of the practice of piety."[11] As part of this study, he includes examples of medieval texts that advocated enumeration and arithmetic for the purpose of pious practice. More recently, Albrecht Classen's *Handbook of Medieval Culture* includes a lengthy section on "number" by Moritz Wedell that describes medieval engagement with a variety of mathematical concepts.[12] Many studies on number, enumeration, measurement, and quantitative reasoning in specific religious, pastoral, devotional, and visionary texts have also been published, many of which have helped to shape my argument and conclusions. These include M. Teresa Tavormina's early essay on perfect numbers in *Dives and Pauper*,[13] and more recently, essays emphasizing the role of enumeration and quantitative reasoning, including Nicholas Watson's "The Making of *The Book of Margery Kempe*," Martha Rust's "The *Arma Christi* and the Ethics of Reckoning," Rachel Fulton's "Praying by Numbers," and Margaret Connolly's "Preaching by Numbers" and "Practical Reading for Body and Soul."[14] When it comes to the extent that quantitative reasoning appears in late medieval religious texts, these essays have not come close to exhausting the topic. Whereas these studies emphasize that number and quantitative reasoning are important for particular texts, my book demonstrates how widespread the phenomenon was—it occurred at a remarkable rate in sermon literature and reached wide lay and clerical audiences. Ultimately, because of the popularity of spiritually enhanced quantitative reasoning in sermons, I am able to assert that it fundamentally shaped the way medieval people thought about number. I therefore go beyond the specific studies already published to make a wider argument about a genre and a culture as a whole.

In setting out to study how texts capture assumptions about numbers and quantitative reasoning, I found another broad area of scholarship, on numeracy, particularly influential. Whereas "litteratus/a" was a Latin term used in the Middle Ages indicating somebody with an ability to read Latin or with a familiarity with Latin grammar, "numeracy" was coined in 1959 by an English education committee.[15] Originally intended to serve as a mirror of literacy, the term was expanded in 1982 by the Cockroft Committee report titled "Mathematics Counts," which argued that "a numerate person should ... understand some of the ways in which mathematics can be used as a means of communication," and this required "the possession of two attributes": first, "'at-homeness' with numbers and an ability to make use of mathematical skills which enables an individual to cope with the practical mathematical demands of his everyday life," and second, "an ability to have some appreciation and understanding of information which is presented in mathematical terms."[16] As it has been defined more recently by the New South Wales Department of Education and Communities and employed in many contexts, "numeracy involves using mathematical ideas efficiently to make sense of the world. . . . Each individual's interpretation of the world draws on understandings of number, measurement, probability, data and spatial sense combined with critical mathematical thinking."[17]

Scholarly studies on numeracy have emerged from a variety of fields, notably education, anthropology, and sociology. Their focus on exploring "vernacular numeracy" or nonformally acquired numeracy led me to question how popular medieval religious texts advocated numeracy. An early and influential anthropological study is Thomas Crump's *Anthropology of Numbers*, which examines how numbers are learned and articulated across cultures.[18]

Specific studies on numeracy that have shaped my thinking on calculation include those that examine informants' vernacular practices.[19] Although of course I cannot interview medieval people about what they thought about mathematical concepts and how they performed them, I can argue that these sermons present for us a new way of looking at medieval numeracy—we can now appreciate how sermons build on and combine the audiences' practical idea of counting, arithmetic, measurement, and so on with a spiritual understanding of number. Medieval sermons demonstrate that people could work simultaneously in both realms of number, the practical and the spiritual. I assert that certain participatory elements in these sermons created and invited practices of devotional math and that we can see evidence of quantitative reasoning being promoted as a mode of veneration.[20]

Last but not least, the scholarly literature on medieval sermons has been of the utmost importance to my study. The literature on this topic is vast, and my book would not have been possible without the dedicated work of Veronica O'Mara and Suzanne Paul, whose multivolume *A Repertorium of Middle English Prose Sermons* offers the incipits, explicits, and summaries of hundreds of Middle English sermons, many of which only appear in manuscript form and are currently unedited. When I started this project, I planned only one chapter on sermons, and the *Repertorium* guided my way to finding the richness of these texts, as well as numerous side projects along the way. Two sermon scholars of note have been of particular importance to my study, Siegfried Wenzel and Holly Johnson, without whose editions, translations, and analyses I could not have written chapter 1 and chapter 4. As more editions of previously unedited sermons are produced, scholarly attention to medieval sermons will certainly only increase.[21]

The specific texts addressed in my study—namely, a number of individual sermons from a range of English manuscripts, as well as the sermon cycles of *Jacob's Well* (Salisbury Cathedral MS 103), Warminister, Longleat House MS 4, and Robert Rypon's collection found in London, British Library, MS Harley 4894—all share something in common: they employ number and quantitative reasoning to express something important about God or humankind's relationship to God, or what drives them from God—sin. They also share something else in common: they have attracted relatively little sustained scholarly attention. Scholarly access to the majority of medieval English sermons has been limited by the relatively few editions available. Moreover, late medieval sermons are not usually included in the readings for literature and history classes, so they have a relatively limited modern scholarly audience. If my book can do one thing, I hope it convinces readers of the value of studying sermons.

This book weaves together two strands of medieval understanding of numbers: the practical sense of number used in a medieval person's daily life and activities, and the spiritual sense of number that appears in numerological discussions. The book demonstrates how medieval sermons draw on and combine both the practical and the spiritual understanding of number. More specifically, I argue that sermonists present their audiences with numerical and mathematical ways of understanding or approaching God that are different from, and at times more efficacious than, literary or sensorial paths. Medieval sermons modeled for their audiences a numerate practice shaped by both pragmatic and spiritual associations, which formed a significant part of their devotional practice. My study also suggests that in some situations, because of numbers' spiritual associations, medieval people could apply a different sense of "accuracy" when it came to calculating numbers. A sum or calculation might not be numerically accurate or fully calculable, but it could still be valuable and therefore "accurate" because it reveals a significant spiritual truth.

A lack of attention to medieval numeracy in current scholarship on sermons has caused us to miss something fundamentally important about this period—that the medieval laity would have been far more numerate, and in ways that we have not appreciated, than we might otherwise imagine. Those of us who focus on literacy must not forget its mathematical sibling.

Chapter 1, "Encountering the Divine Through Number in Middle English Sermons: An Overview," explores the ways in which preachers used number in vernacular sermons to engage and educate their audiences—namely, through sermon division and enumeration, number theory, numerology, and arithmetical examples. Late medieval sermonists relied on their audiences' pragmatic sense of number and expanded that with a spiritual understanding of number. Sermonists, therefore, encouraged in their audiences a hybrid numerate practice that was both pragmatic and spiritual, formed by practical experiences of number infused with numerological meanings. Sermonists capitalized on this hybrid understanding as a way to teach audiences how to live more Christian lives, to improve their Christian practice, and to understand more deeply God's universe.

Chapter 2, "Numbers in *Dives and Pauper* and the Sermons of Warminster, Longleat House MS 4: Models for Spiritual Understanding and Practice," examines two early fifteenth-century pastoral texts by an anonymous

Franciscan author that use numbers to represent divine truth and offer a way for audiences to approach God. I argue that the sermon is a particularly ripe and welcoming place for vernacular discussions of number and that the quantitative reasoning modeled in these sermons is both performative and collaborative. For this author, the goal of the pastoral tradition—with his use of number and math—is to offer an alternative model for thinking about one's relationship to God and the world. The author drew on this audience's practical, numerate understandings to show how one could apply that knowledge to abstract religious ideas like "forgiveness" to create a new, deeper understanding of the divine. The math in these texts offers a framework for making the unfathomable fathomable.

Chapter 3, "'Knowing Thyself' and God Through Number in *Jacob's Well*," addresses scholarly arguments that this sermon cycle trusted its lay audience to be involved in sophisticated choice-making and decisions in their education as they learned to "know themselves."[22] I argue that these sermons' extended discussion of number, arithmetic, measure, and geometry is intended to contribute to the audience's religious education. The sermonist sees discussions of mathematical concepts as a useful way for audiences to learn to "know themselves" spiritually and to understand better what God expects from them. Ultimately, numbers and numerate acts allow the sermon audience to approach God more closely, because contemplation and engagement with quantitative thinking impel the audience to become more obedient and virtuous. However, in contrast to the sermons of Warminster, Longleat MS 4 discussed in chapter 2, in *Jacob's Well* God can be approached through number but not fully comprehended. In this case, the unfathomable remains unfathomable.

Chapter 4, "Quantitative Reasoning in the Latin Sermons of Robert Rypon in London, British Library, MS Harley 4894," examines the Latin sermons of an English master sermonist, the Benedictine Robert Rypon of Durham. I argue that Rypon's sermons offer several intense, extended allegories of number that demonstrate how important spiritual calculation had become in the early fifteenth century. In Rypon's example, the number used to describe God, as well as God's expectations for human behavior, is fully fathomable but quite complex. Of particular note is how he allegorizes the act of counting money to explain difficult theological concepts. Other sermons addressed in this book discuss proper tithing practices and basic monetary problems; Rypon's money allegory directs his audience's focus toward accounting—what scholars have argued fueled the late medieval arithmetical mentality—as he delights in demonstrating exactly how counting money can be used as a model of spiritual improvement. In Rypon's deft hand, counting money models exactly what God expects of Christians. For Rypon, even the most mercantile enterprise can be put to good use for devotional and spiritual contemplation.

The conclusion, "Practical and Spiritual Numeracy in *The Book of Margery Kempe*," argues that despite scholarly efforts to label Kempe's attention to number in her book as wholly mercantile in nature, her memory and discussion of number and arithmetical acts are shaped in large part by the hybrid numerate practices that sermons like those of Robert Rypon promote. Kempe of course was an avid sermon attendee, as well as a reader/listener of other religious works and a practitioner of late medieval piety, much of which focused on calculation. Her text shows this hybrid sense of numeracy at work, which I link to her consumption of sermons as well as other religious literature.

Because I argue that medieval people were encouraged to count and calculate during sermons and that sermons were participatory on many levels, I include an appendix outlining the ways in which medieval people counted and performed acts of arithmetic, as well as other mathematical practices. In all, *Spiritual Calculations* offers a reconsideration of what Alexander Murray and others characterize as the "arithmetical mentality" of the later Middle Ages, as my study argues that discussions of number, numerology, and mathematical concepts offer sermonists a way to explore and express fundamental doctrinal and theological concepts. Thus, this "arithmetic of salvation" can be expanded to include many more related concepts, including the quantitative reasoning of devotion and veneration, as well as that of blessedness and of sin and repentance.

CHAPTER 1

Encountering the Divine Through Number in Middle English Sermons
An Overview

The fifteenth-century Italian writer Poggio Bracciolini relates the following anecdote in his Latin collection of humorous stories and jokes, the *Facetiae*: "A Priest was expounding to his congregation the passage of the Gospel wherein is recited that our Saviour fed five thousand people out of five loaves, and, by a slip of the tongue, instead of five thousand, said five hundred. His clerk, in a low whisper, called his attention to the mistake, reminding him that the Gospel mentioned five thousand:—'Hold your peace, you fool,' said the Priest; 'they will find it hard enough to believe even the number I said.'"[1] In Bracciolini's humorous account, the priest's lay listeners are thought to be unable to comprehend the Gospel miracle, no doubt because of their fully pragmatic sense of number. How could five hundred people be fed by five loaves, let alone five thousand? Indeed, the priest wonders, how can a lay person's practical experience of number allow him or her to understand this miraculous biblical event?

In this chapter I am interested in just this issue—how vernacular sermon authors modeled numerate acts for their audiences, and how they imagined that their lay audiences encountered and understood these practices. My argument is that in contrast to the priest in Bracciolini's joke, who doubted his audience, late medieval sermon writers and preachers (or sermonists) actually trusted their audiences to appreciate the significance of number, number theory, and arithmetical operations in Scripture and other religious writings.[2] In their sermons, late medieval priests relied on their audiences' pragmatic sense of number, derived from counting and arithmetic, and expanded that with a spiritual understanding of number derived from numerology, which was often combined with basic number theory. Sermonists, therefore, encouraged in their audiences a hybrid numerate practice that was both pragmatic and spiritual, formed by practical experiences of number infused with theological and spiritual meanings. Sermonists capitalized on this hybrid understanding as a way to teach audiences how to live more Christian lives, to improve their Christian practice, and to understand more deeply God's universe.

PART I: SERMON STRUCTURE—ENUMERATION AND DIVISION BY NUMBER

Late medieval sermonists wove discussions of numbers into the basic fabric of their sermons and used number as an organizing principle. Thirteenth-century regulations about preaching to the laity encourage this focus on number. Many scholarly studies of medieval English sermons begin by quoting canon 9 of the archbishop of Canterbury John Peckham's Lambeth Constitutions of 1281, which sets forth the educational program for priests and their parishioners. This very text invites a discussion of number in sermons. According to the canon, priests are required to explain at least four times a year "the Fourteen Articles of the Faith, the Ten Commandments, the Two Precepts of the Gospel, . . . the Seven works of Mercy, the Seven Deadly Sins with their branches, the Seven principal Virtues and the Seven Sacraments of Grace."[3] Many sermonists, therefore, expounded on this doctrine and built their sermons around these numbered tenets. Margaret Connolly argues for the importance of enumeration in religious texts, specifically that "in the case of religious instruction, this habit of quantifying and categorizing those elements deemed most essential for the faithful to know and understand had a very long history, and whilst the Lateran councils of the twelfth and thirteenth centuries were influential in promoting such methods of teaching, ultimately the origins of this approach lay in the Bible itself."[4]

A clear example of how one's preaching could be structured to teach this doctrine is offered in the *Modus sermocinandi*, a popular *ars praedicandi* (art of preaching) manual originally composed in fourteenth-century Catalonia by the Franciscan Francesc Eiximenes. The writer describes a preaching wheel that allows the sermonist to visualize how the topic he is speaking of that day directly addresses doctrine (as well as another topic, the five senses) and how the wheel helps to generate the sermon:

When you want to examine the preaching matter, you should place the thema or the matter you want to preach about, as it were, in the centre of a circle, and then around it arrange in order the Ten Commandments, the articles of the faith, the gifts of the Holy Spirit, the eight beatitudes, the five bodily senses, the seven works of mercy, the seven virtues, and the seven vices. And then relate the matter you want to preach about in due order with some distinction concerning the material mentioned according to whether they agree with each other or are opposite to each other, or according to something relevant that comes to your mind, until you have enough material for the sermon.[5]

In this schema, every topic (or matter) can be directly linked back to these basic doctrinal tenets, many of which are specifically numbered, such as the seven works of mercy or the Ten Commandments. Teaching the specific number of the particular tenet (for example, the eight beatitudes) acts as an aid to memory for audiences.

Late medieval sermon practice also encouraged the organizing of individual sermons into numbered parts, a process that is known as *divisio*.[6] As Siegfried Wenzel and others describe, there are two main types of sermons in the later Middle Ages, the "ancient form" (the "sermo antiquus" or homily) and the "modern form" (the "sermo modernus," "university," "thematic," or "scholastic" sermon).[7] The general distinction, as discussed by *artes praedicandi* manuals as well as sermon scholars, is that in the ancient or homiletic form, the sermon explicates a scriptural passage (the *pericope*, or biblical passage for the day) line by line or word by word. The homily may develop the typological significance of the passage (how the Old Testament relates to the New), but generally the homily is not hortatory in nature.[8] In the modern or university form, the sermon has recognizable, distinct sections, and more often than not it is hortatory in nature. The sermonist also begins with a scriptural passage (usually from the day's pericope, which could be several lines long, shortened into a *thema*), but he then moves further afield by dividing the sermon into related topics to be discussed.[9] This division into numbered sections or parts structures the rest of the sermon, as the sermonist proceeds to develop the argument through the process of *dilatio* (addressing things outside the text) or *distinctio* (addressing things inside the text). Of course, it would be a mistake to assume that all sermons can be easily classified as ancient or modern. Wybren Scheepsma, for example, describes how scholars suggest there is no need to make a clear distinction between the two, as many sermons are a hybrid of both forms.[10]

The division of sermons into numbered sections is recommended by many preaching manuals and practiced by a large proportion of late medieval sermonists. As Wenzel observes in his *Medieval Artes Praedicandi: A Synthesis of Scholastic Sermon Structure*, "Nearly all *artes* here considered speak of a *divisio*," the function of which "is to unfold the meaning of the chosen thema and thereby to provide the preacher with ample material for his discourse."[11] Each of the divisions could be subdivided further if so desired, either within the sermon or in an extended sermon cycle. There was some debate over the ideal number of divisions that a sermon should include.[12] According to several popular preaching manuals, the thema of the sermon must "yield at least three (or more) members for the division."[13] For example, in his preaching manual, the fifteenth-century Spanish Augustinian Martin of Cordoba asserts, regarding divisions, that there should be "at least three but no more than six"; as Wenzel characterizes, "The consensus is that three is best . . . though two and four are allowed," whereas four is "the most beautiful," according to a fourteenth-century treatise by the Augustinian Thomas of Todi.[14] Other manuals recommend that sermonists use no more than four divisions, although they can subdivide; as the anonymous author of the *Ars copiosa* explains, however, "A term or notion should not be subdivided into more than four parts 'lest it causes confusion in the preacher and boredom in his audience.'"[15]

Exactly how the division is to be formed is also addressed by sermon manuals. The *Ars copiosa* describes the many ways that this division can take place. The division could occur "according to the four senses of Scripture" (the literal meaning and the allegorical, moral, and anagogical senses), or could occur according to the allegorical sense alone.[16] Moreover, the thema could be divided by verbs or nouns.[17] Pseudo-Bonaventure's *Ars concionandi* identifies a distinction between "divisio extra," which "takes a *notion* suggested by the thema, explains it, and then divides it into parts," and "divisio intra," which "pays close attention to the actual *words* of the thema."[18] According to the anonymous (probably Franciscan) "Nota pro arte faciendi collaciones et sermones," when the preacher introduces the division of his thema by saying, for example, "'In these words two things are indicated,' this is called 'numeracio.'"[19] Of course, a great many other terms may be used to describe the rhetorical moves of the sermon, and interested readers are encouraged to consult Wenzel's *Medieval Artes Praedicandi* for clear descriptions and detailed analysis.

Memory is the primary reason for sermon division. In her work *The Book of Memory: A Study of Memory in Medieval Culture*, Mary Carruthers refers to "the passion of many late medieval preachers for numbering sermon divisions," relating their enthusiasm and practice to the use of numerical grids as aids to memory.[20] Carruthers gives the example of the Dominican theologian Thomas Waleys, who saw the practice of division as helpful for the comprehension and retention of both sermonist and audience. In his treatise *De modo componendi sermones* from the 1340s, he writes,

> Indeed if only one division of the theme be made, still that division will be beneficial as to those subjects, as much for the preacher as for the hearer. For the moderns began not just because of a vogue, as others believe, to divide the theme, which the ancients did not customarily do. Especially it is useful for the preacher, because division of the theme into separate parts affords an opportunity for dilation in the later development of the sermon. For the hearer truly it is most useful, because when the preacher divides the theme and afterwards develops the parts of the division in order and clearly, both the matter of the sermon and the form and manner of the preaching is more easily understood and retained.[21]

This passage emphasizes how *diviso* aids both the preacher's and the audience's memory, as the "matter of the sermon" is more easily retained, thus aiding all the many purposes that sermons fulfill, including explicating, teaching, celebrating, exhorting, condemning, chastising, and encouraging.[22]

Examples abound in sermons of how division and development involving number create an engaging and educative experience. An excellent example of division and subdivision can be seen in a sermon on the occasion of Palm Sunday in the fifteenth-century manuscript Cambridge, Corpus Christi College, MS 392. The sermon writer describes how Christ entered Jerusalem on an ass "as an example of meekness" and to show how humankind "was bound 'wiþ bestyal condiciones' [with bestial conditions] like an ass." The writer then uses the concept of the ass as a way to organize the sermon, stating that "three features of the ass" correspond to sinful people, and three other features to the virtuous. As the sermonist explains, the ass is similar to a sinful person because it is "vile," "rude," and "foolish." However, the ass is also "meek," "hardworking," and "useful," making it akin to the virtuous. The sermonist asserts that these divisions will be the matter of his sermon: "And in declaryng of þese propertes shal stonde þe processe of my mater os tyme wol ȝyue me lycense" (And in the declaring of these properties shall stand the process of my matter as time will give me license). Although the sermonist does not expand on all subdivisions, he returns in the conclusion to the image of the bound ass, suggesting that "ȝif hit [the conscience] be bonde wiþ fonnednes of wordly wysdom and be febul byfore and ful strong byhynde, vnbyndeþ by strong loue to God and to ȝoure neȝsbore and feblyng of ȝour fleshely concupiscence"[23] (If the conscience is bound with fondness for worldly wisdom and is feeble before and very strong behind, unbind it with strong love for God and your neighbor and the weakening of your fleshly desire). Only then will Christ "bryng ȝow into þe temple of his faderes kyndom into blys of heuen"[24] (bring you into the temple of his father's kingdom into the bliss of heaven). The ass, therefore, in all its metaphorical and allegorical splendor, is an animal that can be rhetorically manipulated to fit the complexities of human experience; as the sermon emphasizes, a person's conscience can turn toward the trio of vileness, rudeness, and foolishness, or it can be turned with concentrated love toward meekness, hard work, and usefulness. The example is at the same time memorable, educative, and hortatory, trying to urge audiences' conscience toward love; the vivid image of the ass, with its negative and positive attributes, makes clear the idea that men and women have contradictory impulses within themselves and must make a choice to focus on God's love.

The process of *divisio* could be accomplished in a variety of creative ways in sermons, all with the overall purpose of reforming the audience and leading them closer to God. A sermon for the day of Saint Nicholas in the fifteenth-century manuscript Cambridge, Pembroke College MS 285, uses *divisio* with rhyming to emphasize three reasons why people should fear God: first, "þe uncerteyne tyme of bodily deynge"; second, "þe orible doome at þe general vprysynge," and third, "euerlastying body and soule presonynge"[25] (First, the uncertain time of bodily dying; second, the horrible doom [judgment] at the general uprising, and third, everlasting body and soul imprisoning). Regarding the first point, the sermonist warns that one must prepare oneself for death by thinking on the passion, giving alms, praying, and so forth. Even the great King Solomon and King Edward are now "only worms' food," he warns. Regarding the second point, he cautions that the devil writes down everyone's sins and that "people should remember this when they are in the tavern drinking, swearing, and boasting of their sins." Regarding the third point, the sermonist asserts that at the final judgment, the "sinful goats" will be divided from the "righteous sheep," and that "hell is a prison without redemption."[26] The striking imagery—of kings as worms' food, of the devil writing down sins, and of the sinful goats in hell—only serve to reinforce more strongly in audiences' minds the three reasons to fear God.

A sermon on the First Sunday in Advent in the mid- to late fifteenth-century Hatfield House Cecil Papers 280 uses *division* and *subdivision* as a way to emphasize the important role that Christ plays in people's lives; according to the sermonist, "Three questions may be investigated concerning Christ's coming: its condition, manner, and cause." The sermonist then asserts that Christ came to earth in three ways: "as a doctor to heal; as a king to overcome humankind's enemies; as a friend and intercessor between God and people."[27] Similarly, a sermon on the First Sunday in Lent, also in Hatfield House Cecil Papers 280, delights in sets of three as it describes how "Christ was led into the wilderness by the Holy Spirit for three reasons: as an example of penance, of prayer, and of contemplation and resisting temptation." Christians, the sermonist asserts, can come to Christ through the three parts of confession and thus "enter the wilderness (this new life)" by three means: "through penance for their sins, prayers for help with thanks and worship, and preparation to withstand the devil's temptations."[28] As with this discussion of why Christ was led into the wilderness, many sermons use *divisio* to expand on the reasons why a biblical event took place. The Ascension Day sermon from the fifteenth-century British Library, MS Harley 2247, discusses the five reasons why Christ ascended: first, "for humility" so that the Holy Spirit could descend; second, "so that he could be an advocate for humankind in heaven"; third, "for the sake of dignity" so that human nature could be "joined to divinity, sitting on the father's right hand in heaven"; fourth, in order for Christ "to show the way to everlasting bliss"; and fifth, so that Christ could "open up the gates of perpetual bliss."[29]

As I have demonstrated, division, subdivision, and enumeration are important tools in structuring late medieval sermons. They are aids to memory for both preacher and audience, and perhaps more importantly, division and enumeration allow the sermonist to emphasize Christ's role in the audiences' lives, to explain the reason underlying scriptural passages, to teach people to recognize their sinful natures, and to urge them away from sin and toward righteousness and virtue. Last but not least, *divisio* and enumeration are entertaining and meant to grab and hold an audience's attention. They create vivid and elaborate analogies that enliven listeners and readers. In a fifteenth-century Latin sermon on "Alleluia," for example, which describes the ancient history of King Lear, the audience must have listened closely to learn how Lear could signify the five senses, as well as how the priest would equate Lear's three daughters with "the flesh, the World, and Christ." Even more intriguing, they would have heard about the eight husbands or "kinds of men" that the eight daughters of the devil married.[30] As Alan J. Fletcher, who edited this sermon, observes, "The late medieval popular sermon, then, needed to engage its audience if it were not to remain an arid exercise and wither on the vine."³¹ The combination of enumeration, sermon division, and numerology allowed sermonists to accomplish this.

PART 2: NUMEROLOGY AND THE SPIRITUAL SENSE OF NUMBER

Sermons rely heavily on number in another way—they often incorporate number symbolism or numerology, or the association of a number with a spiritual, scriptural, or otherwise religious sense. This is also sometimes referred to as "allegorical numerology."³² The word "numerology" was coined in the early twentieth century, and it is often thought of in the pseudoscientific occult sense of a numerical system of divination that reveals personal meaning.³³ For example, this includes the practice of adding up the digits of one's birthday, month, and year to reach a single number that supposedly indicates something significant about that person's nature or future, or assigning number values to letters of one's name and adding those to reveal a number that represents an inner truth.³⁴ My study is not concerned with these modern pseudoscientific ideas.

However, the belief that numbers can convey a deeper spiritual sense has been traced back through a number of centuries and cultures and finds much ground in early scriptural studies. As John Scott Lucas argues in his study *Astrology and Numerology in Medieval and Early Modern Catalonia*, "The fathers of the Catholic Church, so dutiful in their pursuit of non-Christian forms of magic, encouraged their faithful to scrutinize the Bible for underlying numerological meaning."³⁵ Lucas explains how the New Testament was written during "a time when Neo-Platonic and Gnostic philosophies were common currency," meaning that "early Christians found" the links between numbers and letters "pregnant with theological implications."³⁶ Those studying Scripture were also deeply interested in another aspect of numerology—namely, the meaning behind specific numbers referred to in the Bible: for example, the forty days and nights of the flood, Christ's forty days in the wilderness, God's creation of the world in six days, and so forth. Many scholarly studies have addressed the biblical use of numbers; for a thorough accounting of the numbers mentioned in the Bible, see Heinz Meyer and Rudolf Suntrup's comprehensive encyclopedia, *Lexikon der mittelalterlichen Zahlenbedeutungen*, as well as Ethelbert W. Bullinger's classic study originally published in 1894, *Number in Scripture*.³⁷

Medieval sermon writers were particularly sensitive to the presence of numbers in Scripture and used those numbers as part of their flexible interpretive process. Sermonists reveled in how productive this spiritual sense of number could be. For example, a sermonist might describe how something that numbers five could signify or betoken the five wounds of Christ, or he might equate the number with something more negative and extrabiblical, such as the five senses, which invite sin into the body. Seven of something could indicate the seven deadly sins or the seven virtues; twelve of something could signify or betoken the twelve tribes of Israel, the twelve apostles, and so on. Many numbers in medieval Christian discourse have spiritual associations: three with the Trinity, six or seven with the days of creation (depending on whether or not the day God rested is included), eight with baptism, and so forth.[38] In many ways, we have already seen hints of this in the *divisio* section of this chapter, for it is a very short step from dividing a sermon into meaningful sections to then allowing the numbering to become significant in and of itself, invoking some kind of spiritual, allegorical resonance.

There are hundreds of examples of this numerological practice to choose from in Middle English sermons, and I shall limit myself to just a few. A sermon on the Seventh Sunday after Trinity in the fifteenth-century Wycliffite sermon collection in Cambridge, St. John's College, MS G.22, equates an Old and New Testament occurrence: before the feeding of the multitude, the crowd followed Christ for three days; similarly, the Israelites traveled three days in the desert after leaving Egypt. As the sermonist describes, the Israelites defeated seven tribes to reach the promised land; this represents the seven deadly sins, as well as the "seven-headed beast of the Apocalypse." The Beast, he asserts, "is the devil and its ten horns represent the breaking of the ten commandments."[39] Spiritual associations allow for the sophisticated allegorical development of religious concepts, wherein numbered objects can be related to spiritual practices as well as other scriptural passages. Through number, the sermon encourages listeners to see themselves as similar to the Israelites, needing to leave Egypt (i.e., representing "sin and ignorance") and defeat the seven deadly sins in order to reach heaven.

Similarly, a startlingly vivid deterrent against sin is offered by a sermon with the thema "Timor mortis conturbat me" in the fifteenth-century manuscript Lincoln Cathedral Library MS 133, which describes how the seven properties of dead bodies are akin to the seven deadly sins. Dead bodies are: one, stiff (i.e., proud); two, cold (i.e., envious); three, unpleasant (i.e., angry); four, heavy (i.e., slothful); five, swollen (i.e., gluttonous); six, rotten (i.e., lecherous), and seven, in possession of a tight grip (i.e., covetous).[40] Motivated by a similar numerological impulse, the sermonist in a Wycliffite sermon on Septuagesima in the fifteenth-century British Library, MS Additional 40672, discusses the New Testament parable of the laborers in the vineyard. The sermonist equates the five different hours that the owner hired laborers for the vineyard with the ages of the church before the second coming of Christ—first, the time "fro Adam to Noe" (from Adam to Noah), second, "fro Noe to Abraham" (from Noah to Abraham), third, "fro Abraham to Dauid" (from Abraham to David), fourth, "fro tyme of Dauid to passyng into Babiloyne" (from the time of David to the exile into Babylon), and fifth, "fro þat tyme til þe natyuite of Crist" (from that time until the birth of Christ), which will usher in the sixth and final age until judgment day.[41] In this example, the sermonist explains the underlying meaning behind what might have originally seemed to lay readers to be an arbitrary number in the Bible (i.e., five hours), equating this work with the significance of the five ages of the church.

Sermons could also break larger numbers into smaller segments with numerological significance, thereby allowing for more flexible interpretations. For example, a sermon for the Twenty-Fourth Sunday after Trinity in the late fourteenth- to early fifteenth-century manuscript Oxford, Bodleian Library, MS Bodley 806, asserts that the woman who was healed of a twelve-year hemorrhage by Christ "signifies those who are publicly in a state of sin who are often healed through shame." The length of time of the blood flow—the twelve years—"signif[ies] the ten commandments, the law of nature, and the Christian covenant with God established at baptism." The woman "suffered the flow of sin," as does anyone who trespasses against these commandments, covenant, and law of nature.[42] In this case, the sermonist preferred to break apart the twelve years into the Ten Commandments plus two other elements—the law of nature and the baptismal covenant with God—rather than to use another spiritual or scriptural association readily available for the number twelve (for instance, the twelve apostles). Similarly, an Easter Day sermon in the fifteenth-century manuscript Dublin, Trinity College 241, describes how Mary Magdalene represents people who repent: as the sermonist describes, "Magdalene" means "tower," which "represent[s] the tower of Siloam which collapsed crushing eighteen people." These eighteen people who were crushed signify "how sinners crush the ten commandments of the old law and eight of the new with the tower of pride."[43] The sermonist reveals his ongoing fondness for numerology when he describes how the Three Marys brought three ointments (standing for penance, devotion, and perfect charity). Ointment, he describes, is made of three spices (contrition, confession, satisfaction); furthermore, devotion is made of three spices (compassion, patience, and perseverance).[44]

A sermon on fasting in the fifteenth-century British Library, MS Additional 36791, also known as the *Speculum Sacerdotale*, demonstrates the flexible, productive energy of the writer's numerological associations. As the sermonist explains, in addition to fasting for forty days of Lent, fasting is also required at four other points during the year, with three days in each of those four seasons. The sermon writer describes how the four fasts represent the four elements and also the four humors; the three days represent the "thre powers of the sowle"—namely, "yre, concupyscencye, and reson"[45] (the irascible, the desiring, and the rationale). He then goes on to discuss the groups of four or tetrads that structure the world and govern the people within it, including the four seasons, the four elements, and the four ages of humankind (childhood, adolescence, maturity, and old age), all of which he relates back to fasting and the ability of fasts to cleanse the body and soul and "help to quell" sin.[46] Thus, through the flexibility of numerological associations, the sermonist effectively grounds the practice of fasting in the very nature of the world and the people in it.

Other forms of numerological figuring can be found in medieval sermons, such as the practice of associating letters with numbers. A sermon in Dublin, Trinity College 241, on Christ's circumcision, describes how Jesus shed blood five times in order to redeem mankind. The sermonist points out how Scripture says that the just will be saved "vix" (i.e., "with difficulty," in Latin). The sermonist then offers an interpretation based on the transnumeration of the letter V into a Roman numeral: "'V' means 'five,' 'I' stands for 'Ihesu' and 'X' for Christ, that is, they will be saved by the five wounds of Jesus Christ."[47]

In this brief section I have offered just a few examples excerpted from a multitude of sermons that rely on numerological associations to develop their arguments. Through repeated exposure to numerological analogies, audiences were trained by sermonists to entertain and no doubt recognize on their own the spiritual associations of numbers. In the next section we shall see how elementary number theory was also incorporated into sermons, often coupled with a numerological sense, to create a hybrid way of understanding number—one that is at the same time both pragmatic and spiritual.

PART 3: NUMBER THEORY IN SERMONS

Elementary number theory, or the study of "the properties and relationships of numbers, especially the positive integers" (*OED*), was often incorporated in late medieval sermons, usually in combination with numerological interpretations. Sermonists united these two ways of looking at number to create vivid means of describing the nature of the divine. Number theory, in combination with numerological meaning, became a useful way for sermonists to explain God's creation, as God made the world with certain "measure, number, and weight."[48]

Boethian number theory was an important part of a medieval mathematical education, and it has a strong influence on many of the examples I discuss in this book. In the Middle Ages, "arithmetic" was the term used for the study of the philosophy of number (and is now known as "number theory"), whereas "algorism" (or reckoning, as discussed in the following section) was the term for practical computation.[49] Boethius's very popular text *De institutione arithmetica* (On the Properties of Numbers) was a foundational text of the university *quadrivium* because it discussed proportions, the basis for the other sciences of music, astronomy, and geometry.[50] Boethius's *Arithmetica* adapted and augmented the second-century arithmetical text of Nicomachus of Gerasa, a mathematician who built his work on Pythagoras.[51] Boethius's text "became the standard reference book for arithmetic in the West for a millennium,"[52] meaning that university-educated writers would have encountered and explored this text for at least several weeks in their studies.[53]

At its very basic level, number theory, as described by Boethius, is concerned with the properties of natural numbers (otherwise known as the positive integers, or one, two, three, and so forth). Boethius begins his *Arithmetica* by defining even and odd numbers and then describing the many properties that these numbers display. He explores the various ways that numbers can be grouped (for example, as "evenly even" like eight, which can be divided by two or four and still remain even, or "evenly odd," like fourteen, which can be divided by two and become an odd number, seven) and then classifies those numbers depending on the sum of their factors. For example, he points out that the number eight is a "diminished" number, because it can be halved (four), or divided into fourths (two) or eighths (one); when these factors are added (four plus two plus one), they equal seven, a number that is contained within the number eight.[54] In addition, Boethius examines (among other things) prime, perfect, and superabundant numbers, and he also considers pentagons, triangles, circles, spheres, truncated pyramids, and so on, before finishing with an extended description of proportions applicable to music. Central to his discussion of number theory is the idea of "unit" and "unity"; all numbers are created from the joining of units into unities.[55]

Number theory was also developed in other influential medieval sources. In the early Middle Ages, Cassiodorus modeled a section in his sixth-century

Institutiones on Boethius,[56] and Euclid's *Elements*, which were translated from Arabic into Latin in the twelfth century, addressed number theory in books seven, eight, and nine,[57] as did Fibonacci's early thirteenth-century *Liber Abacus*, a book that explained Hindu-Arabic numerals and included mathematical and arithmetical examples for merchants, as well as quadratic equations.[58] Thus students of the *quadrivium*, as well as merchants in Renaissance Italy, may have had access to texts other than Boethius that explored number theory.[59]

Boethian number theory also made its way into popular medieval encyclopedias and other reference works. Isidore of Seville included a discussion of number theory adapted from Boethius in his encyclopedic work *Etymologies*; from this work many other texts drew their discussions of number theory.[60] For example, in the thirteenth century, the Franciscan Bartholomaeus Anglicus borrowed heavily from Isidore's *Etymologies* to write the mathematical section of *De proprietatibus rerum*.[61] This text was then translated into Middle English by John Trevisa as *On the Property of Things*, which probed number theory in some depth.

In writing about number theory, these encyclopedists did something that would prove extremely influential for later vernacular writers—they combined traditional number theory with a way of looking at numbers as symbolic of religious truth, or what Faith Wallis has described as a combination of "philosophical numerology" (which "derives the meaning of numbers from their mathematical properties") with "allegorical numerology."[62] Whereas "pure" number theory only expands on the properties of numbers (e.g., four as a square number), a numerological understanding of number focuses on the spiritual, biblical, and other theological connections underlying numbers (as in "four" signifying the four gospels). As I argued in the previous section of this chapter, numerology offered writers a compelling way of connecting numbers with theological concepts and spiritual practices. We see in the discussions of Isidore, Bartholomaeus, and John Trevisa, as well as others, the value of the combination of number theory and numerology. For example, in speaking of the number three, Trevisa writes, "The nombre of þre ... is most holy among nombres"[63] (The number three ... is the most holy among numbers), both because it represents the Trinity and because it is the first number made by adding an odd and an even number together. Thus, whereas "pure" number theory only addresses the properties of the numbers (for example, the assertion that the number three is the union of the first odd and even numbers), when a numerological understanding is added (for example, the assertion that the number three represents the Trinity), the number takes on a theological or spiritual significance that points directly to the divine identity of God. It is this combination of number theory and spiritual meaning that is so appealing to late medieval vernacular sermonists, as we shall see later in this section.

Encyclopedists like Isidore of Seville of course drew from early church fathers, who themselves expounded on the value of numbers and created spiritual associations to explain their properties. Perhaps no writing on this topic was more influential to later medieval authors than Augustine's discussion of the perfection of the number six, which he develops at length in *De Genesi ad litteram*: "We have called the number six perfect in view of the fact that it is the sum of its parts; in fact, these parts when multiplied produce exactly the number of which they are the parts." Augustine continues his analysis of the number six, asserting, "I am even more intrigued by this number when I consider the order of the works of creation."[64] In this case we see the use of number theory (the idea of six as a perfect number, because its factors, when added, equal its value), in combination with a spiritual association of the number six with the creation. Many other such examples from early church fathers abound; Bede, for instance, incorporated numerologically infused number theory into his explication of the measurements in works including *On the Tabernacle*, *On Genesis*, and *On the Temple*.[65]

Late medieval sermons, as well as other religious texts, draw heavily on discussions of numerologically infused perfect numbers. The four most commonly recognized perfect numbers are six, twenty-eight, 496, and 8,128, and they are called "perfect" because the number's factors add up to equal the number itself. For example, as Augustine explained, six can be factored into one, two, and three, which, when added, equal six; twenty-eight can be factored into one, two, four, seven, and fourteen, which, when added, equal twenty-eight. It is important to recognize the extent to which medieval religious literature in general, not just sermons, drew on perfect numbers in their discussions. For example, in a recent essay by Natalie M. Mandziuk on a late fifteenth-century text that describes the length of the wound in Christ's side, she claims that because the text states the wound in Christ's side was one twenty-eighth the length of his body, the original author must have thought of this as a "true" or accurate measurement of the wound, because, as Mandziuk argues, twenty-eight is not spiritually meaningful in a numerological sense. Thus, she asserts, the measure of one twenty-eighth is meant to be "more factual than symbolic."[66] However, Mandziuk fails to recognize that twenty-eight is a perfect number whose factors add up to its total, and therefore the wound is "perfect" in size; it can therefore be both symbolic and "true" at the same time. Accuracy in this sense does not necessarily mean a measurement that can be confirmed with a ruler;[67] for a medieval Christian, what could be more "true" or accurate than a number that reveals a greater spiritual truth? Thus, appreciating how medieval writers relied on number theory can help us understand how authors and texts may be operating in a symbolic realm of number when we have assumed they were being entirely "practical."

At the same time that medieval texts define six and twenty-eight as perfect, texts can also label as "perfect" the numbers ten and its square, cube, tetrad, and so forth, affording further occasions to expound on God's perfection. Boethius refers to "the perfection of the number ten" in his *Arithmetica*.[68] Similarly, according to Hugh of St. Victor, "ten signifies perfection because by extension it is the end of computation."[69] In other words, "ten" contains within it all the single digits involved in computation.

The perfection of ten and its exponents fuels a wealth of medieval religious discussion. Bede in *De tabernaculo* dwells on the perfection of the number one hundred, explaining how, when someone is finger counting (see appendix), the number is "transferred from the left hand to the right"; it "often contains a figure of the heavenly life," since the fingers make a circle, which can indicate infinity. Similarly, in his treatise on calculation by hand, Bede writes that when transferring the number between hands, a person makes "the crown of virginity by making a circle."[70] Moreover, in *De tabernaculo* he argues that the number one hundred is frequently found in Scripture: Noah finished his ark "in a hundredth year," and Isaac "was born in Abraham's hundredth year."[71] This idea of one hundred as perfect is later discussed by John Trevisa, who writes, "Ten siþes ten makiþ a parfit nombre, þat is an hundred"[72] (Ten times ten makes a perfect number, that is, one hundred).

Other medieval texts offer alternative definitions of why ten is perfect, which rely on a long tradition of explicating number properties. For instance, a fifteenth-century Middle English translation of the *Secreta Secretorum* asserts, "tene is a perfite nombyr, and hit contenyth in hym-Sylfe foure nombres, that is to witte, one and two, and thre and foure; the whyche yf they bene assemblet, makyth tene"[73] (Ten is a perfect number, and it contains in itself four numbers, namely one and two and three and four, which, if they are added together, make ten). This reason for ten being perfect—because it is the sum of the first four digits added (one, two, three, and four)—can be traced to the ancient Greeks; ten, its square, and its cube are considered perfect numbers because they form equilateral triangles when their digits are arranged so that each consecutive row increases by one.[74] The fifteenth-century *Orcherd of Syon*, a translation of Catherine of Siena's *Dialogue*, offers a different reason for the perfection of the number one hundred when explicating Jesus's promise in Matthew 19:29 that everyone who has given up homes or families for him "schulen resceyue an hundrid & euerlastinge liff"; as the Lord explains, "Certein for an hundrid is a parfiȝt noumbre, & to þat may no moore be addid to, but if þou bigynne at oon" (Certainly for one hundred is a perfect number, and that nothing more may be added to it, unless you have to begin again at one). The Lord then elaborates to Catherine on a spiritual connection that can be made from this perfect number, comparing one hundred to the virtue of charity, "þe moost parfiȝt vertu" (the most perfect virtue). He explains, "þou comest parfiȝtly to þis hundrid, bi multipliing of oþire vertues in knowleche of þisilf"[75] (You come perfectly to this hundred, by multiplying the other virtues in the knowledge of yourself). Number theory and multiplication, therefore, also become useful ways to describe how virtues are not just accumulated (or added up) but rather function in ways that compound one another.

As we might expect, the idea of one hundred and one thousand as perfect numbers also finds its way into sermons, for these are numbers frequently encountered in Scripture. Oxford, Bodleian Library, MS Holkham misc. 40, a late fourteenth- or early fifteenth-century translation of Robert de Gretham's Anglo-Norman *Mirror* cycle, invokes the idea of the square of ten as a perfect number; in this sermon, the perfect number then becomes a means to appreciate not the perfection of God but rather the enormity of one's sin. As the sermon on the occasion of the Ninth Sunday after Trinity describes, the debtor who owes one hundred measures of wheat, described in Luke 16:7, signifies a person in "perfect" sin: "for hundred is a [parfyt] noumbre. & [parfyt] synne confoundeþ þe soule. Þan is [his synne parfyt] when he ne doþ it noȝt awey witþ word ne wiþ dede. & þerfore he oweþ to suffre ful turment"[76] (For one hundred is a perfect number, and perfect sin harms the soul. Then is a person's sin perfect when he does not do away with it by word or deed. Therefore he must suffer torment completely). In this case, "perfect" modifies sin; "one hundred" would seem to indicate "pure" sin or "entirely sinful," the ultimate state of sin beyond which nothing can be added.

In contrast, a Holkham misc. 40 sermon on the Fourth Sunday in Lent, on the feeding of the five thousand, relies on one thousand as a perfect number to betoken those saved by Christ: "þe fyue þousand men þat were fed of þe fyue loues beytonkenþ alle þat schal be saued. Ffor þousand is noumber parfyt ... & we haue oure v wittes, þat is, herynge, smellynge, seinge, tastynge, felynge & wiþ al þis we owe to seruen God"[77] (The five thousand men who were fed the five loaves signify all who should be saved. Because one thousand is a perfect number . . . and we have our five wits [senses], that is, hearing, smelling, seeing, tasting, and feeling, and with all these we are obligated to serve God). Another sermon on the Fourth Sunday in Lent, in Dublin, Trinity College 241, asserts much the same thing with "Five thousand people were fed with these five loaves; a thousand signifies perfection and five represents the five senses. Those who keep their five senses perfectly will be fed these five loaves."[78] Number theory in these sermons is incorporated with a numerological sense to create an arithmetical problem (five times one thousand) that is designed to reveal deeper spiritual truths. In this case, "perfect" is equated with "saved," with the implication being that in order to be saved one needs to focus his or her senses on serving God.

Late medieval sermonists, therefore, infused their sermons with imagery and examples drawn from both number theory and numerology in order to explain the perfection of God—both the perfection of his creation and the perfection encouraged of humankind in their worship of him. Sermon audiences had a good understanding of the practicalities of whole numbers or positive integers; they used them every day, in the home and the workplace. Discussions of elementary number theory in sermons expanded audiences' understanding to demonstrate that certain numbers functioned in special ways: for example, as mentioned earlier, six is thought to be "perfect" because its factors all added up to equal six, and "ten" is perfect because it is a combination of the first four numbers added together, as well as the number that contains all the single-digit positive integers. Number theory therefore supported and underpinned the truths of the world and Scripture as medieval people understood them, and sermonists coupled this number theory with numerological interpretations in order to emphasize the interpretations of scriptural passages and spiritual practices. In the following chapters, we shall return again to number theory, in combination with spiritual understanding of number, to see how and why this functions so productively in sermons.

PART 4: ARITHMETICAL OPERATIONS AND OTHER BRANCHES OF MATHEMATICS IN SERMONS

As I have argued in this chapter, late medieval sermons are a fertile place for discussions of number and number theory, especially when combined with numerology. But that is not the extent of sermons' engagement with number. The focus of this section is how sermons actually set up arithmetic problems and model calculation for their audiences; they might even invite, either implicitly or explicitly, their audiences to calculate along with them. One obvious place in sermons to find arithmetical operations is in descriptions of pardons. Although I will discuss pardons in more depth in chapter 3, I include an example here to demonstrate the kinds of calculation pardons can encourage. In the fifteenth-century Syon Pardon sermon of British Library, MS Harley 4012, the sermonist details the pardon amounts that can be gained by visiting Syon:

> Firste, euery day in þe ere hosomeuer cometh to the saide monastary deuotly geuyng sumwhat to the reperacions of the saide monastery and say fiue *Pater Nosters* and fiue *Aves* and a *Crede*, shall haue CCCCC daies of pardon. And alsoo hosumeuer saith deuotely owr Lady sauter in the saide monastery, shall haue CCCCC dayes of pardone. . . . Item whosumeuer will come to the saide monastery in the fest of Cristismas, Estren, Whitsonday, Ascencion shall haue euery daie, and euery daye within the vtas of them, shall haue for euery *Pater Noster*, *Ave Mare* and *Crede*, or geuith any almes or goodes . . . shall haue CCCCCCC dayes of pardon and forte.[79]

> First, every day in the year whoever comes to the said monastery devoutly giving something to the reparations of that monastery and says five Our Fathers and five Aves and a Creed shall have five hundred days of pardon. And also whoever says devoutly Our Lady's psalter in this monastery shall have five hundred days of pardon. . . . Whoever will come to the monastery during Christmastime, Easter, Whitsunday, and ascension shall have every day, and every day with the octave (i.e., the days including and following a feast day, totaling eight), shall have for every Our Father, Ave Maria, and Creed, or gives any alms or goods . . . shall have seven hundred and forty days of pardon.

The listener or reader could easily add days of pardon by calculating how many Paternosters, Aves, and Creeds they could say during the specific time of the year that they were able to make the pilgrimage. Some of the specific pardon numbers could also be interpreted numerologically, as in five times one hundred days of pardon for visiting, saying prayers, and donating funds at any time during the year. As we saw in the previous section, five is often invoked in sermons to signify the five wounds or Christ, the five senses, the five loaves of bread multiplied by Christ, and so on, and one hundred was considered to be a "perfect" number indicating divine perfection. Thus, not only could audiences easily add the amounts of pardon, but they could also interpret them spiritually as well, as a way to understand the meaning behind the specific number of days of pardon offered.

This kind of arithmetic problem, in combination with a possible numerological interpretation, is invoked in many sermons. For example, an invitation to subtraction is included in a Wycliffite sermon by William Tayler on the Twenty-Fifth Sunday after Trinity, in the fifteenth-century collection Oxford, Bodleian Library, MS Douce 53. The sermonist proclaims, "According to Augustine, the world will last no more than eight thousand years; according to chroniclers, seven thousand six hundred and five years have passed."[80] This sermon writer tempts his audience to subtract how many years are left before the world ends: 8,000 minus 7605, or 395 years. Figuring out how many years are left before the Apocalypse would no doubt be too tempting to resist for many members of the audience. Furthermore, if were are to imagine that numerologically based factoring was then employed by a few in the audience, the answer, 395, would also have been attractive to those who could factor, as (other than one and 395), it can only be factored into two prime numbers, five and seventy-nine. For those audience members who were numerologically inclined, the arithmetic problem is compelling because it could be interpreted, for example, as the number of Christ's wounds times seventy-nine, which is seven (days, virtues, sin) times ten (a perfect number) plus nine (the Trinity times the Trinity). Or, if that was too difficult, an audience member might have rounded up 395 to 400, which could be more easily factored into significant parts, such as four times one hundred, or forty times ten. Of course, I have no direct evidence that this factoring actually took place in the minds (and hands) of medieval audiences, but the practices modeled in these sermons allow for this supposition. In examples like these, I believe sermonists took advantage of their audiences' practical numerate skills as they strove to link the pragmatic with the religious. Arithmetic becomes a way to help focus the audiences' minds on the lessons at hand, rather than a way to turn them away.

There are many examples of how sermon writers model multiplication and division to generate numerological and symbolic value. As the sermon writer of British Library, MS Harley 2276, a translation of an earlier Latin collection, *Filius Matris*, explains in a sermon on the First Sunday in Lent, "Christ fasted for forty days. This signifies that people from the four part [*sic*] of the world should arm themselves with the ten commandments to combat the devil or use the ten commandments to control stirrings in the four humours of the body."[81] Another sermon that relies on this symbolic factoring, British Library, MS Cotton Claudius A.ii, also introduces the factor of ten. This sermon on the occasion of Sexagesima from John Mirk's *Festial* states that "for sum tyme men lyued nyne hundred ȝere and more, bot now he þat lyueth iii schore ȝere or sumwhatte more it is takon for a long lyfe" (for some time men lived nine hundred years and more, but now he who lives three score years [i.e., sixty years] or somewhat more is thought of as having a long life). As the sermonist explains, "For sixti ben syx sythe ten, so þat be þe syxe ȝe schul hundurstande þe syx werkys of charite þat cometh oute of þe x commandementes of God"[82] (For sixty is six times ten, so that, by the number six, you shall understand the six works of charity that come out of the Ten Commandments of God). Moreover, the original lifespan of nine hundred years is easily divided by sixty; it calculates to fifteen, or three times five. Those audience members inclined to factor with numerological influences might perhaps have been tempted to divide the original lifespan into six works of charity, times Ten Commandments, times the five wounds, times the Trinity. Such symbolic factoring then becomes a devotional practice in and of itself, as the audience is encouraged to dwell on the deeper spiritual value of each number.[83] Yet another sermon relies on division and addition to reach the proper number of fast days in Lent: a sermon on Quadragesima in British Library, MS Additional 36791, argues that "a tenth part of the year [is] given to God through fasting"; thus, "the fast consists of a tenth part of the year, thirty-six days, plus four 'clensynge dayes,'"[84] or forty, a number that audiences had been taught to connect with Christ's tribulations in the desert.

These are just several examples of the kinds of spiritual meanings that can be generated by offering arithmetical problems to audiences who are trained to calculate in both pragmatic and symbolic ways. I would like to suggest that when sermons present arithmetical operations, we can imagine their vernacular listeners and readers would have been encouraged to participate to the extent of their ability. Sermons could set up simple story problems that are familiar to us today. For instance, a British Library, MS Royal 18.B.xxiii sermon on Epiphany describes the journey of the Magi to see the infant Christ, stating, "It was no wonder that they could arrive in thirteen days because they came on dromedaries, which can cover one hundred miles a day."[85] This problem asks its audience to multiply one hundred (which suggests a "perfect number") times thirteen to arrive at the correct distance.

What evidence do we have that medieval audiences engaged in personal acts of calculation when confronted with arithmetic problems in religious settings? As I have mentioned, I have no direct evidence of vernacular audiences calculating while sermons were read or delivered; however, I would not expect to find this. But sermons clearly encouraged this kind of spiritual arithmetical practice in their audiences. For example, in British Library, MS Additional 36791, a sermon on the occasion of All Souls, the sermonist describes how "as in the Old Testament, the Church's offices for the dead last seven and thirty days." He then breaks down the number thirty-seven into its numerologically significant components, using calculation: this thirty-seven signifies "the three powers of the soul and four elements of the body, and the Trinity and the ten commandments respectively."[86] In other words, one can add the three powers of the soul and the four elements of the body to reach seven, then multiply the Ten Commandments by the Trinity to reach thirty, and then add those together.

Moreover, Thomas Lentes has argued convincingly that European Christians in the later Middle Ages engaged in profound ways with the "arithmetic of salvation," which suggests that audiences were quite practiced in calculations intended to profit them devotionally. Evidence is plentiful for devotional calculations in monastic settings; for example, Lentes describes a manuscript from a religious house in Cologne that sets up calculations and corresponding prayers that should be said on such topics as how long (in number of months, weeks, hours, days, and even hours) "Jesus spent in the womb" and then "spent on earth," as well as the number of steps Jesus took during the Passion, how many "drops of blood he shed," "the number of thorns in the Crown of Thorns," "the number of tears wept by Mary," and so on. The manuscript then works through the arithmetic, emphasizing the calculations' numerological importance and thus strengthening the reader's engagement with the accompanying prayers. As Lentes argues, "The various projections and sum totals demonstrate how very seriously the compilers of such lists took the precise recording of the figures."[87] As many lay people wished to participate in spiritual practices similar to those of religious, it seems reasonable to expect that both clerical and lay audiences of sermons would have wanted to engage in devotional calculations as well.

As I have demonstrated, arithmetical operations can rely heavily on numerological understandings of number. Sometimes errors can occur in sermons because the numbers are overdetermined by numerology. Thinking of Christ feeding the multitude leads the author(s) of MS Harley 2276 to suggest in his Seventh Sunday after Trinity sermon that "Christ miraculously multiplied [the loaves] ... to feed seven thousand," the seven of which is said to signify "the seven clasps on John's book."[88] This passage therefore takes the "perfect number" one thousand, multiplies it by the numerologically significant seven (also the sum of five loaves plus two fish from the feeding of the five thousand, or the seven loaves from the feeding of the four thousand), to arrive at seven thousand, arithmetically correct but not scripturally accurate. Indeed, if the sermon writer were adding the two instances of the feeding of the multitude, he would arrive at the feeding of nine thousand (the five thousand from plus four thousand), not seven thousand.

Many sermons also draw on the symbolic value of ratios. To form a ratio is to make a division problem, and medieval audiences were frequently exposed to this concept in sermons. One such example is found in the late fifteenth-century Westminster Abbey Library, MS 34/20 sermon on Lent, which proclaims that a fiend "would rather climb up and down a tree full of sharp razors for a thousand years than endure an hour in hell."[89] Of course, "one thousand years" is often employed in medieval literary texts to mean "an extremely long time," and one might be tempted to make the ratio of one thousand to one. However, the actual ratio is greater than this, for it compares hours to years. It therefore invites the audience to figure out how many hours are in a thousand years. Of course, probably very few if any would stick with the calculations to figure out that there are almost 9 million hours in a thousand years. What matters is the impression of a ratio that compares extremely large to finitely small, not necessary that someone arrives at a specific number.

A less complicated ratio is expressed in MS Holkham misc. 40, in which a sermon for an unidentified occasion on the theme "Multi sunt vocati set pauci vero electi" (Matt. 20:16) (Many are called and few are chosen) claims that "some say that numbers in heaven and hell will be equal; since a tenth of the angels fell from heaven, heaven will be nine part angels and one part people while hell will be the opposite."[90] If the angels in heaven number nine-tenths and people one-tenth, and hell has the inverse, then hell is peopled by one-tenth angels and people therefore must make up nine-tenths. The sermon gives the audience two of these figures and leaves the last calculations, the number of fallen angels and people in hell, to the audience's own discretion. Perhaps when this sermon was delivered, the preacher elaborated this for his audience; however, it is also possible that the sermonist trusted his audience to be able to calculate this terrifying ratio. The staggering number of people in hell certainly could provoke a kind of "math anxiety" in the sermon audience![91]

In the late Middle Ages there appears to have been a tension between texts that promote numbers as a way to comprehend divine truth and those texts that assert numbers actually draw one's attention away from God. In contrast to these sermons that emphasize how practical arithmetic, in combination with numerological understandings, helps to focus one's attention on God as well as on one's own moral behavior, Paul Acker notes that on occasion arithmetic could be associated with sin or evil. As evidence, Acker gives the following example drawn from the *Ancrene Wisse*, the early thirteenth-century guide for anchoresses: "a covetous man is like a fire-tender; in the ashes he makes 'figures of augrim, as þes rikeneres doð þe habbeð muche to rikenin.'" Acker then elaborates, "These 'figures of augrim' are Arabic numerals, and here we find our earliest known Middle English reference to them. But in this passage they serve only to improve the reckoning abilities of the devil's accountant; such associations with the mercantile world only added to the taint suffered by arithmetic."[92] This example appears to draw on the association of mercantile activities with greed, as well as the popular belief that the devil keeps an account book in which he records people's sins; the *Ancrene Wisse* author warns the reader that the devil is always adding up one's sins.

Perhaps motivated by a similar impulse to associate arithmetic with non-godly pursuits, the author(s) of the Life of Saint Edmund in the early fourteenth-century *South English Legendary* imagines the holy man giving up his arithmetic for a higher calling. At first, Edmund applied himself to the practice of arithmetic (arsmetrike) and "cast" his numbers in dust, probably on a dust board:

> To arsmetrike he drouȝ,
> & arsmetrike radde in cours : in Oxenford wel faste
> & his figurs drouȝ aldai : & his numbre caste.—
> Arsmetrike is alore : þat of figures al is
> & of drauȝtes as me draweþ in poudre : & of numbre, i-wis.[93]

> To arithmetic he drew; he pursued arithmetic at Oxford and drew his figures all day, and cast numbers. Arithmetic is a lore (a thing to be studied) that deals with figures and with drafting/drawing and of number, as men draw in the dust, I know.

One night in a vision, however, Edmund's mother comes to redirect his attention away from arithmetic and toward the study of God:

"Sone," heo seide, "to what figurs : woltou nou entende?"
"Leoue moder," quaþ þis oþer : "such as we iseoþ."
"Leoue sone," quaþ þe moder : "betere figurs þer beoþ,
wherto þu most þinr hurte do : & þenche her-on nomore!"
heo nom forþ his riȝt hand : & wrot þer-on his lore :
Þreo rounde cerclen heo wrot : in þe paume amidde,
In þe tueye heo wrot fader & sone : & holigost in þe þridde.[94]

"Son," she said, "to what figures are you now attending?" "Dear mother," said the other, "such as we see." "Dear son," said the mother, "there are better figures, where you should concentrate and think on it no more!" She then took forth his right hand and wrote this learning on it: three round circles she wrote in the middle of his palm. In the two she wrote Father and Son, and then she wrote Holy Ghost in the third.[95]

As described in the passage, Edmund's mother rebukes her son by telling him that there are "better figures" to study than numbers. She then takes his right hand and in the middle of his palm draws three circles, symbolizing the Father, Son, and Holy Ghost. These figures, although drawn just with touch, are more permanent and more pressing than those figures in the dust he was attending to. It seems that in this example, the geometry of the divine becomes a higher calling than the arithmetic of the mundane. As Paul Acker notes, however, when this story is recounted in the sermon collection of Mirk's *Festial*, Mirk gives "no mention of arithmetic: for him it serves as an exemplum illustrating the point 'be bysy to lerne þe beleue of þe Holy Trinite'"[96] (apply yourself to learning the belief of the Holy Trinity). Mirk may have been reluctant to include a negative example of calculation because he emphasizes how important number is for appreciating divine truth elsewhere in his collection.

These concerns that arithmetic can distract someone's attention from God and that it does not represent the divine accurately, are elaborated on in an entertaining fifteenth-century Latin sermon by John Felton that plays on his audience's familiarity with the seven liberal arts. Felton was a priest at St. Mary Magdalene in Oxford, and it is thought his audience was a mixed lay and clerical one.[97] In a sermon for Easter or Corpus Christi, Felton cleverly demonstrates why the liberal arts are not capable of explaining the mystery of the Eucharist. Arithmetic, he writes, "is concerned with numbers" and is "mistaken" about the sacrament because "Isidore, in the third book of his *Etymologies*, has a chapter on infinite numbers. But for Christ, who is in this sacrament, there is no infinite number. Matthew 10[:30] and Luke 12[:7] declare: 'The hairs of your head are all numbered.'"[98] This paradox, when unpacked, suggests that the infinite God has declared there are no infinite numbers to *him*. Felton's sermon emphasizes that God is the master of all number, the supreme counter. As the fourteenth-century theologian and mathematician Robert Grossteste stated, "Whenever you see something with measures and number and order, look for the craftsman. You will not find one, except where the supreme measure, the supreme number, and the supreme order are: that is, with God."[99] Arithmetic and number, therefore, offer a valuable way of understanding God, with the caveat that number (and therefore God) can also be beyond comprehension. Thus, these arithmetical discussions in sermons become a way of capitalizing on audiences' pragmatic sense of number at the same time as they challenge that purely pragmatic sense.

CONCLUSION

As I have argued in this chapter, medieval sermons rely heavily on numbers—first, as a way to divide and structure the modern or scholastic sermon, and second, as a subject for discussion to educate audiences about Scripture and religious practices. Sermon writers draw on numerology, number theory, and arithmetical operations to create a world in which numbers operate on both a practical and spiritual level. These sermons rely on their audiences' pragmatic understanding of number and calculations, but they enrich their audiences' understandings by adding layers of spiritual interpretation over their pragmatic knowledge, thereby training their listeners and readers to think about numbers in a more complicated and spiritually beneficial way.

I began this chapter with a joke by Bracciolini, in which a priest does not correct his mistake (misspeaking that Christ fed five hundred instead of five thousand) because he seems to fear his audience of lay people will not believe the miracle. His hesitancy suggests that he judges his audience to be too practical to believe that Christ could feed even five hundred, let alone ten times that. However, as we see in sermons that address the feeding of the multitude, just the opposite is true: late medieval sermonists develop elaborate allegorical interpretations of the feedings and trust their audiences to understand and internalize their numerical and numerological discussions. Indeed, certain scriptural topics (like the feeding of the four or five thousand) offer special opportunities for discussion of numbers and related arithmetical operations.

The Gospel passages concerning the feeding of the multitude provide many opportunities for numerological expansion. The *Glossa Ordinaria* suggests several interpretations that are later incorporated into these sermons.[100] Moreover, sermonists often stretch and develop their numerical interpretations. When discussing these verses, late medieval sermonists frequently associated the five loaves with the five books of Moses or the old law, which is suggested by the *Glossa Ordinaria*.[101] This concept of the spiritual importance of the number five is then developed further in several sermons, including Cambridge, Sidney Sussex College, MS 74, which states, "Thus his [Christ's] later disciples, especially priests, are obliged to feed both bodily and spiritually with five loaves"—namely, "the bread of wisdom" and the loaves of pity, truth, mourning, and devotion.[102] Another sermon, on the Seventh Sunday after Trinity, in Cambridge, St. John's College, MS G.22, also associates the seven loaves with spiritual meanings: the seven loaves that Christ fed the crowd "spiritually represent the bread of sorrow mentioned in the psalms," with the first loaf "love and fear which leads to wisdom," the second "remembrance of sins," the third "hatred of them [sins]," the fourth "the sorrow of repentance," the fifth "shame for one's sins," the sixth "the effort of carrying out penance," and the seventh "perseverance in good works."[103]

The two fishes also offer a wealth of interpretations for sermonists, including "the orders of kingship and priesthood," as well as "the books of the prophets and the psalms,"[104] "the books of wisdom and prophets,"[105] and the "love for God and humankind."[106] In addition, the two fishes can also signify "faith which is nourished in the water of baptism. Prelates must feed the people with these loaves and the two fishes (old and new testaments)."[107] In the Dublin, Trinity College, MS 241 sermon for the Twenty-Fifth Sunday after Trinity, the five thousand people represent the five senses that "one must keep under control," and the twelve leftover baskets become the "words of scripture gathered up by the four doctors of the Church."[108] Another sermon on the feeding of the multitude, in British Library, MS Additional 40672, states that there are two miraculous feedings in Scripture, because "as two is the number which first departs from unity or oneness, so these two feasts signify that people who have departed from unity with God by their sin are hungry and need to be fed."[109] As we saw earlier in the chapter, these sermons could also draw from number theory with the idea of one thousand as "perfect" and then offer what I call spiritual factoring (the five senses times the perfect number one thousand). Thus, my overarching point of this discussion of the multitude sermons, and of this chapter as a whole, is that number in these sermons is at the same time both practical (for memory, for the *divisio* of the sermon, and for the purposes of enumeration) and symbolic (both numerologically and allegorically). Sermonic discussions of number take on all these resonances, and it is virtually impossible to divorce number from the spiritual understanding of number therein.

Why is this significant? I believe that this understanding of medieval sermon's hybrid method of reading numbers can help us appreciate the complexity and ingenuity of medieval sermons. The allegorical and numerological discussions of number, coupled with arithmetic and number theory, offer countless ways of doing what sermons are meant to do: exhort, encourage, scare, warn, lead, teach, and so forth. Furthermore, an appreciation of how and why this works in sermons can also help us appreciate how multivalent a medieval person's understanding of number was. I therefore conclude my book with the example of Margery Kempe, whose fifteenth-century visionary text describes an engagement with number that is usually interpreted in scholarship as entirely mercantile. However, I argue that often when she includes discussions of specific numbers, she has superimposed a spiritual value on those numbers. Her text also includes several examples of arithmetical discussions that reflect the influence of sermons. Based on examples like these from Kempe, I believe that medieval people listened to these sermons and carried this hybrid numerate practice, this spiritual calculation, out into the world.

CHAPTER 2

Numbers in *Dives and Pauper* and the Sermons of Warminster, Longleat House MS 4

Models for Spiritual Understanding and Practice

In the previous chapter, I offered an overview of the kinds of numerical and arithmetical examples with which sermon writers engage for the edification, education, and enjoyment of their audiences. In this chapter and the following, I focus on two specific sermon cycles in Middle English and their extended discussion of numbers, in order to argue that these texts educate their audiences in a kind of religious or spiritual numerate practice, one that combines both pragmatic and spiritual understandings of numbers. In these sermon cycles, sermonists encourage their audiences to comprehend the divine through number and mathematical operations. If God created all things in number, weight, and measure (Wis. 11:20), then sermons demonstrate just how that world was thought to function through the use of that number.

One early fifteenth-century author of both a sermon cycle and a pastoral treatise stands out for his sustained engagement with number: the anonymous author of the early fifteenth-century sermon cycle in Warminster, Longleat House MS 4 (hereafter Longleat 4), and the pastoral treatise *Dives and Pauper*. Both texts, likely written by a university-educated Franciscan deeply invested in religious education, engage with number in significant ways to facilitate that education for his audiences.[1] Longleat 4, composed between 1409 and 1413, contains "a complete Sunday gospel collection, together with sermons for certain Christian festivals,"[2] and *Dives and Pauper*, written in the first decade of the fifteenth century, is an extended treatise on the Ten Commandments, in the form of a dialogue between a rich layman named

Dives and a learned mendicant named Pauper. Whereas *Dives and Pauper* is extant in several manuscripts and has been edited by Priscilla Heath Barnum for the Early English Text Society, the sermon cycle of Longleat 4 exists in only one manuscript, of which there is no published edition.[3] Fortunately, a detailed summary of each sermon, including their incipits and explicits in Middle English, is included in Veronica O'Mara and Suzanne Paul's multi-volume *A Repertorium of Middle English Prose Sermons*, which has opened up access to this remarkable sermon cycle.[4]

Due in part to the ease of access to *Dives and Pauper*, as well as to the current scholarly focus on pastoral prose treatises rather than sermons, more attention has been paid to *Dives and Pauper* than to Longleat 4, and scant few essays address them both. Scholarship on the separate texts displays some similarities: both texts are understood to be pastoral works meant to educate, engage, and inform their lay and clerical audiences about the nature of God, the meaning of Scripture and doctrine, and how one should conduct oneself morally (with "right action") in the world. Scholars have also addressed the relative orthodoxy or heterodoxy of the texts, in particular the author's approach to lay, vernacular education around the time that Arundel's Constitutions limited access to the Bible in the vernacular for the laity,[5] as well as the author's defense of the vernacular as a language for religious education.[6]

One particular essay is of great importance to my argument. In 1994, a brilliant study by M. Teresa Tavormina examined the discussion of perfect numbers in *Dives and Pauper*,[7] and in this chapter I extend Tavormina's treatment by looking at both *Dives and Pauper* and Longleat 4's attention to numbers, number theory, arithmetic, and numerology. As Vincent Gillespie argues, "Dissenters, like the preacher of sermons in MS Longleat 4 (who also wrote the important treatise *Dives and Pauper*) passionately defended their right to instruct the laity in the vernacular (and the laity's right to be instructed)."[8] My argument picks up on this idea of vernacular instruction in the field of mathematics, and I assert that it is valuable to look at *Dives and Pauper* alongside Longleat 4 because together the texts demonstrate how a writer could draw on a basic level of numeracy in his audience, as well as model mathematical problems, in order to explain and teach religious truths. For the anonymous author, math is a critical part of his pastoral project, and he infuses his audience's practical understanding of number with a numerological or spiritual sense of number.

Specifically, I argue that both texts—*Dives and Pauper* and the sermon cycle of Longleat 4—use numbers to represent divine truth and offer a way for audiences to better understand and venerate God. The sermons, however, offer even more access to God via number than that of the dialogue between *Dives and Pauper*. This is due to the nature of the sermon—it is more hortatory in nature and more active and engaging than a set dialogue between a questioner and a wise man. My assertion is that the sermon is a particularly ripe and welcoming place for vernacular mathematical discussions. The mathematical operations modeled in the sermons of Longleat 4 are both performative and collaborative. The sermonist drew on his audiences' practical, numerate understandings, which he infused with numerological meaning, to show how one could apply that knowledge to abstract religious ideas like "forgiveness" to create a deeper understanding of the divine. Conversations about number in these texts offer a framework for making the unfathomable fathomable.

PART 1: NUMBER AND PERFECTION IN *DIVES AND PAUPER*

Not much is known of the circumstances that produced *Dives and Pauper*. It was written by an anonymous Franciscan, most likely from "southwest England (perhaps Bristol)," between about 1405 and 1410.[9] This text, written in the "fashionable early fifteenth-century form of dialogue," is extant in eleven manuscripts, eight of which are complete. We know more about the readership of the text than we do about the author: the manuscripts' ownership demonstrates the text's wide audience, as they were "owned by wealthy lay people," universities, and monasteries.[10] The treatise also appeared in printed editions in 1493, 1496, and 1536 and no doubt reached an even wider readership in print than it did in manuscript form.[11]

In *Dives and Pauper*, the author explores a wealth of information about God and his creation in the far-ranging discussion of the Ten Commandments. The author contemplates the nature of number in several places: first, in his discussion of the Third Commandment, when Pauper explains why God created the world in six days; second, in his discussion of the Fifth Commandment, when he explains the perfection of the number ten; third, when, in his discussion of the Seventh Commandment, he addresses the need for accurate tithing; and fourth, when, also during the discussion of the Seventh Commandment, Pauper seeks to educate his audience about the value of offering Masses for the dead.

During a dialogue about the Third Commandment, Dives asks Pauper why God made the world in six days rather than in some other number.[12] Pauper offers a lengthy response focused not only on the value of six as the first "perfect" number but also on the remaining perfect numbers, all of which reveal the perfection of God. Drawing on both Augustine and Boethian number theory, the author has Pauper explain: "þe numbre of sexe is þe firste numbre efne þat is perfyth. . . . For alle his partys þat metyn hym ȝif þey ben takyn togedere makyn efne sexe, as i, ii, iii makyn efne sexe, and þese þre numbris metyn hym. For sexe sithis on is sexe, & thryys two is sexe, and twyys þre is sexe"[13] (The number of six is the first number that is perfect. . . . For all its parts that make it if they are taken together make exactly six, as one, two, three make six, and these three numbers make it. For six times one is six, and thrice two is six, and twice three is six). As Pauper defines it, a perfect number is a number whose parts add up to the original number. That he develops the definition with a description of factoring in two different manners suggests that the author wishes to model factoring for his audience. First, he describes how all of six's parts (or factors)—that is, one, two, and three—when added together make six; and second, he describes how factors can be multiplied to equal six: six times one is six, three times two is six, and two times three is six. The attention paid to these actions also suggests that the author expected the audience to be particularly interested in the idea of factoring and that he thought they would benefit from (or perhaps even enjoy) seeing the problem modeled for them. Pauper then explains that for numbers between ten and one hundred, there is another perfect number, twenty-eight: "And þis perfeccioun is in non numbre withynne ten but in sexe, & from ten to an hondrid is non but xxviii" (1:1.284) (And this perfection is in no number within ten but in six, and from ten to one hundred is it in nothing but twenty-eight).

In describing the perfect numbers six and twenty-eight, the *Dives and Pauper* author is echoing the claims of a number of extremely influential earlier religious texts.[14] As mentioned in chapter 1, Augustine explored the value of six as perfect;[15] Bede also invokes this when he writes in *De tabernaculo*, an extended commentary on Exodus 24:12–30:31, that "it is well known that six, the number [of days] in which the world was made, designates the perfection of works."[16] Furthermore, regarding the perfect number twenty-eight, the length in cubits of the curtains in the tabernacle, Bede writes, "If you will count the whole succession of numbers between one and seven, you will reach the sum of twenty-eight, for one plus two plus three plus four plus five plus six plus seven make twenty-eight."[17] Here we see that the perfection inherent in twenty-eight is not limited to adding its factors; Bede argues that it is also special because the numbers from one to seven, when added, reach twenty-eight. Thus, the writings of these early medieval authors promote number theory as valuable because it reveals important truths about Scripture as well as the nature of the world.

Pauper, however, does not stop with the perfect number twenty-eight. He goes on to suggest that for each power of ten, there is a perfect number found within. In the hundreds there is 496: "And fro an hondrid to a þousand is but þis on numbre: cccclxxxxvi" (And from one hundred to a thousand is only this one number: 496), and between one thousand and one hundred thousand there is the number 8,128: "The neste is viii.m.c.xxviii, an þan no mo swyche but on withynne an hondrid þousand, & hoso wil fyndyn þat he must stodyyn" (The next is 8,128, and there are no more than within one hundred thousand, and whoever will find that must strive hard). He then suggests that there is a perfect number for each time a power of ten is added, even if it is an impossible task for clerks to perform: "Aftir an hondryd þousand arn mo swyche þan alle þe clerkys vndir sonne conne telle, mo þan ony herte may þinkyn or tunge tellyn, and þouȝ it is wol hard to fyndyn on" (1:1.284) (After one hundred thousand are more than all the clerks under the sun can tell, more than any heart may think of or tongue tell, although it is extremely hard to find one).

Although I will not rehearse here in full Tavormina's essay, which explores the mathematics behind finding perfect numbers, I will emphasize her assertion that "what is unusual here is the mathematical depth of Pauper's comment on the perfection of six."[18] Whereas other pastoral authors do not usually venture beyond six or twenty-eight, the author has Pauper state that perfect numbers continue for each power of ten to infinity. Tavormina traces this assertion back to Nicomachus of Gerasa, via Boethius's *De institutione arithmetica*, which she suggests university students may have studied alongside another short student text, Thomas Bradwardine's *Arithmetica speculativa*.[19] But why explore this subject of perfect numbers in a prose treatise focused on pastoral care? As James Davis suggests, "Dives personifies the newly literate, worldly, yet pious layman, striving to understand theological injunctions."[20] I would add that Dives also personifies the numerate layman, one who the author knows can appreciate the nuances of his numerical argument. This passage therefore indicates both the author's and the audience's interest in this discourse, a willingness to see the order of the universe through number, a belief that mathematical conjecture can express that perfection.

When Pauper returns to the number six after his brief foray into the concept of infinity, he lays out a string of perfect sixes that underlie the world as medieval Christians understood it, starting with how God made man on the sixth day "as for a perfyth & a noble creature" (as for a perfect and noble created being). God then became man (as Christ) "in þe sexte age of the world" (in the sixth age of the world), and on the sixth day, Good Friday, at the sixth hour, he redeemed mankind. The writer connects these sixes with humankind's duty to God: "And þat same numbre of dayys God hat grauntyd us to warkyn ynne in tokne þat al our warkys schuldyn ben perfyth & good & noþing don omys" (1:1.285) (And that same number of days God granted to us to work in, in token that all our works should be perfect and good and nothing done amiss). In this discussion of the Third Commandment, the writer has moved from the perfection of the world (as mirrored in numbers), to the perfection of God's creation (mankind), to Christ's crucifixion and redemption, to mankind making sure to work "perfectly" and not to sin. The number six, which represents the perfection that underlies God's world and his presence in it, becomes a model with which audiences can understand what their own behavior ought to be.

This discussion of the perfection of six leads directly into the following chapter, which features an elaborate explication of the meaning of the number seven. This passage demonstrates how flexibly the author wields his number symbolism to try to describe both God's perfection and the perfection that humankind strives for. Dives begins by asking why God rested on the seventh day rather than any other day. Pauper answers with a lengthy explanation involving how seven comes after the perfection of six: "so aftir perfyth warkys in þis world schal folwyn perfyth reste in þe oþer world" (so after perfect works in this world shall follow perfect rest in the other world) and links this perfect rest to "endeles reste, boþin of body & of soule" (1:1.285–86) (endless rest, both in body and of soul). However, he quickly turns to a negative association of the number seven with the seven deadly sins and describes how seven "pasyth þe perfyth numbre of sexe, so euery synne pasyth perfeccion & is out of perfeccion of alle goode warkys" (1:1.285) (surpasses the perfect number of six, just as every sin passes perfection and is out of perfection of all good works) before returning to his positive associations once again. Drawing on symbolic calculation, he expands, "For why seuene is mad of four & thre: four betoknyth bodely þingis mad of four elementis, thre betoknyth manys soule & womanys mad to þe lyknesse of þe holy trinite, and þerfor he bad rest in þe seueþe day þat men shuldyn þan restyn boþe body & soule" (1:1.285–86) (Because seven is made of four and three: four betokens bodily things made of the four elements, and three betokens man's and woman's souls made in the likeness of the holy trinity, and therefore he [God] bade rest on the seventh day so that men should then rest both body and soul). He then compounds this by introducing the "seuene blyssis whyche we shul han for perfyth warkys þat we don here in sexe dayys & sexe agis of þis world" (1:1.286) (seven blisses which we shall have for perfect works that we have done here in six days and the six ages of this world), before detailing those blisses and concluding with the assertion that this world is commingled with woe, but in heaven all shall be bliss: "In tokene of þese seuene blyssis þat we schul han in endles reste for our perfyth warkys þerfor God bad reste in þe seueþe day" (1.1.286) (In token of these seven blisses we shall have in endless rest for our perfect works, therefore God bade rest on the seventh day). The number seven, therefore, serves as both a model of perfection and a warning against sin.

The *Dives and Pauper* author is deeply invested in how both number theory and numerological associations with number can help explain to audiences the meaning underlying Scripture as well as how people ought to conduct themselves to please God. This plays out in another discussion of a "perfect" number, that of the number ten and its powers. As described in chapter 1, the number ten is not perfect in the sense of its factors adding up to its whole but rather is considered perfect in medieval number theory because it contains all the single digits within it. During the explication of the Fifth Commandment, *Thou shalt not kill*, Dives asks why there are Ten Commandments, rather than twelve or nine. Pauper responds, "God ȝaf his hestis in þe numbre of ten, for as ten is a numbre perfyth & contenynyth alle numbrys, so Godis lawe is perfyth & al is comprehendit in ten hestys" (1:2.28) (God gave his commandments in the number of ten, for as ten is a perfect number and contains all numbers, so God's law is perfect and all is understood in the Ten Commandments). Pauper then explains that if someone commits one sin, they are actually engaging in all seven, and if that person breaks one commandment, they are actually breaking all the others as well. At this point, the author turns to spiritually infused addition via numerological association by describing how, in Revelation, the woman sitting on the red beast that has seven heads and ten horns can be interpreted as the seven deadly sins and the breaking of the Ten Commandments, "in tokene þat whan man or woman fallit in ony dedly synne opynlyche he fallit in alle seuene pryueliche in Godis syȝthe, & whan he brekyt on comandement he brekyt alle" (1:2.31) (in token that when man or woman falls into any deadly sin openly he falls into all seven secretly in God's sight, and when he breaks one commandment he breaks them all). Because this passage states that ten is a perfect number containing all of the digits within it, this threat of breaking all the commandments if a person breaks one is made concrete—ten is perfect because it contains all the numbers up to nine; breaking one commandment, therefore, means that a person breaks the entire sum of the commandments. As Pauper asserts, perfection can only be attained when one avoids *all* sin.

The perfection of the number ten is introduced yet again in the discussion of the Seventh Commandment, *Thou shalt not steal*, during a section addressing proper tithing. Dives asks, "Why should people pay one tenth part and not another part?" Pauper answers that this one tenth comes directly from the meaning of ten as a perfect number, thereby associating the act of tithing with one of the "perfect works" that all Christians must perform:

> For ten is a numbre so perfyt þat it contynyth alle numbrys, for alle numbris aftir ten ben mad of ten & of numbrys withynne ten. And nyne is a numbre vnperfyt, & alle numbris withynne ten ben vnperfyt in regard of ten. And þerfor God bad þat men schuldyn ȝeuyn to hym þe tente part & kepyn to hemself nyne partis in tokene þat al our perfeccioun comyth of God & to hym it muste be arettyd be preysynge & þankynge, and al [our] inperfeccion comyth of ourself, & þerefor we withholdyn nyne partys to ourself & ȝeuyn to God þe tente part, so knowlechyng þat al our perfeccion & goodnesse comyth of hym & al our inperfeccion comyth of ourself. Also in tokene þat he is our lord & lord of al & al þat we han comyth from hym, as alle numbrys ben contynyd in ten & comyn of ten. (1:2.172–73)

> For ten is a number so perfect that it contains all numbers, for all numbers after ten are made of ten and of numbers within ten. And nine is an imperfect number, and all numbers within ten are imperfect in regard to ten. And therefore God bade that men should give to him the tenth part and keep to themselves the nine parts in token that all our perfection comes from God and to him it must be attributed by praising and thanking him, and all our imperfection comes from ourselves, and therefore we withhold nine parts to ourselves and give to God the tenth part, in acknowledgment that all our perfection and goodness comes from him and all our imperfection comes from ourselves. Also in token that he is our Lord and Lord of all and all that we have comes from him, as all numbers are contained within ten and come from ten.

Several times the author defines why ten is perfect (because it contains all the single digits), as well as how the tenth part comes from the perfection of God; recognizing that "all our perfection and goodness comes from him," he reasons, is the right thing to do. Note in this passage how the author circles back to the significance of the number ten—several times he emphasizes what makes ten perfect, and how that number should become a model for people to internalize. The audience, he insists, should understand that God is a ten and humans are imperfect nines who must strive to be like the number ten.

The discussion of ten as a perfect number in the section on the Seventh Commandment soon gives way to a more concrete exploration of number, which is introduced in a chapter in which Pauper offers some practical advice about offering Masses. In attempting to educate the audience about the most efficacious use of one's donation for intercessory masses and prayers, Pauper explains how many people are mistaken in thinking that they must wait until a certain time in the liturgical cycle for the masses to be the most useful. As he advises,

> betere it is for to han four scor messys songyn togedere day be day for twenty schillyngis, þan to han but þretty messys songyn in þe longe ȝer for twenty schillingys for why ȝe mon for twenty schyllyngis don syngyn a quarter of an anuel & don þe soulys han part nout only of þretty messys but of as many messis as comyn penyys to twenty schillyngis, for þou ȝe ȝeuyn a þousant pound for a messe þe preste may nout aproprychyn þat messe to no soule but only preyyn for hym aftir þat he is boundyn. (1:2.190–91)

> It is better to have four score (i.e., eighty) Masses sung together day by day for twenty shillings than to have only thirty Masses sung in the long year (i.e., on special feasts during the liturgical year) for twenty shillings, because you can for twenty shillings sing a quarter of an annual (i.e., services lasting one quarter of a year) and the souls have part not only of the thirty Masses but of as many Masses as come pence to twenty shillings, for although you give a thousand pounds for a Mass, the priest may not attribute that Mass to any soul but only pray for him after that he is bound.

In this section, Pauper argues that it is better value for money to spend twenty shillings for four score (twenty times four Masses, or eighty Masses), to be sung day by day in a row, rather than spend twenty shillings for only thirty Masses that are sung on particular days in the "long year." Souls, he asserts, will have part of as many Masses as come in pennies or pence in twenty shillings, or twelve times twenty, or 240. This is plain and simple spiritual economy—a donor can get more from for his or her money if he or she follows the formula offered by Pauper.

As Tavormina first suggested in her 1994 essay and I have argued further, the author of *Dives and Pauper* directs his attention to number in this text because he finds number to be a helpful, concrete way of explaining the divine, Scripture, and particular religious practices. Elaborations on number and number theory in this text are coupled with numerological interpretations as a way to help shape the moral compass of the audience, whether that audience encountered the text during private reading, public sermons, or even in confession.[21] We now turn to a sermon cycle composed by the same author; these sermons are particularly rich in numerical and mathematical examples. Whereas *Dives and Pauper* is concerned with modeling perfection for audiences, the sermon cycle is significant in that it addresses a much wider array of numerate models and incorporates both number and mathematics more deeply into its hortatory argument.

PART 2: NUMBER IN WARMINSTER, LONGLEAT HOUSE MS 4—
PERFECTION PLUS

The author of the sermon cycle in Longleat 4 is the same as that of *Dives and Pauper*,[22] and the mathematical discussion introduced in the earlier text is expanded upon in these sermons. Longleat 4 was written circa 1409–13, just a few years after *Dives and Pauper* was composed, and contains a sermon cycle as well as several other religious treatises, including *The Charter of the Abbey of the Holy Ghost* and *Pore Caitif*. The sermon cycle is composed of fifty-six temporale sermons, from the First Sunday in Advent to the Twenty-Fifth Sunday after Trinity, in addition to sermons on the assumption, the visitation, and the nativity.[23] The manuscript is thought to have been written by a scribe with a dialect from the "central east midland" in the area of Ely or Cambridge.[24] Whether the audience was a reading or a listening one,[25] it is clear that the author wished to educate and enlighten his audience in what he felt was a valuable way of expressing difficult religious concepts; this sermon cycle offers an even more extended discussion than does *Dives and Pauper* of number in its spiritual sense. My argument is that the sermons show a masterful range of equivalences, which can be both negative and positive. Mathematical operations model for audiences a way to grasp the content of the sermon by referring to their practical knowledge, which is then closely linked with spiritual understandings. It is this connection of the practical and the spiritual that makes number such a powerful device and discourse for promoting faith and devotion—number makes the abstract graspable and understandable.

Similar to many other late medieval sermons introduced in chapter 1, the Longleat 4 sermons use number and enumeration as an organizing principle. For example, the second sermon in the cycle, on the Second Sunday in Advent, enumerates the "fifteen signs that will occur on the fifteen days before the last judgement," as described by Jerome,[26] as well as the four types of generation the world has witnessed, the last of which will pass before the final judgment: Adam from the earth, Eve from a man without a woman, Christ from a woman without a man, and the typical experience of generation, from a woman and a man.[27] Another sermon, for the Tenth Sunday after Trinity, describes the five times that Christ wept: at his birth, for compassion, when he raised Lazarus, for Judas, and then on the cross.[28] Time and time again throughout the sermons the author shapes his content and argument around enumeration; one would be hard pressed to find a sermon in the cycle that has not been formed like this.

This author devotes much attention to the spiritual meaning of numbers in order to explain specific scriptural references. As I argued in the previous chapter, scriptural passages that contain specific numbers are attractive to sermonists who enjoy capitalizing on the spiritual and/or allegorical meanings of those numbers. For example, in a sermon for the Fourth Sunday in Lent that addresses the feeding of the multitude, the Longleat 4 author draws from the *Glossa Ordinaria* by equating the feeding the multitude with two fishes that signify the prophets and psalms.[29] In his Fifth Sunday after Trinity sermon, he equates the Gospel's two miraculous catches of fish with two time periods: before Christ's passion, when people were idolaters, and then after Christ's passion, when the saved are gathered in heaven.[30] When elaborating on the number five, the sermonist makes similar associations in several sermons, which suggests that once audiences or readers were introduced to this way of allegorizing they could then recognize the "numerical moves" the preacher might make. For instance, in the sermon for the Fourth Sunday in Lent, he relates how Christ fed five thousand people by multiplying five loaves that "signify Christ's five wounds and the five elements of repentance"— namely, "contrition, confession, almsgiving, prayer, and fasting."[31] However, in another sermon on the feeding of the five thousand, for the Twenty-Fifth Sunday after Trinity, the five loaves signify the five senses that are fulfilled by Christ: one's sight "by the sight of Christ," one's smell and taste "by the sweetness of his divinity," one's hearing "by the sound of his voice," and one's touch "by spiritually kissing and embracing Christ," all of which represent five joys.³² In contrast, the number five could also signify strikingly negative concepts, as in the sermon for the Second Sunday after Trinity, on the parable of the great supper, in which the three guests symbolize the sins of pride, covetousness, and lust. The second guest, who "was concerned with his five yoke of oxen," is interpreted by the sermonist as "signifying covetous people whose five senses are yoked to worldly affairs."³³ Just as one's five senses could lead to spiritual understanding and delight, one's five senses, when "yoked to worldly affairs," lead a person away from God.

In contrast to *Dives and Pauper*, in which the author largely limits his attention to number to the perfection of six and ten, in the Longleat 4 sermons the author ranges much further in the numbers he addresses, including references to two, four, five, seven, eight, nine, and twelve, all of which demonstrate great flexibility in their spiritual meanings. Take for example the number six. In his sermon on the Annunciation, the sermonist argues that on the sixth hour of the sixth day in March that Mary conceived;³⁴ his repeated sixes invoke the idea of perfection, as they also do in another sermon, for the Fifteenth Sunday after Trinity, in which he associates the six leaves on the lily with the six deeds of mercy.³⁵ Similarly, in his sermon on the Second Sunday after the Octave of Epiphany, in an explication of the wedding of Cana, the sermonist describes how Jesus changed six jars of water into wine. At the wedding of Cana, he writes, "the six jars signify six sacraments through which God turns grace into love. . . . The six jars also represent the six ages of the world." The "sinful souls" who are wedded to the devil need "six jars of water to cleanse them and inspire repentance."³⁶ In another sermon, echoing *Dives and Pauper*, he elaborates on the six days in which the world was made: humankind, he adds, was remade through six works of redemption.³⁷ Similarly to *Dives and Pauper*, he describes in his Palm Sunday sermon how Christ died on the sixth day to reform mankind, who was created on the sixth day; Christ was nailed on the cross "at the sixth hour," and Adam ate the apple "at the sixth hour." The sermonist then connects these important sixes to the significance of the number nine: "Christ died at the ninth hour," and "Adam was banished from paradise at the ninth hour."³⁸

However, in the Seventh Sunday after Trinity sermon, the sermonist uses the number six in a negative sense: "Spiritually all who reject sin come to Christ from far away. The sinner travels six days' journey from God: from disliking to consent to sin; from consent to action; from action to habitual sin; from habitual sin to addiction to sin; from addiction to sin to contempt for God; from contempt for God to despair which is the journey to hell."³⁹ The writer thus associates numbers with spiritual and/or allegorical meanings so frequently that we can assume his audience was deeply familiar with the practice. Any number repeated or emphasized could be allegorized positively or negatively. Even the number three, which has so many positive associations (such as the Trinity or the Holy Spirit's three forms of dove, cloud, and fire),[40] could be interpreted negatively, as in the sermon for the Third Sunday of Lent, in which he identifies the three devils that were cast out as lechery, covetousness, and pride, the root of all sin,[41] or the sermon for the Eighth Sunday after Trinity, in which he identifies three false prophets: "the devil, the world, and the flesh."[42] A similar contrast can be seen with the number ten: it can of course signify the Ten Commandments or even ten thousand talents; however, we can also see it being used negatively, as in the example of the ten lepers whom Christ healed, who signify "those who sin against the ten commandments."[43] Thus we see how versatile these comparisons can be to explain a wealth of scriptural references, as well as a way to enlighten audiences about both virtue and sin.

The sermon writer also models some basic addition and multiplication problems that demonstrate how a number can be divided into its spiritual parts. The practice of factoring allows for flexibility in how the numbers can be impressed in the service of theological discussion. For example, in his Quinquagesima sermon, he describes why Christ chose twelve apostles: Christ wanted men to preach the Trinity (representing the number three) in the four parts of the world.[44] In another sermon, on the First Sunday after the Octave of Epiphany, he employs the "three times four" formula again by identifying the twelve apostles as men "dependent on faith in the Trinity expanded in the four gospels."[45] The sermonist obviously enjoys the educative possibilities afforded by multiplication. The sermon on the Sexagesima, on the parable of the sower, presents the following example of spiritual factoring and arithmetic: "Married people produce thirtyfold fruit, that is, the ten commandments multiplied by the three goods of marriage (faith, children, and the sacrament of matrimony); widows produce sixtyfold fruit from the commandments and the six works of mercy; virgins produce a hundredfold fruit, ten multiplied by itself."[46] The ten times ten of virginity of course invokes the idea of the perfection of the number ten. Virgins produce perfection, as they produce the Ten Commandments times the Ten Commandments. Married people and widows can actually share in part of that perfection, as they produce the Ten Commandments times another tenet.

On one occasion in the Longleat 4 cycle, the sermonist's arithmetical example leads to an answer that is spiritually true, although not "accurate" in the practical sense. In his sermon for the Third Sunday after Trinity, he relates how Christ left his ninety-nine sheep to look for the one lost sheep: this, he factors, is "nine orders of angels keeping the ten commandments," which when multiplied is ninety and not ninety-nine.[47] In this case the concept of spiritual factoring is the important point, not the accuracy of the numbers when multiplied together. This, however, is the only example I have found in the cycle where the numbers do not "add up" correctly. For the sermonist, this spiritual factoring and subsequent multiplication become a kind of interpretive devotional act, when one adds and/or multiplies numbers to uncover the spiritual truths they reveal.

The sermon writer also models the practice of a different kind of numerological addition, that of assigning number values to letters, in order to explain the practice of fasting. For the First Sunday in Lent, he provides a sermon addressing the temptation of Christ by the devil. The writer ends the sermon with an explication of the meaning of the number forty-six, for he asserts that Christians engage in forty-six days of fasting in a year, which he explains to be made up of thirty-six days, six Sundays, and four days before Lent. Following a centuries-old numerological practice, he assigns numbers to the letters of the name Adam to explain why Christians fast forty-six days during the year: "In þis maner we fastyn xlvi dayys in tokene þat for þe synne of Adam we fellyn in nede and myschef of fastynge for synne. For þe name of Adam is euene xlvi, for in Gru and in Ebru alle letterys tokenyn certeyn numbris: A is i, d iiii, a i, m xl, and so þat name of Adam betokenyth xlvi, þat is þe numbre of þe dayys of our fastynge"[48] (In this manner we fast forty-six days in token that for the sin of Adam we fell in need and hardship of fasting for sin. For the name of Adam is an even forty-six, for in Greek and in Hebrew all the letters signify certain numbers: A is one, d is four, a is one, m is forty, and so the name of Adam betokens forty-six, which is the number of days of our fasting). The writer plays on the idea of factoring the number forty, arguing that its factors, when added, number fifty, which is "the age at which a man can take his inheritance; thus through fasting Christians may obtain their spiritual inheritance (heaven)."[49] The factors of forty do indeed add up to fifty (one, two, four, five, eight, ten, and twenty), and in asserting that they add up to fifty no doubt provoked at least some of the members of the reading or listening audience to make certain. By connecting this arithmetical problem with religious fasting, the sermonist demonstrates how the factors of forty, when added, surpass their original number, just as achieving one's spiritual inheritance surpasses one's earthly inheritance; the sum is more than its individual parts.

Longleat 4's sermons draw quite heavily on basic number theory to describe both God's creation and how the liturgical cycle functions. As we saw in *Dives and Pauper*, the author incorporates the idea of the perfect number six and its factors; in the sermon cycle, however, he chooses to elaborate on another popular idea from number theory, that of the circularity of the number five. His sermon for the Twenty-Fifth Sunday after Trinity features this popular idea of five's circularity. In his discussion on the feeding of the five thousand with five loaves, the sermonist expounds on the value of five by combining both number theory and the numerological significance of the number five. He uses five's circularity to support the idea of the coming of Christ and the never-ending liturgical cycle. "Christ came after five ages and five thousand years to save humankind.... It is right that the church should mention Christ's coming on the last Sunday of the year since the liturgical year is circular, as is the number five which multiplied by itself gives twenty-five and this is the twenty-fifth Sunday."[50] The sermonist seems to assume that the audience was familiar with the properties of the number five as well as its numerological significance. He then connects this understanding with the circular quality of the liturgical calendar, reminding his audience of all the significant fives there are to support this celebration: the five ages, the five thousand years, the five thousand people fed by Christ, the twenty-fifth Sunday, and so on. The audience may have understood these connections immediately if they were familiar with the idea of five and its circularity, or they may have been surprised by the way the sermon weaves these topics together. Either way, the lesson would not have been easily forgotten, as a reader or listener looking at his or her hand would have been reminded of the properties of the number five with their fingers, which, when closed, make a circle.

This particular sermon is drawn to a close by the sermonist with a gesture toward infinity. In heaven, he writes, there is "endless satisfaction" in the compounding of fives: "This is þe ende þat we schulden alle sekin: to comyn to þe kyngdam and to þe blisse þat hath non ende and to ben fed and fild in oure fyue wittis wiþ þese fyue blissis, tokenyd be þe fyue louys wiþ whiche Crist fedde fyue þousand of men"[51] (This is the end that we should all seek: to come to the kingdom and to the bliss that has no end and to be fed and filled in our five wits with these five blisses, betokened by the five loaves with which Christ fed five thousand men). Thus, all the number fives have a purpose and are intimately connected; the number serves as a way to connect various parts of Scripture for audiences. In contrast to the joke by Bracciolini that began chapter 1 of this study (how a priest doubted his audience would believe in the miracle of five hundred loaves, let alone five thousand), this sermonist is speaking to an audience who he expects will appreciate all the numerical and spiritual resonances of this scriptural passage.

This idea of five's circularity is an aspect of number theory that derives from Boethius's *Arithmetica*. Boethius explains in his chapter "Concerning circular or spherical numbers" that the number five is circular because of its particular multiplication properties, which are comparable to a circle:

> When the numbers of cubes are so extended that from any number of cubic quantity a side begins, and the extremity is terminated at the same point of height, then that number is called cyclical or spherical. Such are the multiplications, which begin from five or from six. Five times five, which make 25, having progressed from 5, ends at the same 5. If you extend this five out again, its terminus will again come to 5. Five times 25 makes 125 and if you bring this number to five times more, it will be terminated in a five number. And this will always happen the same way, all the way to infinity.
>
> These numbers are called cyclical or spherical because spheres and circles are always formed by a turning about of their own principal number. A circle is a figure which, with one point put down, and another placed at a distance from it, that placed at a distance is brought around, all along with an equal space from the middle point constantly maintained so that it ends at the same point again from which it began to move.[52]

Similarly, albeit more concisely, John Trevisa defines circularity of number by emphasizing the squaring and cubing of five: "Þe numbre *spericus* and *circularis* comeþ of a nombre þat is multiplyed by itsilf and efte by þe nombre þat comeþ þerof, and torneþ into itself in a cercle wise and makeþ a spere al rounde, as fyue siþes fyue, fyue siþes"[53] (The spherical and circular number comes of a number that is multiplied by itself and also from the number that comes thereof and turns in to itself in a circle and makes a sphere all round, as five times five, times five). For both Boethius and Trevisa, therefore, the circular number has the particular quality of always returning to and signaling itself. God himself is frequently described in medieval texts as circular; he contains all within him, and nothing exists outside him. He is never-ending and infinite, just as a circle. How better for a sermonist to encourage his audience to picture infinity than to have them imagine a circle and to play with multiples of the number five?

Medieval English writers enjoyed capitalizing on the idea of five as circular, as it proved to be a vivid image to express the notion of infinity. This concept is directly invoked in a late fourteenth-century or early fifteenth-century Wycliffite sermon in British Library, MS Additional 40672, intended for a "common of a Virgin not a Martyr." The sermon addresses the parable of the wise and foolish virgins and relies on the idea of five's circularity to indicate priests and other religious experiencing a never-ending state of bliss in heaven as well as those experiencing the never-ending damnation of hell:

> Crist seiþ þus atte bygynnyng: *Þe rewme of heuene is lyʒk to ten virginus... but fyue of hem were foolus, and fyue of hem were warre.* ... Þis reume of heuene is þis chyrche; þes ten virgynes ben þo þat ben spiritual, as ben preestus and religious and mony oþre in þe chyrche.... But þes ten virgynes ben partid in two, in fyue foolis and fyue wyse.... And boþe þes partus ben in fyue, for þe wyse schal ben in heuene euere in a sercle of blisse, as fyue ys noumbre in a sercle, and þe toþur fyue foolus schal be dampnyde in helle wiþowton ende; and as a sercle haþ noon ende, so schal not peyne of þese ypocrites.[54]

> Christ said thus at the beginning: *The realm of heaven is like ten virgins... but five of them were fools, and five of them were wise.* ... This realm of heaven is this church; the ten virgins are those who are spiritual, as are priests and religious and many others in the church.... But these ten virgins are divided into two, into five foolish and five wise.... And both these parts are in five, for the wise shall be in heaven ever in a circle of bliss, as five is the number in a circle, and the other five fools shall be damned in hell without end; and as the circle has no end, so shall the pain of these hypocrites be endless.

In this example, the five wise virgins indicate those people in the circular—that is, endless—bliss of heaven, while the five foolish virgins represent those in the never-ending damnation of hell. The never-ending circular five is well known to medievalists from the late fourteenth-century *Sir Gawain and the Green Knight*'s "endless knot" or pentangle that appears on the front of his shield.[55] As Geraldine Heng has argued, "Never requiring to be tied, untied, or retied," the pentangle is "the sign for Gawain and his perfect knighthood."[56] Thus, the pentangle in this case functions in a circular manner suggesting both incorruptibility and infinity.

Whereas the Wycliffite sermon in British Library, MS Additional 40672, on the ten foolish and wise maidens associated the number five with those experiencing the endless bliss of heaven and endless damnation, Longleat 4 extends the allegory of never-ending bliss to also include the five "wits" or senses that are fed with five blessings or "blisses," which are betokened by the five loaves. The number five could therefore be useful for a variety of allegorical readings that serve as models for how to reach heaven as well as how to avoid hell.

As mentioned at the close of chapter 1, many sermonists use the occasion of the feeding of the multitude to introduce a discussion of number. Longleat 4's sermonist also takes advantage of this occasion to do the same. However, he takes it one step further. A sermon in this cycle that addresses the feeding of the multitude, intended for the Seventh Sunday after Trinity, draws on number theory and its interest in the stability and instability of numbers four and five, as well as the "roundness" or circularity of five, in order to assert the priority of the new law given in the New Testament: "There were two miraculous feedings, of five and four thousand people, signifying the old and new law.... Under the old law the people lived by their five senses; under the new, Christians are governed by the four cardinal virtues. Four is a stable number while five is an unstable 'round' number (multiplied by itself it always ends in five)."[57] Here, the text relies on the numerological understanding of five as the five senses and four as the four cardinal virtues. But then the sermonist contemplates the specific properties of the numbers four and five, by stating that four is stable and five is an unstable round number that multiplied by itself always ends in five. The introduction here of "stable" and "unstable" numbers is derived from Boethius, who in turn based his text on Pythagoras's association of the cube with earth, as it was stable and immobile.[58] According to Trevisa, the number four is a square and therefore stable;[59] this stableness betokens the stability of the church as founded by Christ in the New Testament, whereas the Old Testament relies on the five senses, which are linked with instability, and here, circularity. Thus, in one sermon, the number five can represent Christ and the liturgical cycle; in another, the relative instability of the Old Testament when compared with the New. In the Seventh Sunday after Trinity sermon, (in)stability is equated with gender and age, for the sermonist argues that "women and children were not included in the figure of four thousand; by nature they are unstable and weak, although through grace they are often more stable than men."[60] The writer suggests that number theory can reveal a fundamental truth about the nature of men and women, although grace of course can override or "correct" nature.

The idea of "stability," as it refers to several numbers and their squares, is an important concept in number theory.[61] Sermons elaborate on other spiritually significant numbers and their properties in order to explain to audiences significant moments in Christ's life and the life of the church and its members, as well as the mystery of the Trinity. For example, a sermon on the circumcision of Christ also found in Longleat 4 explains why the circumcision took place on the eighth day. In addition to describing how Christ's circumcision signifies "the final circumcision from sin in the eighth age at the last judgment," the sermon writer refers to the number eight as a 'sad square numbre . . . for it is twyys twyys two' and it is equal in height, width, and depth, thus it signifies faith in the Trinity and the equity of righteousness."[62] Eight, therefore, is a cube (two times two times two) that invokes the duo of faith and equity. "Sad" in this sense means "fixed" or "rigid," or firm and steadfast, unyielding; thus eight is stable in the numerological sense as well.[63] Many baptismal fonts in medieval parish churches were octagonal in shape; these fonts offered a physical representation to parishioners of the number two cubed.

This focus on the square and cube of ten as perfect may also have led medieval authors to connect ten and its square with the idea of round or circular numbers, which often indicate perfection through never-ending bliss. The mid-fourteenth-century *Ayenbite of Inwit* (The Prick of Conscience) declares that one hundred is a round number, the fairest of all: "Ac þe tale of an hondred . . . betokneþ ane rounde figure. Þet is þe uayreste amang alle þe oþre figures" (The tally of one hundred betokens a round figure; it is the fairest among all the other figures). This description occurs in the midst of exploring the fruits of the virginity, in which the author likens the virgin's hundred fruits to "þe coroune þet þe wyse maydynes : ham corounede" (the crown that the wise maidens wore), for just "ase ine þe rounde figure : þe ende went ayen to his ginninge / and makeþ ase an coroune : alzuo þe tale of an hondred : ioyneþ þan ende to þe ginning. uor tenziþe ten : makeþ an hondred"[64] (as in the round figure the end turn again to its beginning and makes itself a crown; also the tally of one hundred joins the end to the beginning, for ten times ten makes one hundred). The never-ending circle of the crown suggests images of the unbroken circle, or the *hortus conclusus*, of the Virgin Mary. This idea of circularity, which we also saw in our discussion of number five, is of critical importance—it signifies the unbreakable, never-ending kingdom of God.

Longleat 4 also incorporates another element of number theory to describe God's plentitude when it refers to the number twelve as a superabundant number. Boethius's *Arithmetica*, as well as other texts, describe superabundant numbers, or those numbers whose factors add up to more than the number itself. An example of a superabundant number would be twenty-four, since we can add its factors (one, two, three, four, six, eight, and twelve), which at the sum of thirty-six are greater than the original number; Boethius sees the "superfluous" or superabundant number as an example of "immoderate plentitude."⁶⁵ In contrast, as we saw earlier, the Longleat writer points out that the factors of forty actually add up to fifty, making it a remarkable number because one fasts for forty days in Lent, and one is rewarded with the spiritual inheritance of heaven; one gains so much more than what one puts into the fasting. The number eight, however, would be considered "deficient" because its factors add up to less than eight (one plus two plus four equals seven). This thinking of numbers as superabundant or deficient proved to be quite influential for medieval writers. For example, in the late eighth century, Alcuin of York wrote that the second creation stemming from Noah and his family in the ark was deficient, because they were eight in total (namely Noah, his wife, three sons, and their three wives).⁶⁶

The Longleat author takes the occasion in a sermon to discuss the number twelve as a superabundant number. In the sermon for the Twenty-Fourth Sunday after Trinity, which describes the healing of a woman with a hemorrhage, he asserts, "The woman had suffered for twelve years, signifying that this is the age at which men and woman are first tempted by lust, and, as a 'plenteous number,' that people are tempted by riches and plenty."⁶⁷ Of course, "plenteous" could mean simply "copious" or "a great number," but given the familiarity of the sermon author of the Longleat cycle with number theory, "plenteous" here can likely be translated as "superabundant."⁶⁸ Twelve, elsewhere such a positive signifier of the apostles, is here used to represent the excesses of sin; sins not only add up to reach a particular number (here, twelve), they compound to exceed that number with sixteen or $1 + 2 + 3 + 4 + 6$.

The tenth-century Latin play *Sapientia* by the German playwright Hrotsvit of Gandersheim demonstrates how the concepts of superabundancy or deficiency could be incorporated in a both entertaining and fruitful manner to explore the idea of God's measure. In the play, Sapientia and her three daughters (Fides, Spes, and Karitas) arrive in Rome as missionaries. Emperor Hadrian attempts to test their faith by questioning and torturing them, to no avail.⁶⁹ When Hadrian asks how old Sapientia's three daughters are, Sapientia takes the opportunity to introduce some Boethian number theory by asking her daughters, "Would it please you, children, if I fatigued this fool / with a lesson in arithmetical rule?" She then offers up a riddle of the ages of her children: "O Emperor, you wish to know my children's ages; Karitas has completed a diminished, evenly even number of years; / Spes, on the other hand, a diminished evenly uneven number; and Karitas [*sic*] an augmented unevenly even number of year." Hadrian of course is flummoxed, stating, "Your reply leaves me totally ignorant as to the answer to my question," which results in Sapientia defining the mathematical terms for him.[70] After a lengthy lesson on numbers and number theory (including perfect, diminished, and augmented numbers, as well as denominators and quotients), Sapientia praises God for Wisdom verse 11:20 (that God ordered everything according to number, measure, and weight) before Hadrian remarks that he has listened to her lecture long enough and she must pray to his gods or be tortured.[71] As Sandro Sticca observes, this scene of Sapientia explaining number theory to the emperor is meant to show the "ludicrous ignorance of the persecutors," which is set against "the subtle and refined knowledge of the Christian martyrs."[72] For this statement to be true, we would need to assume that the Latin reading and/or speaking audience was comfortably familiar with number theory, so much so that they would find Hadrian's ignorance "ludicrous" and not personally familiar.

As Sapientia describes, her eldest daughter is twelve years old; the number twelve, she states (following Boethius), is superabundant or "augmented," for its factors add up to greater than itself (one, two, three, four, and six when added yield sixteen). The number twelve is perhaps the most popular example of a superabundant number in vernacular literary discussions. Twelve is also numerologically significant, as it suggests the twelve apostles, the twelve tribes of Israel, and so forth. Numerological references to twelve are quite commonplace in sermons; for example, as the sermon on the First Sunday after the Octave of Epiphany in Longleat 4 describes, Christ "began teaching at the age of twelve signifying that there are twelve articles of faith, preached by the twelve apostles."[73] Moreover, in the sermon on the Quinquagesima, or the Sunday before the beginning of Lent, which is mentioned earlier in this chapter, the sermon writer comments on Luke 18:31–43, verses in which Christ prophesies and then heals a blind man. As the writer describes, Christ "chose twelve (four times three) disciples so that they might preach the faith of the Trinity to the four parts of the world, and replace the twelve patriarchs of the old law. The gospel can be divided into three parts: a prophecy of Christ's passion, a miracle, and a thanksgiving."[74] In this sense twelve is useful because two of its factors, four and three, could be allegorized a number of ways.

What is so useful about twelve apostles is that the number twelve can be divided in multiple ways. This is seen in the fifteenth-century *York Play of Pentecost*, which asks audiences to consider how factoring led the apostles to more fruitful proselytizing. The play, likely produced by the Potters yearly in York, opens with a discussion of the prime number eleven, which is not divisible by any other number other than one and itself, and the superabundant number twelve, which is the preferred number of apostles because they can be broken into smaller groups of two, three, four, or six.⁷⁵ After the death of Judas Iscariot, the apostles only number eleven. Peter argues that they need to be twelve for the sake of easy division into smaller groups. Peter opens the play with a call to the apostles to find a twelfth member, which he elaborates in twelve lines of verse:

> Brethir, takes tente unto my steven,
> Thanne schall ye stabily undirstande
> Oure maistir hende is hente to hevyn
> To reste there on his Fadirs right hande.
> And we are leved alyve, ellevyn,
> To lere his lawes lely in lande.
> Or we begynne us muste be even
> Ellis are owre werkis noght to warande.
> For parfite noumbre it is none,
> Off elleven for to lere,
> Twelve may be asoundir tone
> And settis in parties seere.⁷⁶

> Brothers, pay attention to my speech,
> Then you shall understand me firmly
> Our gracious master is carried to heaven
> To rest there at his Father's right hand.
> And we are left alone, eleven,
> To teach his laws faithfully in the lands.
> Before we begin we must be even
> Or else our works won't matter.
> For perfect number it is none,
> In eleven to teach,
> Twelve may be taken apart
> And set in several parts.

Peter here laments that he and his fellow apostles number eleven with the loss of Judas. As Augustine states in *The City of God*, "numerus undenarius... transgressionem legis ac per hoc peccatum significat" (the number eleven stands for trespassing against the law and consequently for sin). He explains in his *Tractates on John* that "'Judas did not damage the number twelve' by his betrayal, for the apostles were not allowed to remain at eleven."[77] Furthermore, the editor of the TEAMS edition, Clifford Davidson, comments that "as a prime number, eleven has no divisible parts. Twelve, on the other hand, would enable the disciples to go out two by two, as Jesus suggested (see Mark 6:7), or by threes, fours, or even sixes, that is, 'settis in parties seere.'"[78] Peter declares, "We are left alive eleven" (And we are leved alyve, ellevyn) and then advises that they need instead to be an even number so that they can divide into smaller, even groups to fulfill their preaching missions; a prime number, which would have to be divided into uneven groups such as five and six, or four and seven, just would not do.

This biblical cycle play draws on the idea of eleven as a prime and undesirable number, for it cannot be divided into smaller, even parts. Prime numbers are an extremely important element of medieval number theory. As Boethius defines it, "The prime and incomposite number is that which has no other factor but that one which is a denominator for the total quantity of that number so its fraction is nothing other than unity, and such are 3, 5, 7, 11, 13, 17, 19, 23, 29, 31. In these numbers, there is only one factor found, and each is a denominator of itself and that only once." Boethius concludes this statement with the assertion that only the "mother of all numbers," or "unity," can be a factor of those prime numbers.[79]

The *York Play of Pentecost* also invokes the idea of a "perfect number" to demonstrate how deficient and unstable their numbering eleven is. Peter states that "parfite noumbre it is none" (line 9), thereby asserting that eleven is not ten (a perfect number, as defined by many medieval texts) or twelve.[80] In the twelfth century, Hugh of St. Victor notes in his *Exegetica de scripturis et scriptoribus sacris* that the number eleven "denotes transgression outside of measure";[81] the fourteenth-century poem *Piers Plowman* also seems to incorporate this understanding when it is noted that when something occurs "out of measure," it occurs eleven times.[82] The number eleven has even been referred to as "the most monstrous of all numbers" to medieval people.[83] Moreover, Peter in the *Play of Pentecost* invokes the idea of "stability" described in number theory by promising to the other apostles, "Thanne schall ye stabily undirstande" (line 2) the situation if they comprehend what he has to say. "Stabily" in this context suggests "faithfully" and "resolutely," as well as suggests the sense of "stable" number.[84] Thus, when the apostles form the stable number twelve (that is, four times three), the followers of Christ will also understand and perform their mission more steadfastly.

The opening lines of the *York Play of Pentecost* demonstrates that these discussions were not just happening in late medieval sermons, but also in other popular religious texts and performances. One could even suggest that the discourse about numbers occurring in sermons influenced other literary genres, or at least that sermons and other religious texts shared the same impulse—to show how useful both theologically and spiritually it was that numbers like twelve could be divided in so many ways. After all, this is a culture that uses the shilling as its currency; as the shilling is worth twelve pennies, its division can yield all sorts of units that can be added up to reach a shilling, as we see in later (i.e., postmedieval) centuries with the tuppence and thruppence. The Longleat 4 author is not concerned with how pennies add up, but he does take advantage of his audience's knowledge to demonstrate how the apostles can be the Trinity times the Gospels, or the four corners of the world times the Trinity. As the author defines, twelve is the age that Christ first started teaching; twelve therefore signifies the spreading of Christ's word and his ministry in the world. Once again, we see how the sermonist puts the practical understanding of number in the context of religion. How does an audience imagine Christ's ministry spreading in the world? They can imagine the number twelve. When they see something that numbers twelve, what are they to imagine? Christ's ministry spreading in the world.

Discussions of number and mathematical operations appear and are performed for audiences in a variety of religious texts. The Longleat 4 sermonist is not doing anything new in this sense, but what is remarkable is his repeated and sustained treatment of number. Time and time again he returns to the topic of number, numerology, number theory, and arithmetic to express his core message: look to numbers as a way to pattern a Christian's life in God. In a particularly brilliant sermon for the Ninth Sunday after Trinity, the author introduces certain measurements that appear in the Bible. During his explication and analysis of the parable of the unjust bailiff from Luke 16:1–9, he advises his audience, "It is difficult to know what measure of oil and wheat the bailiff remitted since measures are different in different countries. God leaves the measure of forgiveness to the discretion of his confessors who must take into account the contrition shown, the strength of the individual sinner, and his or her status."[85] Here we note that instability of measure becomes a positive model for the sinner, whose forgiveness by God is measured in different amounts. The sermonist insists that just as concrete, actual measures differ from culture to culture, so too does the measure of God's forgiveness differ, depending on the circumstances of the confession. Whereas usually the idea of different measures (and the instability expressed therein) in other texts can indicate the challenge of inconsistency (for example, in descriptions of currency in pilgrimage manuals), in this sermon the preacher reverses this idea to demonstrate how different measures actually represent forgiveness. This appeal to measure provides a very concrete, practical way for audiences to understand God's forgiveness. The audiences' practical numeracy, therefore, can be put to good use to help them understand a more abstract spiritual concept.

As I have argued in this section, Longleat 4 includes enumeration, numerology, number theory, and arithmetic to help audiences visualize spiritual truths and explain abstract concepts such as virtue, the perfection of God, and the infinite nature of heaven, as well as negative concepts such as the depth of sin and the infinite nature of hell's punishments. Both *Dives and Pauper* and Longleat 4, whether reformist texts or orthodox, trust in their audiences to comprehend and appreciate the discussions of number. Both texts teach audiences to interpret numbers symbolically as well as practically. *Dives and Pauper* may suggest the higher perfect numbers are out of the reach of clerks, but in Longleat 4 nothing seems to be out of the reach of the audience; the sermons argue that God's truth is completely understandable and approachable and that God is within their reach, if they just interpret number in the correct manner. Even the instability of measure across countries, times, and cultures becomes a positive model—one can "increase" one's measure with more contrition.

A fundamental concept of numeracy is that numerate practices differ from culture to culture. This chapter has demonstrated how an early fifteenth-century sermon cycle encourages a particular kind of numerate practice, one that combines a practical understanding of numbers with a spiritual understanding, and one that also is quite flexible in the associations it promotes between religious knowledge and numerical reflection. According to the anonymous author of *Dives and Pauper* and the sermon cycle in Longleat 4, number and mathematical operations offer easy access to scriptural, theological, and spiritual meaning. Only the higher perfect numbers remain outside clerics' grasp, but even then, we are told those numbers exist and, no matter how high the number, point to God's perfection in the same way that the numbers six and twenty-eight do. In the next chapter, however, we shall encounter a sermon cycle that challenges this sense of fathomability of the divine through mathematical operations, as we explore a sermon cycle that relies on and extols number as a way to approach the divine while at the same time resisting quantification of the divine.

CHAPTER 3

"Knowing Thyself" and God Through Number in *Jacob's Well*

The previous two chapters have focused on how sermon writers rely on their audiences' practical understanding of number and mathematical operations—that is, their practical numeracy—in order to make abstract religious and spiritual concepts concrete. Sermonists do this by yoking their audiences' practical sense of numeracy with spiritual understandings of number, thereby encouraging in their audiences a kind of hybrid numerate practice for contemplating the divine in the world and humankind's relation to the divine. Thus far we have seen examples of how number confidently represents the divine. In this chapter, however, we shall see how a sermonist uses number to demonstrate that although much of how a Christian is supposed to conduct themselves is best represented through number, sin itself is difficult to quantify. Furthermore, God himself resists quantification and is ultimately unfathomable.

The focus of this chapter, an extended sermon cycle found in the mid-fifteenth-century manuscript Salisbury Cathedral Library MS 103, otherwise known as *Jacob's Well*, is startlingly rich in numerate practices, as its ninety-plus sermons offer a sustained engagement with number and mathematical operations throughout.[1] The sermons invoke the practices we have seen in the first two chapters of this book—discussions of number theory, numerology, arithmetic, and measure (here combined with geometry) to invite audiences to consider the benefits that a spiritually infused numeracy can provide. At its most basic level, *Jacob's Well* models math to explain both godly virtue and humankind's sin. First, *Jacob's Well* serves as an instruction manual offering practical arithmetical models about how to calculate tithes properly so that the audience does not cheat God and the church. Second, it offers instruction in how numerologically infused arithmetic can be an active form of spiritual devotion. Third, the cycle uses the idea of measurement and mismeasurement to model one's proper behavior in the eyes of God. And fourth, the sermon writer employs geometry as a way to encourage his audience to visualize sin and virtue, and particularly to appreciate sins' horrors and virtues' benefits.

Jacob's Well negotiates the tension between the practicality of number and its spiritual uses. It exploits audiences' understanding of practical measurement of lengths, distances, and weights by describing the depth of the body and conscience's *wose* (the "ooze" of sin), which must be purged to reach the "living waters" and a "pure well" of virtue. With its foregrounding of measurements, *Jacob's Well* encourages its audience to add up the various lengths, widths, and depths to plumb fully the depth of their sin. At the same time, however, the cycle resists easy quantification and repeatedly asserts that spiritual calculation does not necessarily operate within our received notions of practical accuracy. This tension between calculability and incalculability creates room for audiences to engage directly with the arithmetical and spiritual practices and concepts; this direct engagement encourages audiences to discover the behaviors, beliefs, and attitudes that are most pleasing to God.

Scholarship on *Jacob's Well* has explored how the text focuses on trying to teach the audience to "know thyself." Leo Carruthers's essay "Know Thyself: Criticism, Reform, and Audience in *Jacob's Well*" attempts to define the audience of the text and argues for a mixed audience of clerics and laity.[2] Moira Fitzgibbons's "*Jacob's Well* and Penitential Pedagogy" responds to Carruthers's earlier essay in a brilliant examination of how the sermon cycle author educates his audience. Imagining his audience as students, he encourages them to "know themselves" through discussions of the articles of the faith, the deadly sins, the seven gifts of the Holy Spirit, and so on. The *Well* writer continues a tradition of interpreting the gift of knowledge as a gift of self-knowledge, or the gift of understanding the role of Christian knowledge in one's life; as the *Well* writer states, at the ascension Christ gave everyone "his ȝyfte of kunnynge for to knowe þe-self to gouerne þe in vertuys"[3] (his gift of knowledge to know yourself in order to govern yourself in the virtues). Fitzgibbons explains, "the Christian knowledge set forth by the *Well* writer ideally will facilitate conversation, remonstrance, and genuine contrition within his community." Fitzgibbons points to an important tension in the sermons: on the one hand, the sermonist presents a "disparagement of academic learning," and on the other hand, "his own sermons expose the laity to the learning and rhetoric of the friars."⁴ Despite this tension of "value[ing] submissiveness over academic training," the *Well* writer "remains open to intellectual and pedagogical activity on the part of lay people themselves," or what Fitzgibbons terms "lay inquiry."⁵

In sum, Fitzgibbons argues the *Well* writer trusts his lay audience to be involved in sophisticated decision-making in their education as they learn to "know themselves," and offers a twofold approach to formal knowledge—the sermons both question the value of formal education and also uphold it. My argument in this chapter picks up on Fitzgibbons's focus on "knowing thyself" by examining how the sermons' treatment of number, numerology, arithmetic, measure, and geometry contribute to the audience's religious education. I argue that the author sees mathematically enriched discussions as a useful way for audiences to learn to "know themselves" and to understand better what God expects from them. Ultimately, numbers and numerate acts allow the audience to approach God more closely, because numbers and numerate acts propel the readers and listeners to become more obedient and virtuous.

OVERVIEW OF *JACOB'S WELL*

Jacob's Well is an extended allegory made up of ninety-five sermons based on the biblical story of the Samaritan woman and Jesus at the well, and the cycle was probably designed to stretch from Ash Wednesday to Pentecost.⁶ In the Gospel of John, Jesus asks the woman to draw him some water and then tells her of the "living water" of God.⁷ In *Jacob's Well*, the sermonist describes how the audience must dig through an enormous pit of ooze that represents the sinful body and conscience, which must be cleansed to become the "fit receptacle of the limpid water of Grace."⁸ First, the audience must remove the "þe dedly watyr of curse" (the deadly water of the curse) that has entered the body by the five senses. Then the readers and listeners must cast out the water with the pickax, spade, and shovel of confession. Once the water has been removed "with a scope of penaunce" (with the scoop of penance), the audience must dig out the seven deadly sins "in whiche þe soule styketh" (in which the soul sticks). With the spade of "clennesse" (cleanness) they must cast out the gravel bed of sin and dig into the ground of virtue, which has seven springs of water representing the seven gifts of the Holy Spirit (ed. Brandeis 2). They must line their well with stones and lime, which represent their works of faith. The audience is also instructed to build a ladder of charity that will lead them to heaven after their death. The author suggests this process will take ninety-four days, or the length of the rest of the sermon cycle, to prepare the well completely. In the cycle, the sermonist breaks down his subjects using an allegory of measurement—of depths, breadths, and widths—as a way to divide and organize his discussion. Whether speaking of the five floodgates of the senses or the specific breadth and depth of lust, the sermons invite audiences to consider the spiritual significance of the numbers incorporated therein.

Scholars have debated the nature of the sermon cycle's audience. In her study *English Preaching in the Late Middle Ages*, H. Leith Spencer suggested that the sermons were more likely intended for private reading than public performance.[9] However, Carruthers presents a convincing argument that the sermons were intended to be delivered orally and thereby designed to reach a sizable parish audience. According to Carruthers, the cycle likely attracted a mixed lay audience from the Suffolk area near Bury St. Edmunds and Ipswich, one full of merchants and tradespeople, as references to the parish, to monastics, and to lay men and women can be found throughout the sermons.[10] This suggests listeners who were highly accustomed to performing calculations for trade and industry. In his essay "The Audience of *Jacob's Well*: Problems of Interpretation," Atchley both reconsiders Carruthers' linguistic data and posits a slightly different audience "consisting mostly of farmers and lower-class inhabitants," a "rowdy bunch" whom the preacher "took his responsibility to educate . . . quite seriously."[11] More recently, Fitzgibbons has argued that it is not known if the sermon cycle was ever delivered, for the manuscript is not the author's autograph copy, although she does support Atchley's argument that the cycle was written for a "socially mixed group of listeners."[12] Fitzgibbons suggests that the sermons continued their work long after the audience had left the church, for she sees the parish "as a space of spiritual and intellectual exchange" in which "active individual consciences must search for truth both within and outside the church's walls."[13] I argue that discussions of number and numerate acts in the sermons become a way for the audience to search for that truth. For listeners and/or readers, therefore, these sermons functioned either as a kind of educative tool that taught numbers and arithmetical concepts or, more likely, as an invitation to practice numerate skills that the audience had already acquired, in combination with numerological associations, so that the audience could apply these lessons and skills to moral living, spiritual practices, and devotion in general.

PART 1: "KNOWING THYSELF" THROUGH NUMBER—BETTER LIVING THROUGH PRACTICAL MATH

Jacob's Well introduces into its early sermons a detailed treatment of tithing practices, with particular focus on how one should calculate a tithe properly. The first step of "living well" and knowing thyself is to give to God and the church what is due. In elaborating on this, the sermons cover poor tithing practices as well as "evil tithers"—those who cheat and those who try to hide their inadequate tithing (ed. Brandeis 44). Number and calculation offer a clear path to being a good tither and to avoid being like Judas, who is called out in the text as *the* most egregious example of bad tithing.

The third sermon of *Jacob's Well* offers an extended discourse on tithing that relies on arithmetic. Amid an exploration of good and bad tithing practices, the author models an example of proper tithing, one in which a farmer does not deduct his expenses from his yield before offering this tenth. The sermonist then introduces the example of Judas and his problematic tithing practice, therefore forging a connection between those tithers who are simply poor at calculation and those who purposefully cheat God and the church. First the author begins with a word problem that invites the audience to reckon the tithe along with the preacher:

> ȝif þou hyre an acre of lond for ij. s, and þe tylying þer-of stondyth þe on ij. s., þe seed stondeyth þe on ij. s, þe rente stante þe on vj. d, þe gaderyng & þe repyng standyth þe on xij. d, þou schalt paye þe tythe schef of þat growyth þer-on, or þe tythe part ȝif it be pesyn, or hey, þowȝ all þat growyth þer-on be noȝt worth vj. d. And þou schalt rekene no cost ne expunse. (ed. Brandeis 38)

> If you hire an acre of land for two shillings, and the tilling costs you two shillings, the seed costs two shillings, the rent costs you six pence, the gathering and reaping cost you twelve pence, you shall pay the tithe sheaf on the growth, or the tithe part if it be peas or hay, although all that grows there is not worth six pence. And you shall not reckon any cost or expense.[14]

This example invites the audience to calculate all the costs: six shillings (for rent, tilling, and seed) plus eighteen pence (for the gathering plus reaping), at twelve pence per shilling, equals six times twelve plus eighteen, or ninety shillings. One must pay a tenth part, even if the growth is not worth half a shilling. That the sermon writer walks his audience through a specific example of calculating a tithe suggests one of two things: either he suspected that his audience was not tithing correctly and needed an arithmetical model to instruct them (i.e., he thought of himself as teaching a new skill or refining and reinforcing a previously acquired skill), or he imagined his audience would pay close attention to the hands-on tithing calculation and understand it fully, while reinforcing the point that tithers cannot deduct any expenses. In either scenario, by working through the problem together with his audience, the preacher can highlight the moments where a tither might go astray. He captures his audience's attention with the arithmetic problem and encourages them to calculate with him and participate in a model of good tithing practice.

The sermonist is especially concerned with how to model the reckoning of a proper tithe when faced with different numerical challenges. An important problem that *Jacob's Well* addresses is what happens when a would-be tither does not have ten of an object from which to tithe. The writer offers examples to be worked through with the solution of "rounding up" to the nearest ten. For instance, he describes, if one only has seven sheep or fleeces, one must round up to ten and give one: "And 3if þere be but vij. lambys, or vij. flees, or aboue, þanne owyth j. flees or j. lambe to be payed to tythe" (ed. Brandeis 39) (And if there be but seven lambs, or seven fleeces, or more, then you owe one fleece or one lamb to be paid for the tithe). The sermonist also warns earlier that one must not give the eleventh sheaf for tithing, but rather the tenth, as the tithing ratio means one out of ten (1:10) rather than one out of ten plus one (1:11).[15] Throughout this section, the preacher anticipates the many ways his community might err through improper tithing; only repeated examples and modeling of correct calculations will keep them on the right track. Moreover, he makes it very clear that farmers must not deduct any expenses before tithing, which would serve to decrease their offering. Merchants and tradesmen, however, may deduct "resonable costys" (ed. Brandeis 40–41) (reasonable costs or expenses),[16] and I imagine that the conversation about what "fair portion" meant would have continued long after the sermon had ended.

During his discussion of tithing, the sermonist turns to the story of Judas as a way to explain how understanding proper and improper tithing calculations can help audiences to appreciate particular biblical passages more fully, as well as to learn how not to harm Christ. First, the sermonist begins with the Bible and uses examples of improper tithing as a clear way to explain the link between two events from the Gospels: Judas's protest that Mary Magdalen anointed Christ with oil that could have been sold instead, and Judas's betrayal of Christ for thirty pennies. The sermon discusses how Judas believed the oil Mary used could have sold for three hundred pence: "it my3t a be solde for iij. hundred pens, & haue be 3ouyn to pore folk" (ed. Brandeis 43) (It may have been sold for 300 pence and have been given to poor people).[17] The *Well* writer argues that Judas as "purse-master" wanted to steal the tithe of the three hundred pence, which would have been equal to thirty pence: "Judas was wo, þat he had no3t þat vauntage of þo xxx. pens þat was þe tythe of þe iij. hundreth pens, be-cause þe oynement was no3t solde" (ed. Brandeis 43) (Judas was full of woe that he had not the benefit of thirty pence, which was the tithe of three hundred pence, because the ointment was not sold). Not being able to steal his thirty pence, Judas later sells Christ for thirty pence to recover his lost tithe: "þer-fore he thou3te to rekouere þo xxx. pens, & he wente & solde crist for xxx. pens" (ed. Brandeis 44) (Therefore he thought to recover the thirty pence and went and sold Christ for thirty pence). Identifying Judas as the purse or tithe master, and then presenting the arithmetical calculation (one-tenth of three hundred is thirty), explains the reason behind the specific monetary amounts described in the Bible, as well as reminds audiences of the process of calculating their tithes. However, even though Judas's arithmetic is correct in this instance, he is of course not a good tither, for he is motivated by greed and deceit. Thus, the example warns, one can be a numerically correct tither but also an evil tither and betrayer of Christ if the spirit and intent behind the practice are not pure.

An audience listening to or reading *Jacob's Well* would no doubt have encountered discussions of proper and improper tithing in texts and performances outside of sermons. For example, one of the most significant displays of improper tithing occurs in the Wakefield Master's *Mactacio Abel* biblical cycle play, which features Cain mis-tithing as he miscounts his sheaves. As both *Jacob's Well* and *The Killing of Abel* assert, one must render the appropriate amount to God and the church. Textual models of good and bad tithing therefore reinforce the law, the spiritual concept, and the arithmetic required to perform the tithing. In *The Killing of Abel*, Abel and Cain debate the need to give a tithe to the Lord. Cain then counts out his tithing sheaves from one to ten meticulously, reluctant to hand over any to the Lord. I quote most of Cain's speech although it is lengthy, because it demonstrates his attention to counting, something a performer could have emphasized on stage with various physical movements:

>Oone shefe, oone, and this makys two,
>bot nawder of thise may I forgo:
>Two, two, now this is thre,

yei, this also shall leif with me:
ffor I will chose and best haue,
this hold I thrift of all this thrafe;
Wemo, wemo, foure, lo, here![18]
better groved, me no this yere.

....

ffoure shefis, foure, lo, this makis fyfe—
deyll I fast thus long or I thrife—
ffyfe and sex, now this is sevyn,
bot this gettis neuer god of heuen;
Nor none of thise foure, at my myght,
shall neuer com in godis sight.
Sevyn, sevyn, now this is aght.[19]

One sheaf, one, and this makes two,
but neither of these may I forgo:
Two, two, now this is three,
Yes, this also shall remain with me.
For I will choose and have the best,
of all this grain; I think it's thrifty:
Wemo, wemo, four, lo here!
I grew none better this year.

....

four sheaves, four, lo, this makes five—
"If I deal out quickly thus, it will be long ere I thrive"[20]
five and six, now this is seven,
but God of heaven will never get this;
Nor none of these four, in my power,
shall ever come in God's sight.
Seven, seven, now this is eight.

Just how exactly Cain is counting here has created some debate. George England, the editor of the first Early English Text Society edition of the play, suggested that the reason why Cain repeats many numbers is because he is actually counting to twenty instead of ten (with two sheaves per number), as he really only wishes to give one-twentieth for a tithe instead of one-tenth.[21] Clifford Davidson also argues for Cain's purposeful mis-tithing; Davidson posits that the Wakefield Master's attention to counting sheaves demonstrates how Cain "uses his arithmetic to exclude God."[22]

Cain continues counting, emphasizing his distress at having to give up anything:

we! aght, aght, & neyn, & ten is this,
we! this may we best mys.
Gif hym that that ligis thore?
It goyse agans myn hart full sore.[23]

We[mo]! Eight, eight, & nine, & ten is this.
We[mo]! This (one) we can most easily do without.
Give him that which lies there?
It goes against my heart very sorely.

After this long speech, Cain then seems to miscount his next sheaves: "we! lo twelve, fyfteyn, sexteyn (We[mo]! Lo twelve, fifteen, sixteen), to which Abel then responds, "Caym, thou tendis wrang, and of the warst"[24] (Cain, you tithe wrongly, and [give] the worst). What appears to be happening is that Cain is not counting correctly above ten as he skips eleven and then miscounts "twelve, fifteen, sixteen," perhaps purposefully in order to skip over certain better sheaves that he does not want to include in his count. William G. Marx has suggested that the Wakefield Master may be employing humor here—that Cain is not purposefully miscounting, but rather in his ignorance he does not know how to count over ten and is just guessing.[25] Cain then finishes the count with his eyes closed, and it is unclear how many sheaves he actually has. He indicates, "This hold I thrift of all this thrafe"; according to the *Middle English Dictionary*, "thrafe" is "A measure of wheat, straw, etc., usu[ally] containing 12 or 24 sheaves."[26] Cain, however, only appears to count up to sixteen sheaves (or eighteen sheaves, according to one scholar), and he tithes just two of the worst. Moreover, if there are actually thirty-two sheaves or more in total, then Cain has really shorted God.[27]

Texts like *The Killing of Abel* and *Jacob's Well* emphasize to audiences how arguably two of the worst figures in the Bible, Cain and Judas, manipulate numbers and cheat the Lord through their bad tithing practices; Cain shorts the Lord his tithe either purposefully or because of his innumeracy, and Judas's greed causes him to betray Christ in an effort to seek to reclaim the thirty coins of which he felt deprived. Later in the sermon on tithing, the *Well* writer muses once again on the nature of the number thirty and its link to Judas and bad tithers in general. He argues that in every act of false tithing, a person actually breaks the Ten Commandments three times because of a lack of truth, worship, and love (i.e., by not being true to, holding in reverence, or loving God and the curate). As Pauper in *Dives and Pauper* argues, every time a person breaks one commandment, he or she actually breaks all ten. This leads the sermonist of *Jacob's Well* to calculate: "And þus in þi fals tythyng, for þou brekyst thryes the x. comaundementys, þou hast thryes x. cursys of god, þat is, xxx^{ti} cursys, as iudas hadde" (ed. Brandeis 46) (And thus in your false tithing, for you break thrice the Ten Commandments, you have thrice ten curses of God, that is thirty curses, as Judas had). The sermonist's message is clear: if the audience shorts the Lord on their tithes, they are breaking the Ten Commandments times three, or thirty, the number of coins Judas betrayed Christ for.

By presenting examples such as this, the *Well* writer encourages his audience to factor larger numbers found in the Bible into smaller, more numerologically significant parts, such as ten for the Commandments, and also suggests how basic acts of arithmetic could be incorporated into one's understanding of biblical truths. This problem can be worked out both arithmetically and numerologically, thereby training audiences to calculate using these two related methods. This example serves to highlight how these two practices augment one another and are not mutually exclusive; numerological and practical figuring could facilitate one another. Multiplication is a fruitful way, perhaps even the best way, to show that sins compound more quickly than one might imagine. Thus, for the *Well* writer, "knowing thyself" means realizing how quickly one's sin is multiplied in the eyes of God.

PART 2: "KNOWING THYSELF" THROUGH SPIRITUAL CALCULATION

As we saw in the above example of thirty curses arising from the breaking of the Ten Commandments times three, the *Well* writer warns how quickly sin compounds. But he also uses the occasion of preaching as a vehicle for offering instruction in how numerologically infused arithmetic can be an active form of spiritual devotion. He returns to a discussion of thirty as three times ten again much later in the sermon cycle. In a sermon titled *De ieiunio* (On Fasting), the author urges the audience to "kest out þis spyȝtful grauel of brennyng lust for dreed of þe feend. for loue of god. for mede of soule" (ed. Atchley 119) (Cast out this spiteful gravel of burning lust for dread of the fiend, for love of God, and for reward of soul). He then promises,

> alle weddyd þat makyn hem clene wyth þis spade of contynens fro vnordynat & brennyng lustis schul haue in heuene xxx. corounnys.

þat is xxx folde mede of a specyal ioye. *lucas viij*. Thretty comyth of thre & of ten þerfore ȝif þou kepe in þi wedlock. thre and ten þou schalt haue thryes ten medys.... þanne for þise iij þat þou keypst in þi wedlok. & for þise ten comaundmentis þat þou kepyst þou schalt haue in heuen iij. & x. medys. þat is thryes ten corouns. þat is. xxx specyalle ioyes. (ed. Atchley 119–20)

All wedded folk that make themselves clean with the spade of continence from inordinate and burning lust shall have in heaven thirty crowns or garlands. That is thirty-fold reward from a special joy. Thirty comes from three and ten; therefore if you keep in your wedlock three and ten, you shall have thrice ten rewards. If you keep three in your wedlock and these Ten Commandments that you keep, you shall have in heaven three and ten rewards. That is, thrice ten crowns, that is, thirty special joys.

In this passage, the *Well* writer recognizes how the number thirty is particularly attractive and productive for numerological-based calculation. This conversation about crowns echoes the sermonist's earlier discussion of tithing, reinforcing his point that contemplating numbers and their spiritual associations can encourage a person's right action and obedience to God and ultimately lead to compounded reward in heaven.

Arithmetic that is heavily reliant on numerology appears throughout *Jacob's Well* and invites audiences to make spiritual connections with basic calculations. A notable example is presented in the opening of the sermon cycle, which details the many rungs of the Ladder of Love, which will ultimately allow the penitent sinner to reach heaven. This ladder is made up of the lowest rungs (the dread of judgment and the hope of bliss) plus ten rungs (the Ten Commandments) plus fourteen more rungs (the seven deeds of bodily mercy plus the seven deeds of ghostly mercy), plus one rung for the Ave Maria, plus seven more rungs ("the highest stakes") made from the seven petitions of the Paternoster (ed. Brandeis 3).[28] Added together, the ladder of love has thirty-four rungs, which corresponds with Christ's thirty-fourth year—that is, the year he was crucified and resurrected, thus enabling the worthy to enter heaven. It is clear from this example that the audience is meant to add the rungs to reach thirty-four, since the result is such a significant part of the allegory's meaning. The sermonist, in describing the various parts to add, encourages his audience to participate in the reaching of the final sum, revealing the path to heaven through Christ's sacrifice and love. The author, however, does not reveal the final sum to the audience, no doubt confident that they will achieve the sum themselves.

Pardons offered another path for medieval Christians to redress their sinful choices and actions, and the *Well* writer does not neglect this practice. In a remarkable passage addressing several pardons granted by popes, the sermonist models the specific calculation of the pardon, relying on both arithmetical and numerological skills. As the sermon on the prayer *Ave Maria* describes,

> Pope Urban þe fourth ȝaf & grantyd to alle þo. þat bene on clene lyfe wiþ outen ende þat *seyn*. þis word *Ihesus* Amen in þe ende of þe Marie—xxx dayes of pardoun. Pope Iohun also þerto ȝaf & confermede lx. dayes of pardoun of þe penaunce enioynede. And also he þat seyn euery day þe sautir of oure lady whiche is þre tyme fyfte aueis. schal haue eueryday to pardoun xxxiij. ȝere and. xxx. days. so þat þe summe of pardon in þe wooke is a Clxxij. ȝeer grantyde of þe forseyde popys wiþ oute ende Amen. (ed. Atchley 507)

> Pope Urban IV granted thirty days of pardon to those of a pure life who say the name of Jesus at the end of the *Ave Maria*. Pope John also confirmed sixty days of pardon. Anyone who says the psalter of our lady, which is three times fifty Aves, will have thirty-three years and thirty days of pardon each day so that the sum of pardon in a week will be one hundred and seventy-two years granted by the aforesaid popes.[29]

In this example, the sermonist's audience is invited to perform several acts and skills related to number. First the sermon asks for an act of duplation or doubling; the earlier pope offered thirty days of pardon, the latter sixty. The second act is one of factoring or dividing and multiplying, as the Psalter of Our Lady's 150 Aves are rendered as three times fifty (which audiences would have been trained in other sermons to have thought of as five times ten, or numerologically as the five wounds or the five senses times the Ten Commandments). Next called for is another act of addition and multiplication, but it is not immediately clear how the author has arrived at thirty-three years and thirty days of pardon, or 397 months (4,764 days); some further calculation indicates that this is rendered from Pope Urban's thirty days, times 150 Aves. Then the passage demands yet another act of multiplication in order to arrive at 172 years: thirty times 150 times seven days is 31,500 days, or eighty-six years and about four months. However, using the larger figure of sixty days of pardon (offered by Pope John) times 150 Aves times seven days equals 172 years (plus about six months).

What this long calculation reveals is that the numbers do actually work out accurately to the nearest year, but it is not at all clear how they work out until some extended arithmetic is performed. It is certainly possible that medieval audiences would have concerned themselves with these figures, or it could be that they simply accepted the calculations performed for them without engaging in their own arithmetic. But just because the final sum may have been too difficult to arrive at while listening to the sermon does not mean that the audience could not participate in calculation for at least part of the time. After all, the sermon initially lures the audience into the arithmetic problem with a simple act of duplation (thirty plus thirty), and then factoring (three times fifty). As the problem becomes more difficult, it would have perhaps left behind all but the most tenacious of lay calculators. (For an overview of how medieval people calculated, including by fingers and with memorized tables, see the appendix.) Ultimately, what is important is not that the audience members arrive at the "correct" answer of 172 years but that they appreciate the remarkable length of time—172 years—that God's grace, through pardons and the power of the Ave Maria, can bring to them.

PART 3: "KNOWING THYSELF" THROUGH ENUMERATION (AND RESISTANCE TO ENUMERATION)

Jacob's Well offers several examples that suggest that appreciating number and/or engaging in calculation is a productive way of learning how to venerate God more fully, and how to live a more steadfast and moral life. One such example is the legend of Saint James the Mutilated, which focuses on cardinal and ordinal numbers. This discussion of James falls within a larger section on fortitude and magnanimity, in a section on steadfastness, which is said to form several feet "in wydnesse in þis sqware" (in width of this square, corner, or side) in the well.[30] Best known to medieval English audiences from the thirteenth-century hagiographic collection *The Golden Legend*, the Life of Saint James the Mutilated describes in great detail his loss of bodily parts as he is tortured, with James offering an extended meditation on number as each part is removed. In *Jacob's Well*, as in the *Golden Legend*, the sermonist describes how each finger and toe is cut off; James's responses often incorporate the number of the body part in a numerological or spiritual sense. For example, when his third finger is cut off, James responds, "þise thre braunchys I offere to þe. þat art o. god & personys thre" (ed. Atchley 202) (these three branches I offer to you that are one God and three persons). Likewise, the eighth finger prompts James to speak of Christ's circumcision on the eighth day; the ninth finger, how Christ died in the ninth hour; and the tenth finger, the Ten Commandments.

James demonstrates to audiences how counting in a mundane sense can be easily changed to counting in a numerological sense. When the third toe of his left foot is cut off, James's response, "A ston to be sqware & stable. muste haue strokys to make it able" (ed. Atchley 204) (a stone, to be square and stable, must have strokes to make it able), means that any rough corners (or digits) must be hewn off in order to make it stable—that is, steadfast. However, squareness and stability, as we saw in chapter 2, are related, for they invoke number theory, particularly in association with two and its cubes. In the example of James, however, stability is associated with the number three. Finally, after twenty-eight amputations (twenty digits, two hands, two feet, two arms, and two legs), which invokes the "perfection" of the number twenty-eight, James is decapitated. The writer notes that James's steadfastness is like a stone in one's well, arguing that the audience should "takyth exaumple be hym. & takyth þis thrydde sqware gostly myght in thre fote of wydnesse.... And þis schal be a good sqware & a stedfast in ȝoure welle" (ed. Atchley 205) (take example by him, and take this third square [i.e., side or corner], ghostly might, in the third foot of wideness.... And this shall be a good & steadfast square in your well). Here the author invokes the stability of the square again as he asks the audience to model themselves on James; they are to focus on the stability of the number three, the Trinity.[31] Ultimately, the sermon suggests that "three" represents stability as strongly as, or more strongly than, the number four, an important revision to established number theory.

At the same time as *Jacob's Well* asserts that the divine can be known through number, other examples from the sermons resist the audience's desire and ability to count clearly and definitively. One such instance would be a form of what I call "extreme counting." As mentioned earlier in this study, Thomas Lentes describes how late medieval religious men and women practiced calculating enormous amounts such as the number of Christ's steps on earth, the tears shed by Mary, and the wounds of Christ.[32] This practice had a far reach, for Margery Kempe, an avid sermon listener and reader of other visionary and pastoral texts, calculates Christ's wounds from his scourging: in a vision she sees "sextene men wyth sextene scorgys, and eche scorge had viii babelys of leed on the ende, and every babyl was ful of scharp prekelys, as it had ben the rowelys of a spor. And tho men wyth the scorgys madyn comen-awnt that ich of hem schulde yevyn owr Lord xl strokys"³³ (Sixteen men with sixteen scourges [i.e., each with a scourge] and each scourge had eight balls of lead on the end, and every ball was full of sharp prickles, as if it had been the wheels on a spur. And then the men with the scourges made a vow that each of them should give our Lord forty strokes). When we multiply sixteen by eight by forty strokes, the passion brings Christ 5,120 wounds. In other medieval texts, Christ's wounds were variously calculated as 5,475 and even 6,666.³⁴ However, as Nicholas Watson has noted, the *Book*'s multiplication is complicated by Kempe's vision of the tips "ful of sharp prekelys," for she gives no concrete number for these. Although multiplication allows Kempe and her readers to appreciate the magnitude of Christ's passion, the precise number of wounds cannot be calculated and is actually much greater.³⁵ This passage, therefore, both advocates and resists enumeration. The word problem, with its multiplication of men times lead balls times lashes, encourages the audience to attempt to calculate something that cannot be fully counted and invites extended contemplation of the enormity of Christ's sacrifice. The ultimate lesson offered by Kempe is that the act of calculation leads one close to God, but the appreciation that his sacrifice is incalculable leads one even closer.

Like Kempe's imagining the uncountable wounds of Christ, *Jacob's Well* introduces a exemplum in which extreme counting is invoked but not fully performed. A hermit who lived in the desert had to fetch water every day from a well. The hermit, "for sluggynes & slewthe" (for sluggishness and sloth), wished to move closer to the well, but when he looked behind him, he saw a curious and frightening sight: he "seyȝ an aungyl folewyn hym, & tellyn his steppys" (saw an angel following him, and tallying his steps.) When he asked the angel why he was counting his steps, the angel replied,

> I noumbre þi steppys in þi trauayle for to schewyn þe noumbre þerof a-for god aȝens þe feend, þat þou ther-thrugh mowe haue mede in heuen. for feendys noumbre þe steppys of man & womman to synne warde, & alle rownynges & ianglynges in dyvyn seruyse, for to schewe þe noumbre of hem a-for god to mannys dampnacyoun. (ed. Brandeis 111)

> I number your steps in your toil in order to show the number thereof before God against the fiend, so that through them you will have reward in heaven. For fiends number the steps of men and woman

toward sin, and all the noise-making and janglings in the divine service, in order to show the number of them before God for the purpose of man's damnation.

Similar to Kempe's example of the high (but ultimately uncountable) number of Christ's wounds, this exemplum invokes the idea of a very high, unidentified number of steps. One could calculate the specific number of steps the hermit traveled if the distance and time were given; however, the exemplum resists quantification. Rather, the sermonist gestures toward the inability of men and women to quantify their misdeeds or thoughts in any accurate way. Take care, however, the exemplum warns—for devils are keeping an exact count, as is God.[36] In this context, "knowing thyself" means that one must recognize how quantifiable both one's evil and one's virtuous deeds are to God and the devil, even if a full accounting of them falls beyond that person's grasp.

Jacob's Well also introduces the idea of counting without end, or "numberless" infinity, as a way to invoke a large number to represent the enormity of one's sin while still resisting easy quantification. When the sermonist describes how twelve corbels must bear the weight of the well's walls, he advises that the twelve articles of faith can stand "for þe xij. fote of þi curblys . . . þanne is þi welle weel curblyd & wel groundyd alle abowtyn be nethyn to settyn on owre ston werk ȝif þou kepe þis stedfast feyth in the ground of þi welle" (ed. Atchley 259) (for these twelve feet of corbels . . . then is your well well corbeled and well grounded all about beneath to rest on our own stone work if you keep this steadfast faith in the ground of your well). The author notes that the audience "muste make redy sande & lyme to oure stonwerk" (must make ready sand and lime for our stonework), then likens the sand to human sin: "þe sond must be mynde of oure synne for sande hath manye kyrnelle. wythoute noumbre. . . . Ryȝt so. haue mynde of þi synnes þat arn wythoute noumbre" (ed. Atchley 267) (the sand must remind us of our sin, for sand has many grains without number . . . just as you must have mind of your sins that are without number). This idea of sand or gravel as tiny individual pieces without number is emphasized several times in the text. For instance, in a discussion about how the audience must delve deep in the well to find the spring of grace, the sermonist advises the listeners to cast out the gravel, "þe wose of glotonye," with a spade of fasting. The gravel is uncountable, he warns: "As kyrnellys of grauel arn wyth owte noumbre so arn fleschly desyres in man" (ed. Atchley 93) (As tiny pieces of gravel are without number so are the fleshly desires in man). Later the sermonist returns to this idea, fleshing it out more fully by pointing out the individual and distinct grains of gravel:

"As grauel kyrnellys arn wythoute noumbre & bareyn wyth oute fry3t for þo kyrnellys hangyn no3t to gydere as erthe but arn departyd iche kyrnelle fro oþer be hym self þerfore no fruy3t may growe þer in" (ed. Atchley 114) (As tiny pieces of gravel are without number and barren without fruit, for the pieces do not hang together as earth but are separated each piece from one another, by itself, therefore, no fruit may grow therein). Kernels or grains of sand appear to be infinite, without number, to humankind, but to God they represent finite, countable, and individual lapses.

The sermonist's repeated use of pieces of gravel or grains of sand to describe sin finds a counterpart in *The Book of Margery Kempe*, where a similar image, compounded with many others, is used to describe the praise owed to God. In the closing prayer of the *Book*, Kempe embarks on an extremely long sentence that attempts to list a tremendously large, or perhaps an infinite, number of the smallest items of God's creation. The syntax of the sentence is somewhat loose; the sentence begins with Kempe attempting to describe the number of souls that could fit into her own soul in the world without end, thus invoking infinite multitude, magnitude, and time. By the end of the sentence Kempe suggests that the tremendously large numbers of small objects she has invoked, if they were souls dedicated to praising the Lord and all speaking with Kempe's mouth, would not be able to praise the Lord for the grace he has shown her on earth. It is worth quoting this remarkable sentence in full:

> Here my preyeris, for thow I had as many hertys and sowlys closyd in my sowle as God knew wythowtyn begynnyng how many schulde dewllyn in hevyn wythowtyn ende, and as ther arn dropys of watyr, fres and salt, chesylys of gravel, stonys smale and grete, gresys growyng in al erthe, kyrnellys of corn, fischys, fowelys, bestys and leevys upon treys whatn most plente ben, fedir of fowle er her of best, seed that growith in erbe, er in wede, in flowyr, in lond, er in watyr whan most growyn, and as many creaturys as in erthe had ben, and arn, er schal ben and myth ben be thi myth, and as ther arn sterrys and awngelys in thi syght, er other kynnes good that growyth upon erthe, and eche were a sowle as holy as evyr was our Lady Seynt Mary that bar Jhesu owr Savyowr, and yf it wer possibyl that eche cowede thynkyn and spekyn al so grete reverens and worschep as evyr dede owr Lady Seynt Mary here in erthe and now doth in hevyn and schal don wythowtn ende, I may rith wel thynkyn in myn hert and spekyn it wyth my mowth as this tyme in worschip of the Trinite and of al the

cowrt of hevyn, to gret schame and schenschep of Sathanas that fel fro Goddys face and of alle his wikkyd spiritys, that alle thes hertys ne sowlys cowed nevyr thankyn God ne ful preysyn hym, ful blissyn hym ne ful worschepyn hym, ful lovyn hym ne fully yevyn lawdacyon, preisyng, and reverens to hym as he were worthy to han for the gret mercy that he hath schewyd to me in erth that I can not don ne may don.[37]

Hear my prayers. For though I had as many hearts and souls closed in my soul as God knew from without beginning how many should dwell in heaven without end, and as there are drops of water, fresh and salt, chips of gravel, stones small and great, grasses growing in all the earth, kernels of corn, fish, fowl, beasts and leaves on trees when there is great abundance, feather of foul or hair of beast, seed that grows in plant, or in weed, in flower, on land, or in water when most grow, and as many as have been on earth, are, or shall and might be in your might, and as there are stars and angels in your sight, or other kinds of good that grow upon earth, and each were a soul as holy as ever was our Lady St. Mary who bore Jesus our Savior, and if it were possible that each could think and speak as great reverence and worship as every deed our Lady St. Mary here on earth and now in heaven and shall do without end, I may well think in my heart and speak it with my mouth at this time in worship of the Trinity and of all the court of heaven, to the great shame and ignominy of Satan, who fell from God's face, and of all his wicked spirits, so that all these hearts and souls could never thank God nor fully praise him, fully bless him nor fully worship him, fully love him nor fully give praise, laud and reverence to him as he were worthy to have for the great mercy that he has shown to me on earth. That I cannot do nor may do.

The longest sentence of the *Book* mirrors Kempe's desire to count to a tremendously large number, perhaps toward infinity, as she attempts to describe the number of souls in the court of heaven, who, echoing an earlier chapter (chapter 82), also reside within her own soul. In order to suggest the sheer size of the court and number of souls, she employs the smallest parts of creation, including all the hairs on all the beasts, all the drops of water in the world, all the leaves on trees, and all the "chesylys of gravel, stonys smale and grete." Nicholas Watson perceptively argues that "Read one way, much of the *Book* seems trustingly confident in the adequacy of number as a way of calculating the relation between earth and heaven." However, Watson continues, "all the language of enumeration in the *Book* is there precisely in order to expose its own inadequacy and reveal the absurdity of trying to count to infinity.... Limited as she is, she cannot encompass eternity or yet creation."[38] Watson therefore sees a "failure of number" and "Kempe's personal awareness of limitedness," hence her reliance on the "as if" tag or simile.[39] Through the "as if" simile, "finite humans can aspire to infinitude."[40]

Kempe's example shows how a lay person, an avid listener of sermons, takes an example of extreme counting, like that invoked in *Jacob's Well*, and incorporates it into her own devotional practice. Just as the *Well* writer invokes the grains of sand to demonstrate how unquantifiable sin can be for a person but still quantifiable to God, Kempe shares a prayer in which she attempts to describe how much praise God deserves—something uncountable to humans but still enumerable by God. Kempe's prayer demonstrates how well the visionary "knows herself" through Christian doctrine and devotional practice, which leads to her deeper spiritual understanding of the divine. The *Well* writer uses a similar metaphor, that of grains of sand or gravel, in a negative sense to indicate the enormity of human sins, in order to encourage his audience to reach the grace and knowledge that Kempe has arrived at. For this task, he relies throughout the cycle on the concept of "measure."

PART 4: "KNOWING THYSELF" THROUGH MEASURE

Jacob's Well focuses much attention on the idea of "measure" to help audiences know themselves and God. Discussions of number in medieval texts often invoke the idea of "measure." The *Middle English Dictionary* defines "measure" in two main ways, and many medieval English religious texts play with these meanings. "Measure" can refer to the "act of measuring" or calculation and reckoning, as well as "proper proportion" and balance, including moderation in food and other activities.[41] An example of how these two senses can be invoked can be found in the fifteenth-century poem "A Song of Just Mesure" by the Benedictine John Lydgate, which explores measure as moderation within the practice of mathematical measurement:

> Without mesure may non artificere
> In his wirkyng parfitely procede,
> Peyntour, steynour, mason, nor carpentere,

Without mesure accomplissh nat in dede;
Where mesure fayleth, wrong wrought is euery dede.[42]

Without measure may no craftsperson
In his working perfectly proceed,
Painter, dyer, mason, nor carpenter,
Without measure accomplish nothing indeed (in deed);
Where measure fails, wrongly wrought is every deed.

No craftsman may work without measuring tools and equipment; where "measure fails," every deed is "wrought wrong" because of the failing of tools and the failing of moderation. Another of Lydgate's poems, "Mesure is Tresour," also explores the idea of measure as moderation; "measure" is repeated in the last line of each stanza, emphasizing the value of moderation. Other fifteenth-century texts also invoke the meanings of measure. For example, the morality play *Mankind* includes a lengthy admonition by Mercy to Mankind "that begins 'Mesure ys treasure' and goes on to encourage moderation in all things."[43]

These complementary definitions of "measure" are also treated at great length in popular Middle English biblical cycle plays. Who can forget the *York Play of the Crucifixion*, where the soldiers have mismeasured the nail holes in the cross? "It failis a foote and more" (It fails by a foot and more), declares the Third Soldier before he wrenches Christ's body with ropes to attach the Lord to the cross.[44] Repeatedly this play calls attention to the problem of mismeasurement, to the assertion both that the soldiers are not "in measure" or "in moderation" and that they have incorrectly measured their work. Indeed, as Third Soldier proclaims of the poorly bored nail hole, "In faith, it was overe skantely scored; / That makis it fouly for to faile"[45] (In faith, it was not scored well; that makes it fail foully). Even when the soldiers eventually lift up Christ's body on the cross, they discover that the hole they have dug for the cross is "overwide," which "makis it wave": "Methynkith this crosse will noght abide, / Ne stande stille in this morteyse yitt"[46] (It seems to me this cross will not stand upright / nor stand still in this mortise), say the soldiers before driving wedges into the hole to prop up the cross. Jesus's memorable words to the audience from the cross then call direct attention to the idea of the measure with his admonition:

Al men that walkis by waye or strete,
Takes tente ye schalle no travayle tyne.

Byholdes myn heede, myn handis, and my feete,
And fully feele nowe, or ye fyne,
Yf any mournyng may be meete
Or myscheve mesured unto myne.
My Fadir, that alle bales may bete,
Forgiffis thes men that dois me pyne.⁴⁷

All men who walk by way or street,
Take heed—you shall not lose your toil—
Behold my head, my hands, my feet
And fully feel now, before you finish
If any mourning may be measured
Or misfortune compared with mine.
My Father, who makes all misdeeds better,
Forgive these men who do me pain.

Jesus instructs all those who pass by to take notice of his pain; he then challenges them to see if their pain and/or torment (their "mischief") compares or "measures" to his. Jesus thus offers his own body as a measuring tool for humankind. This idea also appears in the *Towneley Play of the Last Judgment*, in which Jesus "uses the six corporal acts of mercy (Matt. 25:31–46) to measure the goodness and badness of the risen souls." He then "compares this to the number of his wounds which testify to the extant he suffered for the world's salvation."⁴⁸ In both the *York Play of the Crucifixion* and the *Towneley Last Judgment*, Jesus thus invokes the idea of measurement and calculation while demonstrating that what has happened to him is beyond moderation and ultimately unmeasurable.

Other cycle plays also develop the idea of measure as a way to impart biblical truths and discuss humankind's response to God. The Noah plays in particular draw on the dual meanings of *measure*, defining the specific dimensions of the ark to be built while also exploring Noah's family's "measure" and moderation in the face of God's commandment. God instructs the elderly Noah to build the ark and to measure its dimensions correctly and precisely; humankind, however, has been entirely out of measure in its behavior and must be punished accordingly. "Multiplication" also has a double meaning in the Noah plays. God states he told mankind to multiply (i.e., in their number), but their sins have multiplied beyond measure; hence God will give Noah a tangible mathematical problem, the building of a ship to specific dimensions. The Noah plays thus call attention to measure as a way to invite audiences to participate in (and identify with) the process of measuring and calculating while learning about the importance of obedience to God.

As we can see from this brief discussion of Lydgate's poems and several biblical cycle plays, late medieval religious texts often invoke "measure" in both its senses to emphasize how men and women should respond to and venerate the Lord. This is true for *Jacob's Well* as well, as it plays with the two senses of "measure," meaning "moderation" and "to determine size." While discussing Justice, for example, the sermonist asserts, "þis ryȝtfulnes is a rewle. whiche is ryȝtest of alle mesurys" (This rightfulness is a rule, which is rightest of all measures), which also puns on the idea of "rule" (ed. Atchley 208). Likewise, under the section on abstinence, the author asserts that "sobyrnesse & temperaunce is nouȝt ellys but kepyng of mesure" (soberness and temperance is nothing else but the keeping of measure). The author continues to pun: "þe first fote is. holde þou mesure in vnderstondyng. . . . after þe mesure of truthe and desyre he noȝt to se resoun þere non may be" (the first foot is "hold you measure in understanding" . . . after the measure of truth and desire he ought not to see reason where none may be), and he continues to refer to measurement and moderation throughout the section on abstinence (ed. Atchley 106–7).[49]

In the sermon cycle, measurement functions in two different realms: the practicality of measurement and its real-world applications, as well as measurement's spiritual resonances, which cannot be fully calculated. The first exemplum in the cycle occurs immediately after the sermon writer offers a summary of the remaining ninety-four-day cycle. Advising his audience to "lokyth in þe begynnyng of euery werk þat ȝe do, how it schal be perfourmyd, & what schall be þe end!" (ed. Brandeis 4) (Look in the beginning of every work that you do, how it shall be performed and what its end shall be!), the *Well* writer then offers a paradox or mystery, one that would no doubt have been quite interesting to an audience of merchant-class people used to weights and measures. It is the story of King Alexander's precious stone, which was so heavy that when it was weighed on a scale, nothing could equal it. However, when a tiny amount of dust was cast onto the stone, it became so light that anything else placed on the scale weighed more than the stone. The interpretation, the sermonist explains, is that we are mighty while alive and less than the least when in the grave, covered in earth.[50] This exemplum serves to remind the audience that when they are listening to or reading the sermon cycle, they are not entering the secular world of measurement but rather the spiritual world of measurement, one which will challenge their firmly held pragmatic numerate beliefs. The exemplum presents an apparent paradox, and its placement at the start of the cycle invites the audience to consider all numerate acts through this lens. At first glance the stone looks to be something miraculous or magical, but in reality all it does is emphasize God's truth: how worldly measure will be overturned by divine measure after death.

The apparent paradox of Alexander's stone is similar to mathematical paradoxes found in another sermon, the fifteenth-century Latin sermon for Easter or Corpus Christi by John Felton. Felton elaborates why the seven liberal arts are erroneous when explaining the mysteries of Christ. As mentioned in chapter 2, Felton asserts that arithmetic is mistaken because even though Isidore of Seville acknowledges an infinity of numbers, Christ recognizes no such numbers when he declares in Luke 12:7, "The hairs of your head are all numbered." Felton then reveals why traditional geometry cannot explain the mystery of Christ: "Geometry, which is concerned with figures, is mistaken here because it teaches that a circle covers the greatest area, while a triangle covers the smallest, and further, that a larger figure covers a greater area than a smaller one. But here, the triangle covers as much as the circle, because the triangular piece of the host after it has been broken contains as much as the whole host." Wenzel explains that "after consecration and before communion, the (round) host is broken by the priest into three pieces, at least two of which would be roughly triangular."[51] Thus, as Felton describes, arithmetic and geometry may explain the ordered world as it is known, but their insufficiencies can be easily exposed. The Bible promises that God ordered all things in measure, number, and weight, and these paradoxes remind listeners of the essential "three in one" mystery at the center of all being. A medieval lay merchant audience, no doubt a highly competent group of calculators, would feel comfortable and able to do much of the math in the sermon cycle—but exempla such as these remind them that the divine is greater than their limited human comprehension.

Many sermons in *Jacob's Well* encourage audiences to imagine in great detail the specific measurements of sin, but the actual measurements often resist quantification. The ooze of Wrath, for example, is said to be seven feet in depth; the sermonist then elaborates on the nature of each foot (the first foot is secret hatred of the heart, the second foot the malice of the mouth, and so forth), which suggests concrete dimensions; however, the audience is never told how wide across Wrath is, thus frustrating any firm quantification. To make matters more complicated, the sermon writer mixes his metaphors on the following day when he speaks of the "seven branches of wrath" (ed. Brandeis 97). Sloth, however, has breadth but not depth; it is eighteen feet broad, and these feet are divided into three equal parts of six feet, each of which represents an aspect of the sin (ed. Brandeis 103, 107–10). Thus, despite the specificity of the measurements, it is actually impossible to add up easily the daily measures over multiple sermons. Despite the specificity of the measures, they resist sustained quantification.

A particularly complicated example of measurement is offered by the author's elaboration of Cupidity. The *wose* of Cupidity is "three square" or three-cornered or sided—that is, triangular—and is thirteen feet broad (ed. Brandeis 119). As the author describes, the first five feet are usury, which is twelve inches thick. The second five-foot section consists of different pieces. The first foot (simony) is six inches thick (ed. Brandeis 127). The second foot is divided in two (theft is five inches thick; robbery is six inches thick). Sacrilege, the third foot of the second section, is eight inches deep; then false litigation's depth is given as eleven inches deep, and wickedness as seven inches deep. The final three feet are made up of dishonest trade at five inches thick, disreputable crafts at nine inches thick, and gambling at nine inches deep (ed. Brandeis 128–35). Passages like this use seemingly precise measurements to allow sustained discussion of sin through the enumeration and quantification of individual parts, but often the individual sermons, as well as the cycle overall, resist quantification, suggesting that the depth of misdeed or even sacrilege is difficult to define. *Jacob's Well*, therefore, relies on the rhetoric of specificity but is purposefully disorienting, inviting the audience's participation in sustained reckoning while demonstrating how difficult sin really is to fathom and quantify. For instance, in the previous example, it is hard to know if "depth" and "thickness" are synonymous, or if they indicate the measurement of two different directions (vertical and horizontal).

There are also the difficulties of units of measure, for the sermons sometimes combine feet, inches, fathoms, and spans. For instance, we are told that "þis wose of [lecchery] is iij. fadome brode" (The ooze of lechery is three fathoms broad). These fathoms are then enumerated and described; for example, "þe firste fadom brede of þis wose of leccherye, þat is, leccherie in herte, & þat is iiij. fote depe" (ed. Brandeis 158–59) (The first fathom broad of lechery is lechery of the heart, and that is four feet deep). But how do we measure this fathom, which has two understandings in this time period—the span from the elbow to the wrist or the span of an adult man's arms, or six feet?[52] If it is the latter, then Lust is an extremely *broad* sin (like Sloth), for the well has suddenly expanded to eighteen feet across. However, if the fathom is only wrist to elbow, then Lust is only half the size, narrower than Sloth. While it is tempting to imagine the preacher, while delivering the sermon, gesturing and measuring certain units with his arms or hands to emphasize the relative size of sin, this of course is conjecture; it seems more likely that the point of the cycle's discussion of sin is that quantifying the number, measure, or extent of one's sin, like counting grains of sand or gravel, is ultimately impossible for humankind, although it is completely possible for God. While discussing the deadly sins, the *Well* writer makes repeated references to humankind being out of measure; this serves to emphasize that there are just, proper proportions for people and that sin by its very nature is essentially something beyond measure and moderation. To "know thyself," therefore, one has to excavate one's body and mind of sin to reach one's true and proper measure.

PART 5: "KNOWING THYSELF" THROUGH THE GEOMETRY OF SIN AND VIRTUE

Perhaps the most remarkable aspect of numeracy introduced in the sermon cycle is what I call the geometry of sin and virtue. As I have discussed above, the sermonist develops an elaborate geometry based on the idea of digging a well, with the sins and virtues taking on three dimensions. In this section I argue that the *Well* writer is using this novel way of dividing and organizing the sermons because he is drawing from a long tradition of describing God as a geometer. Inviting his audience to see the world in this way—particularly to see sin as imperfect shapes—offers a striking representation of how out of proportion sin is, and how the audience must cast out that sin in order to reach that perfect ladder of love, which will lead to heaven. Just measurement and proportion await at the end of properly excavating and reinforcing one's well.

The *Well* writer's inspiration for building his sermon cycle on the metaphor of digging a three-dimensional well can be found in Ephesians 3:18–19: you "may have power to comprehend with all the saints what is the breadth and length and height and depth, and to know the love of Christ which surpasses knowledge, that you may be filled with all the fulness of God." As a sermon writer in London, British Library, Additional 40672, explains, in these verses Paul "prays that his readers will be strengthened by God's spirit . . . he refers to two trinities, the Holy Trinity and the three gifts of faith, hope, and love. Paul prays that they will then understand the breadth, length, height, and depth of God. These four terms have been interpreted in various ways . . . breadth in God's benevolence to his creation; length in its longlasting nature; height in the extent of God's superiority over his creation;

depth in the variety of creatures God created. The full interpretation will be known in heaven."⁵³ For medieval theologians, geometry was a useful way to describe God. Some medieval people were familiar with the image of God as a geometer; one can see just such an image, of God holding a compass as he creates and measures a fractalized world, in the first folio of the French *Bible Moralisée*, Codex Vindobonensis 2554, in the Österreichische Nationalbibliothek.⁵⁴ The fifteenth-century theologian Nicholas of Cusa developed a spiritual geometry in which he described geometric shapes and their divine significance; as he explains, "the infinite triangle . . . is at once one and three, and symbolizes the trinity," whereas the "infinite circle . . . symbolizes the maximum absolute, which coincides with the minimum absolute, and thus, with the divine unity." Moreover, the "infinite sphere . . . is at once length, width, and depth . . . [and] represents the complete actuality of the divine principle."⁵⁵ According to Nicholas of Cusa, regular geometrical shapes, when stretched to infinity, become a particularly useful way of conceptualizing the divine.

In *Jacob's Well*, however, geometry is employed to show how irregular and misshapen sin is. When the sins are introduced, the sermonist details their dimensions in length, width, and depth; these dimensions are unsettling; they are out of measure, irregular, and not proportional. The *Well* writer emphasizes that the audience must realize their sin puts them out of all moderation. The sins are strange and unsettling shapes and sizes. Several are two-dimensional. For example, as mentioned earlier in this chapter, Sloth is "xviij. fote brede of wose" (ed. Brandeis 103) (eighteen feet broad of ooze), and these eighteen feet are arranged into three groups of six feet; the sermon writer then elaborates on the description of each kind of sloth without assigning any depths. Other sins are described as firmly three-dimensional. Envy at first takes the form of an equilateral triangle, for it has "iij. cornerys of wose" (ed. Brandeis 82) (three corners of ooze); the first is envy in the heart, and it is three feet broad. The second is envy of the mouth, and it is also three feet broad; the third corner is envy in deed, and it too is three feet broad, making this a perfect equilateral triangle, until the audience is told to "Caste out of þi pytt þis wose of enuye in þise cornerys" (ed. Brandeis 84) (Cast out of your pit this ooze of envy in these corners), which suggests that the audience ought to be imagining a three-dimensional solid instead of an object on a plane. Several sins are obviously three-dimensional, although not all their sides are measured. The ooze of Wrath has four sides or corners (it is "foure-square") and extends seven feet deep (ed. Brandeis 91–94), thus making it a cube or rectangular box. In their descriptions, therefore, the ooze of sins can form distinct prisms by extending the various shapes in depth; in *Jacob's Well*, the audience encounters shapes such as the octagonal prism and the triangular prism. Parallel prisms were familiar to a limited array of medieval scholars from book 11 of Euclid's *Elements*, in which a prism is defined as a "solid figure, contained by planes [i.e., faces], of which the two opposite (planes) are equal, similar, and parallel, and the remaining (planes are) parallelograms."[56] Prismatic solids would have been much more familiar to the laity and clergy alike from medieval architecture, as there are a number of examples of octagonal prisms in church columns.[57]

It is with these prismatic descriptions of sin that their forms grow more complicated. The shapes do not remain regular cylinders or prisms all the way to their bottoms, for the depths vary within the solid. The top portion may appear to be a cylinder or regular prism, but the bottom or base is not parallel to the top and ends up looking like a set of stairs, for want of a better simile. An example of this is Lechery, which, as we learned earlier, is three fathoms broad. If we assume Lechery is a circle three fathoms broad, the plane is divided into these three fathoms, but then depth is added, creating a cylinder. The first fathom across is lecherous thoughts or lechery of the heart, which is four feet deep (a foot for each of thought, delight, consent, and burning desire). The second fathom across is formed of lecherous words, manners, and conditions, which is an undisclosed number of feet deep, and the third fathom across is the deed of lechery, which is fourteen feet deep (the first foot is between a single man and a single woman, the second a single man and a woman vowed to chastity, the third a single man and a virgin, and so forth). Thus, the shape of Lechery ends up looking like a solid possessing the top potion of a cylinder but then becoming quite irregular (or even undefined) at the bottom. Another example of this odd-bottomed shape would be the ooze of Covetousness, which has three corners, making it triangular; these three corners are thirteen feet broad, and the various parts have different depths, from usury (at twelve inches) to simony (at six inches), theft (five inches), and sacrilege ("many inches"). This suggests that fully excavating and eradicating one's sin would be extremely difficult, especially as it is unclear just where the sin ends. The example of Pride offers an even more extreme shape. Pride is defined as having eight corners. These corners are measured in breadth. For example, the first "cornere of pride in presumpcyoun is vj. fote of wose in brede" (corner of pride in presumption is six feet of ooze in breadth), and pride's third corner, "vnbuxomnesse, is thre fote brood in wose" (ed. Brandeis 70, 72) (disobedience, is three feet broad in ooze). The octagon is an irregular shape, with other corners measuring two or three feet, except for vainglory, which has no measurement, only "thre manerys" (ed. Brandeis 71). The shape created is essentially that of an irregular octagonal prism, with one part undefined.

As the *Well* writer emphasizes, sin is out of all measure and moderation, and geometry offers a perfect way to demonstrate this to his audience. "Knowing thyself" means recognizing one's misshapen sin. This argument would be very easy to make if the corresponding virtues were described with completely regular shapes in the cycle, for I could then assert that while sin is misshapen and mismeasured, virtue is uniformly regular and completely fathomable. However, virtue is not always clearly measured in these sermons, either. In some circumstances, the sermonist neglects to give all three dimensions. Regarding mercy, for example, the writer expounds a very neat and clean division of the virtue into two equal halves, which would suggest balanced measure with familiar numerological resonances: "þis ground of mercy is vij. fote thycke. þat is to seye it hath vij. degrees. and it is xiiij fote in brede & vij fote brood on þe ry3t syde. & vij. fote brood on þe lyft syde" (ed. Atchley 67) (This ground of mercy is seven feet thick, that is to say it has seven degrees and it is fourteen feet in breath, and seven feet broad on the right side and seven feet broad on the left side). The seven feet on the right side are the works of mercy, and the seven feet on the left side are the bodily deeds of mercy (ed. Atchley 72, 77). However, as each foot is then discussed in terms of breadth but not depth, the sermonist resists describing the three-dimensionality of the virtue, until he eventually moves on to the depth of the "grounde of almes" (ed. Atchley 85).

In other sermons in the cycle, the measurements of virtue and belief can suggest a geometric form that yields clear spiritual guidance. For example, the *Well* writer explains that the well must be four square, with each square three feet wide: "here beforn I telde 3ou þat 3oure welle must be iiij sqware. & yche sqware 3 fote wyde" (ed. Atchley 235) (Here before I told you that your well must be four square, and each square three feet wide). These, when multiplied together, equal twelve:

> þanne iiij. sythe iij. make xij. þanne 3oure welle muste be xij fote abowtyn þanne muste þe curblys þe tabylment þe fundement be nethe. þat is þi feyth & þi beleue be xij fote abowte in wydnesse for to acorde to þe wydnesse of þe foure sqware. þi beleue in xij fote wydnesse is in xij. artycles whiche xij. arn in þi crede. (ed. Atchley 235–36)

Then four times three makes twelve. Then your well must be twelve feet about. Then must the corbels—and the tablement (a foundation structure)—be placed beneath. That is your faith and your belief are twelve foot about in wideness for to accord to the wideness of the four squares. Your belief in the twelve feet of wideness is twelve articles, of which twelve are in your Creed.

The writer seems to be suggesting in this passage that each "square" or side of the well is three feet in length, which would, when added, equal twelve "fote abowte."[58] This example works out perfectly both geometrically and numerologically, for the audience's belief and faith must rest on Christian doctrine, specifically the twelve articles of the faith; the squareness of the shape also indicates the stability of faith and belief. As we saw in the earlier chapters, four times three (as in the four gospels times the Trinity) make for convenient spiritual arithmetic. Through this example, the audience can "know themselves" and be in perfect measure with their squared and stable faith and belief resting on the twelve articles of the faith.

The *Well* writer saves his strongest example of "right measure" of virtue via geometry until he approaches the end of his sermon cycle, when he offers an extended meditation on the Ladder of Love or Charity. As the sermonist explains, this ladder stretches from the deep well to high heaven and has three dimensions, echoing the passage from Paul: "A laddere hath lengthe brede hey3te & depth" (A ladder has length, breadth, height, and depth). In addition, it also has the dimension of time, for he describes how the ladder of love "is long in tyme duryng" (ed. Atchley 349) (is long in time enduring). The writer makes a series of analogies between the dimensions of the ladder and the divine. For example, the ladder is broad and wide like Jesus's love, as well as deep and low like his love, and so on (ed. Atchley 352–54). In discussing the length of the ladder, the writer asserts, "þe lengthe of his [Christ's] loue was betoeynd þat he hyng a long in his body in þe lengthe of þe cros. as he hadde stande ri3t vp" (the length of Christ's love was betokened by his hanging long in his body the length of the cross, as if he had stood upright). He also asserts that "þe hey3te & þe depthe of þe charyte of god þat is þe brede þe lengthe þe hey3te & þe depthe of þis laddre of loue in god to man" (the height and the depth of the charity of God, that is, the breadth, the length, the height, and the depth of this ladder of love in God to man). The charity of God, he writes, is multidimensional, and the scope of it lies beyond humankind's comprehension: it "ys hyere þanne heuene deppere þan helle. lenger þanne erthe & braddere þan þe se. in mesure" (ed. Atchley 354) (is higher than heaven, deeper than hell, longer than earth, and broader than the sea in measure). The sermon writer proposes that God's charity both encourages comparison and measurement (so that audiences can appreciate it) while at the same time resisting quantification, because his love is beyond a person's ability to measure. Yet the scope of God's charity is still "in measure"—that is, in perfect moderation.

This description of man's love for God as multidimensional, that "þi loue to þi god as I telde þe beforn must be longe brode hey3. & depe" (your love to your God, as I told you before, must be long, broad, high, and deep), is extended to love of one's neighbor as well, as the writer explains the allegorical meanings of the measurements as a way to teach his audience how they must believe and act in the world. He also adds another dimension by translating "length" as time: "loke þi loue to thy ney3boure be long in durynge in to þin ende" (ed. Atchley 373) (look that your love to your neighbor be long in duration to your end). "Broad" is translated as loving one's friend and foe on both sides: "In largenes of brede loue hym þus. loue on þi ry3t syde þi freend. loue on þi lyfte syde þi fo" (ed. Atchley 374) (In largeness of breadth love them thus: love on the right side your friend, love on the left side your foe). To love one's neighbor "highly" is interpreted as asking what profits one's brother and "loue his soule bettere þan þi body and þanne is þi love hey to hym" (ed. Atchley 375) (than your body; and then is your love high to him). Last but not least, one must love one's neighbor deeply and lowly: "in lownesse lowly loue hym lowly serue hym. lowly helpe hym lowly worschyppe hym" (ed. Atchley 375) (in lowness humbly [lowly] love him, humbly help him, humbly honor him). In this example, the *Well* writer revels in his description of the geometry of love with all its dimensions (in all senses of this word), culminating in the poetical exhortation to love one's neighbor "in lownesse lowly loue hym." Geometry, with its multidimensionality, becomes a perfect metaphor to use in describing both the love of God and humankind's need to love one another, as God is the ultimate geometer.

One could argue that the *Well* writer only alighted on the idea of the three-dimensional well as a useful *divisio* schema for his sermon cycle; rather than imagining a tree with branches, for instance, he decided to adopt another useful visual schema. However, the time and attention he devotes to the actual shapes and dimensions of sin, virtue, belief, love, and so on throughout the cycle indicate that he is heavily invested in the metaphoric and allegorical possibilities offered by geometry. The irregularity of the shapes of sin shows how they resist easy quantification and also prove themselves to be completely out of measure; they are odd, strange, misshapen forms. Whereas the virtues and qualities that follow are not necessarily definable shapes either, they do appear more balanced and more in "measure" in terms of their numerological meanings. Finally, as we see in the description of the Ladder of Love, the sermon writer is delighted by the opportunity afforded by equating different dimensions—length, breadth, width, and time—with Christ's unmeasurable love, which serves as a model for humankind's love for one another. Thus, only through "knowing thyself" via a deep knowledge and spiritual understanding of virtue and love can one hope to measure up to God's expectations and to appreciate and fathom more fully God's love.

Jacob's Well is a remarkable text full of examples of arithmetic, measurement, and geometrical shapes. The sermons draw from the everyday experience of its audience—merchant-class lay men and women practicing numerate acts in their homes, towns, businesses, and markets—and often combined their practical experiences of number with numerological interpretations. The sermon cycle encourages numerate figuring while often purposefully resisting easy quantification, which emphasizes how difficult it is for people to count or quantify their own sins—the numbers are no doubt too large to comprehend, and the volumes are often undefined. We must also acknowledge or even embrace the frequent breakdown of the extended allegory, as the sermonist moves back and forth from the division of sin into "trees with branches" or two-dimensional figures to a well of ooze that is a three-dimensional solid with depth, breadth, and width.[59] God may have ordered the world in weight, measure, and number, but the sermon writer of *Jacob's Well* shows how difficult it is for humans to appreciate fully that measure. Many of the sermons suggest that mathematical operations and understanding of number are appropriate and useful ways for engaging in spiritual practice, for living a life of right action and obedience, and for learning to love God more deeply. At the same time, however, calculation does not necessarily lead directly to knowing God, as we see in the examples that resist enumeration and counting. Rather, the struggle with number and the appreciation of its spiritual resonances lead one to appreciate the enormity of God's love even if God cannot be fathomed specifically.

Katherine Cooper argues that the author of *Jacob's Well*, in his discussion of penance, tries to define contrition as measurable, but as each step of contrition grows harder, it ultimately proves impossible. Cooper concludes that the tools of contrition are inadequate to excise the *wose* that pollutes the audience's conscience.[60] In this chapter, I have argued that the problem is not that the tools are inadequate but rather the depth of sin that one has fallen into. According to the sermonist, a person cannot truly know the extent of his or her sin, or the extent of mercy that God will extend to any individual Christian upon his or her judgment. The problem of measure lies not with the tools but with the *wose* itself. But just because one cannot specifically measure that sum of sin fully does not mean that one is excused from examining the individual parts in great detail to combat them inch by inch. The sermonist presents an amazing array of measures that point to something fathomable (the depth of sin), even if the sums of those measures cannot be fully determined. Thus, the overall message promoted by the effort of digging out sin and forming a well can be extremely accurate—how to conduct oneself in the way that God expects, and how to love God better—while still resisting easy quantification, for it is the effort of spiritual calculation that leads the audience closer to God.

CHAPTER 4

Quantitative Reasoning in the Latin Sermons of Robert Rypon in London, British Library, MS Harley 4894

In the first three chapters of this book, I examined how Middle English sermons engage with number, numerology, and mathematical operations—including number theory, arithmetic, and even geometry—to explain and model a range of religious concepts and spiritual practices, from how to escape the depths of human sin to how to praise God abundantly for his creation. I argued that these sermons foster a particular kind of numerate understanding and practice in their lay audiences that relies on both pragmatic and spiritual senses of number. In this last chapter, I focus on a Latin sermon collection that reveals a remarkable engagement with number, the collection of a "master" sermonizer, the Benedictine Robert Rypon (ca. 1350–1421/1422) of Durham Priory. Like the Middle English sermons previously discussed, Rypon's Latin sermons assume that the audience, either reading or listening, will comprehend, appreciate, and even enjoy the many moments in which they are asked to participate in spiritual calculation.

Most medievalists will not have read much of Rypon's work, as his sermons have largely remained unedited until recently. In 2019, Holly Johnson's edited collection of Rypon's sermons on feast and saints' days, in Latin with English translations, was published in the Dallas Medieval Texts and Translation series, and a second volume, on Rypon's Lenten sermons, is in preparation.[1] Rypon produced fifty-nine sermons that have survived in one manuscript, London, British Library, MS Harley 4894, which Siegfried Wenzel characterizes as "almost a de luxe" manuscript.[2] As Johnson's editions attest, these sermons are replete with startling imagery, attention to sensory details, and delightful and revealing discussions; Johnson observes how creative Rypon's sermons are, stating that they "develop in detail, sometimes excessive, complex analogies and moralizations."[3] For example, Rypon delves into the five interior and exterior senses across a variety of sermons, as well as incorporates vivid imagery involving the seven deadly sins.[4] Although many of his topics are quite typical for late medieval sermonists, what is so unusual in this collection is his brilliant attention to detail as well as many of his curious examples and analogies that demonstrate both the depth of his learning and his willingness and ability to innovate.[5]

Rypon's career and sermons have attracted the attention of several scholars, including G. R. Owst, Siegfried Wenzel, and, more recently, Holly Johnson. Johnson traces Rypon's university and monastic career and reports that Rypon received his doctorate from Durham College, Oxford, and served as both the prior of Finchale Priory and the subprior at Durham Priory.[6] As Johnson argues, his collection of sermons in Harley 4894 was based on orally delivered sermons that were written down later, with their references expanded and an index added: she concludes that these sermons "retain the flavour of the oral performance but with an eye towards a reader and potential preacher."[7]

Rypon's original aural audiences were both monastic and lay, as "Rypon preached in churches in Durham as well as in the Cathedral, probably often in the Galilee chapter where the monks preached on Sunday afternoons, sermons the laity were granted indulgences for attending."[8] He also preached "at neighborhood churches on Rogation days" and "during processions for the king or for peace."[9] This suggests that at least some of the sermons were originally preached in English, in part if not entirely. It is important to realize that just because a sermon is extant in Latin does not necessarily indicate that it was preached in Latin. It may have been intended as a model sermon to be translated into the vernacular when preached; conversely, of course, vernacular sermons may have been translated into Latin when preached.[10] This means that it is not always possible to make concrete assumptions about a sermon's audience based on the language the sermon was written in; what helps to identify audience, for example, is how the sermons address the listeners and readers, or how the specific content of a sermon might reveal the concerns of either lay or clerical audiences.[11]

I include this caveat because in turning to Latin sermons in this chapter, I do not want to suggest that, because of the language in which they were written, they necessarily required or attracted a completely different audience from the vernacular sermons discussed in the first three chapters. My study focuses on "English" sermons—that is, sermons composed in England, in Middle English and/or Latin—because sermons could easily be translated into either language when orally delivered. Being written in Latin does not necessarily mean that a sermon was delivered in Latin. Certain of Rypon's sermons, however, such as the sermon exploring the different senses of the word for "was" in Latin (making the distinction between *erat* and *fuit*) would have made more sense to someone familiar with Latin, but this does not exclude a certain segment of the laity who may have understood the content. Although scholars have long emphasized the role of the mendicant orders in preaching to the laity, more recent scholarly attention has uncovered the significant role of the Benedictines in public preaching.[12] As Wenzel asserts, Rypon "evidently was occasionally sent out from the priory to preach in the countryside," for the Durham Accounts record that he preached "apud Heghinton, Billyngham, et S'cam. Hildam etc."[13] Several of Rypon's sermons are specifically addressed to priests and curates, but, as Wenzel notes, many have no specific address, and one is even addressed to both priests and parents, which would suggest that the audience for the sermons was often mixed.[14] Thus, we cannot assume that the intensity of Rypon's engagement with number in his sermons is necessarily due to a more literate, Latinate, monastic audience, although certainly monks would frequently have been part of his audience. However, I believe we can say that Rypon's attention to number comes in large part from both his academic training and his work in account keeping as a prior of Finchale Priory and as an almoner at Durham Priory.

In this chapter, I argue that Rypon's sermons offer several extended discussions involving number that demonstrate just how important spiritual calculation had become by the early fifteenth century. Like the writers of the vernacular sermons considered in earlier chapters, Rypon incorporates spiritual calculation into his texts, through the inclusion of number, number theory, geometry, and arithmetic, combined with numerology. In Rypon's examples, the numbers used to describe God, as well as God's expectations for human behavior, are fully fathomable. Extended treatment of the numerological value of Jesus's and Adam's names reveals a sermonist who appreciates the long, learned tradition of exploring number in theology, and his discussions rely on knowledge of both the Greek and the Roman methods of representing numerals as well as the Hindu-Arabic method, with its concept of zero.[15] At the same time, however, Rypon is equally comfortable using a contemporary, practical example of quantitative reasoning drawn from his extensive experience with accounts as prior and almoner when he employs the act of counting money to explain a difficult theological concept. Other sermons examined in this study address tithing practices and basic monetary calculations; Rypon, however, fully capitalizes on the role of monetary calculations in the church by directing his audience's focus toward accounting—what scholars have argued fueled the late medieval arithmetical mentality—as he delights in demonstrating exactly how counting money can be used as a model of spiritual improvement. In Rypon's deft hand, counting money models exactly what God expects of Christians. For Rypon, therefore, even the most mercantile enterprise can be put to good use for devotional and spiritual contemplation.

PART 1: RYPON'S USE OF NUMBER IN SERMONS

As we have seen in the first three chapters of this book, sermonists employ discussions of number in multiple, interconnected ways, by developing sermon division and enumeration and incorporating numerology and number theory, as well as arithmetical acts. Rypon's sermons embrace all these practices as well, and he weaves them together in particularly complex ways. He is especially drawn to the numerological meanings associated with the numbers seven and ten and invokes these meanings in several sermons.

Of course, sermon division and enumeration are of particular importance to Rypon, who was well trained in the scholastic sermon tradition. For example, in the sermon for the Sunday after Epiphany, on the theme "Make his works known among the peoples" (Isa. 12:4), the sermonist divides the theme into three (knowledge, people, and virtues), and he then proceeds to divide each of those into three as well:

> I find in Scripture that the knowledge and also the people and the virtue are threefold. For it is knowledge through signs, words, and deeds: through express signs of inward perfection, through persuasive words of learned preaching, through manifest deeds of salvific action. In addition, [the people] are threefold: the people perfected, the people subjected, and the people gathered from both groups. The people perfected are the clerical people, the people subjected are the lay people, the people gathered from both are the general people. Last it is a virtue physical or natural, a virtue ethical or moral, a virtue theological or supernatural.[16]

Rypon then delves into his division, and during his discussion of the first part, "make known" or knowledge, he turns to the five interior and exterior senses before moving to the five signs of inward perfection. During his elaboration on parts two and three (which he combines), he describes how the office of the curate is divided into six parts, as well as how "to make known the virtues" requires the "four rules in nature"—first, "only a good thing should be loved," second, "every bad thing should be shunned," third, "not every good thing should be loved equally," and fourth, "not every bad thing should be hated equally but each according to the degree of its wickedness."[17] Rypon's sermons rely heavily on division, subdivision, and enumeration, and this is not much different from what we have seen in the Middle English sermons discussed in earlier chapters, except for an increased intensity combined with a special fondness for subdivision. This is not unexpected, however, as several of Rypon's sermons are quite long in comparison to the Middle English sermons in Longleat 4 or Salisbury Cathedral 103. Siegfried Wenzel characterizes Rypon's sermon style as follows: "Such meticulous attention to structure goes beyond the customary division, subdivision, and distinctions of the scholastic sermon; it creates an impression of academic fussiness."[18] It may also have been the result of a process that expanded the sermons in written form from their earlier orally delivered form, as Rypon would have had ample time to develop his arguments more fully.

Whether fussy or merely attentive to structure, Rypon especially enjoys the sensory qualities created by his sermon divisions. For example, in an elaborate allegory of a well in his First Sermon for Rogation Days, he describes how the paths to the well are actually the seven virtues. Four obstacles made of sin block the paths, including "the thorny hedge of avarice" and "the deep ditch of gluttony or lust with which sloth is connected."[19] In his Second Sermon for Blessed Oswald, on the theme of "This man began to build" (Luke 14:30), Rypon expands on the multiple staircases with which different social estates can reach heaven. The sermon progresses through the seven steps of humility by which "all Christians should ascend to the excellence of a holy life, which is the eighth step, which reaches the terrace, specifically heaven, that is, beatitude,"[20] and then later delves more specifically into individual staircases, including the stairs "by which knights will ascend to heaven"[21] and the steps "by which the farmers and citizens will ascend to heaven."[22]

Rypon is a sermonist who enjoys a good *divisio* and makes the most of it. With Rypon's spiritual associations of number, we also see an intensification of focus as he delves deeply into the extended allegory made possible by numerological meanings. In general, in comparison to the sermonists of Longleat 4 and *Jacob's Well* (Salisbury Cathedral 103), Rypon seems to tend less toward the quick numerological association and more toward the developed discussion that relies on layered associations. For example, in his First Sermon for the Blessed Mary Magdalene, with the theme "Strength and comeliness are her clothing" (Prov. 31:25), Rypon elaborates on how the church can be compared to a woman, and therefore "each Christian should be clothed in virtuous strength and comeliness."[23] As evidence of this, he describes how the exterior senses can encourage natural strength in God, and also how they can debilitate that natural strength. He gives the example of Samson, who heard Delilah's false voice and was lured in by her. Rypon explains that when she cut off Samson's hair, he lost his strength, "which was dependent on seven locks of hair."[24] He then equates the seven locks of hair with "the seven gifts of the Holy Spirit in which all the virtues necessary for salvation are included."[25] Furthermore, those seven locks represent those Christians who, like Samson, in giving up the locks—that is, virtues—are "handed over (I say) to the power of the devils."[26] But Rypon does not stop there with the analogy. He continues to elaborate on the multiple meanings of the number seven by asserting that when Samson's hair grew back in, "Samson grew in strength and finally killed the greatest number of Philistines," which Rypon interprets to mean that "someone who, limping in the folly of the world, falls into the evil of sins: when his seven hairs grow again—that is, the seven mortal sins—finally he punishes and kills himself spiritually along with many depraved Philistines, specifically those who fall into evil through him."[27] Thus, as Rypon has explained, these seven locks of hair can represent opposing forces: first, the seven gifts of the holy spirit; second, Christians who give up the truth, and third, the seven deadly sins, in a brilliant allegorical interpretation that completely reverses the interpretations of seven hairs or locks. Rypon is here challenging his audience to be extremely flexible in their numerological interpretations, and the audience would need to be quick on their feet to keep up with the sermonist's evolving implications of the number seven. Whereas for many medieval commentators Samson's betrayal prefigured the betrayal of Christ, in Rypon's sermon he takes the interpretation of Samson in a much different direction, led by the possibilities of the interpretation of the number seven. Rypon's interpretation of Samson as committing suicide with those he has depraved seems to augment Augustine's interpretation of Samson as prompted to suicide by "the Holy Spirit within him."[28]

 Rypon enjoys elaborating on the spiritual meaning of the number seven because of the flexibility offered by its various numerological associations. Another example of this can be found in his First Sermon for the Second Sunday in Lent, on the theme of "You have received from us how you should walk" (1 Thess. 4:1). In this passage Rypon models a complex set of opposing equivalences: "And the Apostle recites in the same place which are the works of the flesh and which are the fruits of the spirit. But the Apostle recites the works of the flesh in the number seventeen which is composed of seven and ten as a sign that the ten works of the flesh are opposed to the Ten Commandments, and the number seven of the works of the flesh agrees with the seven deadly sins which are contrary to the seven gifts of the Holy Spirit or the seven virtues of the sacraments of the Church."[29] Here the sermonist describes how the works of the flesh and the fruits of the spirit are counterbalanced. Seventeen is made of seven and ten, or the ten works of the flesh, which are contrasted to the Ten Commandments, and the seven remaining works of the flesh are equivalent to the seven deadly sins and counterbalanced by the seven gifts of the Holy Ghost or the seven virtues of the sacraments of the church. In this example, Rypon's choice to separate the prime number seventeen into ten and seven is quite productive, for he can then pull in the Ten Commandments as well as significant heptads, suggesting to his audience that numerological calculation can be employed for either the purpose of equivalence or opposition.

Although I have asserted that in general Rypon elaborates on spiritual associations of number less frequently than do the authors of Longleat 4 and *Jacob's Well*, when he chooses to engage, he does so quite intensely. In his Second Sermon for Blessed Oswald, he draws on the verses in Luke 14:31–32, which raise the question of when a king should enter into battle:

> 31 aut qui rex iturus committere bellum adversus alium regem non sedens prius cogitat si possit cum decem milibus occurrere ei qui cum viginti milibus venit ad se
>
> 32 alioquin adhuc illo longe agente legationem mittens rogat ea quae pacis sunt.
>
> 31 Or what king, going out to wage war against another king, will not sit down first and consider whether he is able with ten thousand to oppose the one who comes against him with twenty thousand?
>
> 32 If he cannot, then, while the other is still far away, he sends a delegation and asks for the terms of peace.[30]

As Rypon reflects on this passage, he offers an engaging and extended interpretation involving the preacher and the audience's prideful assumptions:

> Morally, each preacher of God's word, indeed each person, is called a king who should rule the kingdom of his own soul. The other king advancing against him is God, who is the King of kings. The preacher engages in war with God and advances against him with ten thousand when, by preaching the Ten Commandments of the Lord, he presumes to convert the people by his own preaching. Also a person advances against God with ten thousand when he believes that he merits heaven by only fulfilling the Ten Commandments. But certainly God advances against both the preacher and the hearer and any other person with twenty thousand because truly he can say to us, "Whatever good you have done on my behalf, I did doubly more on your behalf."[31]

Rypon explains in this passage that the ten thousand men signify the Ten Commandments; humans, both preacher and audience, are like kings with ten thousand men or the Ten Commandments. In his pride, the preacher preaching about the Ten Commandments thinks he converts by his own power, and the audience members think they only need to fulfill those Ten Commandments to reach heaven. God, however, has double that strength and requires much more effort from his creation. Rypon then equates this act of duplation or doubling with humankind's sin: "Indeed, God opposes us by objecting to every sin that we have done in heart, word, or work, which undoubtedly are twice more than the good works we have done."[32] This then leads to a discussion of the three estates of man, which then leads to the staircases to heaven I referred to above. The point, the sermonist suggests, is that number can lead to heaven, but the effort required to mount steps will be demanding, since the enumerated steps required to get to heaven insist on so much more than just living by the Ten Commandments.

Rypon's sermons also contain several extended commentaries involving arithmetic combined with number symbolism, which he employs to describe the human lifespan as it should be lived for God. In his First Sermon for Easter, he relies on spiritual associations with the number forty, as well as some basic arithmetic, in order to discuss the importance of repenting of sin and doing good works. "Decline from evil and do good" (Ps. 36:27), he quotes, and he first discusses what it means to "pass over spiritually from Egypt,"[33] which invokes analysis of the number forty. He describes how "the children of Israel" left Egypt and remained for forty years in the desert, which he equates with the "sinner passing over from sin," who "should continue his regimen for forty years . . . that is, through his entire life—by rejecting sin." He then continues by discussing how forty signifies "the course of human life" because "we recognize as holy the time of penance for sin."[34] He returns once again to the number forty as the span of a man's life, connecting that with the "forty days in this pasch," before introducing a detailed example of spiritual factoring and multiplication: "But everyone knows that in forty there are four tens; this ten signifies the Ten Commandments, which should be multiplied by four because they should be fulfilled throughout the four parts of the year through which human life moves and in the four complexions of the body in which the bodily powers consist, in a sign that the Ten Commandments should be carried out continuously with all [one's] powers."[35] Rypon's comment that "but everybody knows" (*set constat*) that there are four tens in forty suggests that he expects his audience to be familiar with this kind of factoring on both a pragmatic and a spiritual level. He introduces what would have been to his audience the quite familiar association of the number ten with the Ten Commandments and then moves to the assertion that the Ten Commandments are fulfilled in the Pasch feast, before returning again to the concept of "forty" in relation to Christ: "For as Christ ascended into heaven forty days after the Resurrection, so also we, after passing through the course of life which is signified in this feast, ... finally ascend to heaven."[36] The numerological associations (the four seasons of the year or the four humors, times the Ten Commandments) yield a kind of spiritual calculation that indicates humankind's lifespan in the service of God.

In the following section, we shall see how Rypon moves from assigning the familiar numerological values to numbers (such as equating the number ten with the Ten Commandments) to how he employs a traditional and learned form of numerology, that of assigning number values to letters, in order to convince his audience of the ultimate value of Christ's sacrifice.

PART 2: NUMEROLOGY AND NAMING

Rypon's interest in numerological connections reaches its peak in his Fourth Sermon for the Third Sunday in Lent, where he speaks on the theme of "Jesus was casting at the devil" (Luke 11:14). Before he immerses his audience in numerology, however, the sermon invokes both spiritually infused number theory and geometry as a way to describe demons as well as sinful people. In elaborating on the meaning of the word "devil" or demon, Rypon muses on why there are eleven names of demons in Scripture; the number eleven, he argues, "aptly pertains to the names of the demons because, according to blessed Gregory, while the Decalogue [the Ten Commandments] is in number ten, the transgression of the Decalogue in which is included every sin, is aptly designated by the number eleven."[37] Rypon invokes the Ten Commandments, with their embodiment of the perfection of the number ten, and the imperfection or sinfulness of the number eleven, as we saw with the *York Play of Pentecost* before the twelfth apostle was chosen. Whereas certain sermons I examined earlier in this book imagine a person's transgression as occurring within the number ten of the Ten Commandments (either a person could break all the commandments by breaking one commandment within the ten, or a person is best represented by the imperfection of the number nine), in this sermon Rypon chooses to emphasize how the number eleven represents people's transgression of the Ten Commandments, an act that equates them with the sinful demons named in Scripture.

Immediately after this passage Rypon moves from number theory to spiritual geometry, in which he introduces a discussion of atoms, as derived from the *minima naturalia* theory of Aristotle and revised in the work of Scholastic scholars. Rypon embarks on an exploration of the knowledge the demons had of God; in comparing their wisdom to his, "they grew proud," which of course led to their fall. This leads Rypon to reflect upon how little humans understand the works of God. He invokes the geometry of a circle to suggest that "no one can know the nature of a single atom [i.e., an indivisible element] . . . because the atom is a dimensional body being able to receive a circle around itself." Rypon explains, "In a circle are contained all the figures of a straight line and thus infinite subjects and consequently infinite passions and infinite conclusions and thus infinite knowable things are in it. And hence a certain philosopher said: 'I know one thing—that I know nothing.'" Rypon suggests that because a circle contains infinity within it—infinite subjects, passions, and conclusions—as well as "an infinite number of knowable things," the circle offers too much for one person to know, which led to Socrates's conclusion (or at least Plato's account of Socrates's conclusion). Thus, this passage would seem to suggest that the circle, in representing infinity, is too great for humankind (or indeed, for a fallen angel) to strive for—this knowledge is only able to be known by God. The preacher warns, "And, indeed, it is vanity to be proud about any unstable thing because, of course, that which is unstable is likely to fall. But knowledge, especially wordly knowledge, is most unstable, falling as it does into oblivion by some sudden corporal illness."[38] However, Rypon emphasizes that men and women cannot indulge in the vanity of saying that nothing can be known—they must know some stable things for certain, which are offered by concrete numbers. Rypon then continues by enumerating and interpreting the eleven names of demons.

When he turns to Jesus's name, Rypon offers an elaborate numerological discussion of the numbers that each of the letters in Jesus's name represents. In this passage, the sermonist argues that numerology can now accurately represent the power and perfection of Jesus. Drawing on Saint Bernard, Rypon sets up his equation by describing the letters used to render the name "Jesus" in Greek and Latin:

> With regard to the signification of this name Jesus, it must be noted that among the Greeks, it is written with six letters, namely iota, eta, sigma, o, y, sigma. These letters sound among the Latins as: I, E, S, O Y, a diphthong for which the Romans placed this letter V and sigma. The rest, according to the custom of the Latins, is written with three Greek letters, namely Iota, Eta, Sigma . . . which three letters can morally designate the Trinity. . . .The writing of the three letters is pronounced among us as Jesus.[39]

Having established the number of letters and connecting the number three with the Trinity, Rypon then moves to the general numerological workings of these letters using the classical Greek system of assigning letters to stand for numbers, and quoting Bede as his source. I include the passage in its entirety, to demonstrate Rypon's attention to detail as he describes how number values are assigned to each letter. In this passage, Rypon includes Arabic numerals instead of the more typical Roman numerals, even introducing the idea of zero:

> As far as the writing of this blessed name is concerned, as to the six letters, the venerable Bede says in that passage in Luke 2[:21], "His name was called Jesus," that the number of letters of this name is redolent of the eternal mystery of our salvation. For each letter of this name denotes a certain number denoting a mystery of our salvation. Regarding this, note that according to some there are 24 letters in the Greek alphabet and three figures added to them, so that the letters with the figures are three nines. Thus in the first group of nine, each letter signifies a number, one number per letter and the order of the number up until nine. In the second ninefold each figure is counted for its multiplied number one hundred according to the order of the algorithm.[40] So the first letter of this name, "Jesus,"

namely iota, that is "i," denotes 10 because iota is the first letter in the second group of nine letters of the Greek alphabet. In second place, the letter eta, that is "e," denotes 8. The third letter is sigma which is the second in the third group of nine, and it designates the number 200. The fourth letter is short o, and it is the seventh in the second group of nine, and this denotes 70. Y [i.e., upsilon] is the fourth letter in the third group of nine, and it denotes 400. Sigma, as was said, denotes 200. Thus all these numbers added together, namely 10, 8, 200, 70, 400, and 200, make 888, which number, reduced by 0, agrees with divine figure of the Resurrection of the Lord. For the Lord rose on the eighth day, namely the day after the Sabbath. So also we after seven ages, that is after the Sabbath of souls on the eighth (as it were) age, will rise.[41]

In this technically specific passage, Rypon carefully walks his audience through the steps of his calculations so that the logic becomes clear to them. First, he explains how the twenty-four letters of the Greek alphabet, plus three figures, equal twenty-seven, which can be factored into three times nine (or three "ninefolds"). Second, he describes how each letter of Jesus's name can be replaced with a number, as it fits into one of the three ninefolds. The first ninefold contains numbers one through nine; the second stands for multiples of ten up to ninety; and the third ninefold stands for multiples of one hundred up to nine hundred. Third, he works through the letters individually, stating how he arrives at their number value, and then describes how the numbers can be added together to equal 888, which was traditionally thought to be the number of Jesus.[42] Fourth, he then describes how 888 betokens other significant eights, including the resurrection on the eighth day, if one counts after the previous Sabbath. To make this connection, Rypon imagines taking out the zeroes from the tens and hundreds (800 plus 80 plus 8) so that just the number eights are left, which signify the Resurrection. Number, therefore, fully proves and supports the meaning of the name of Jesus, the Resurrection, and his role in the salvation in humankind, for Rypon asserts that people will also rise in the eighth age. In the passage, Rypon moves from the Greek method of assigning letters to represent numbers to using the Hindu-Arabic numerals, including 0, a "newer" method of representing numbers that was gaining some traction in England at the time but would not become standard usage for at least two centuries.

Having demonstrated how 888 is calculated in detail, Rypon then turns to a more familiar topic, the symbolic resonances invoked by the numbers eight and ten, as he draws on acts of multiplication to enhance the spiritual meaning of his argument:

> Or in another way it can be said that the name of the Savior, namely Jesus, may simply contain 8 because whether 8 is multiplied by 10 or by 100, the resulting number is still 8. For 8 multiplied by 10 equals 80, and 8 multiplied by 100 equals 800. Thus from the multiplication of 8 by 100 our resurrection is understood as before, and in the multiplication of 8 by 10, whence 80 results, denotes that by fulfilling the Ten Commandments, we may reach perfect beatitude. As for 8 multiplied by 100, since the number one hundred in Scripture signifies the reward of the perfect, it is signified that through 8, namely Jesus, we will come to our eternal reward. In a sign of this, the centenarian Abraham begat the first son of the promise, namely Isaac, who means "laughter" or "joy." From all this it appears fully that in the interpretation, naming, and signifying of this name, "Jesus" is a pious remedy and aid. And this is what is written in Acts 4[:12]: "For there is no other name under heaven given to men, whereby we must be saved," except in this name.[43]

Here Rypon contemplates multiplication and spiritual factoring (for example, eight times the Ten Commandments), as well as the perfection of ten and one hundred, all of which, when multiplied, lead back to the power of the name of Jesus. Eight, as we saw in chapter 1, was thought of as a marvelous number because it was two times two times two, or two cubed; the twelfth-century theologian Gerhoch of Reichersberg states, "Eight, as the first perfect cube, imprints us in body and soul with the security of eternal beatitude."[44] The sermon audience is schooled in the numerological meaning of Jesus through the assigning of number values to letters in Greek, as well as those numbers' spiritual resonances (the numerological practices that we have seen most often in this book). Rypon is fully comfortable in this quantitative and numerological world, demonstrating for audiences how calculation can lead them to understand the full significance of Christ's resurrection and the eternal reward offered by God.

Another sermon by Rypon, the Second Sermon for the Sixth Sunday of Lent / Palm Sunday, on the theme of "What shall I do with Jesus" (Matt. 27:22), also reflects on the three figures of Jesus's name and their value in connection with the Trinity. This sermon offers a more familiar numerological assessment of Jesus's name than the previously discussed sermon; in this text, the sermonist begins by exploring how Jesus's name is associated not with 888 but rather with the number three and related trios—namely, the Trinity and the three natures of Christ, as they stand against three evils:

> For it is written, according to the Greeks, with three figures, which are iota, eta, sigma. Iota is interpreted as the perfection of the Lord; eta as a strong mind; sigma as worthy of hearing. Therefore all together, Jesus, that is perfection of my strong Lord worthy of hearing. First by the writing: the fact that it is written in three letters or figures shows to us the faith of the Trinity or of the three natures in Christ, namely the deity and humanity in which are two substances or natures, namely body and soul. Or it is written in three figures through the trinity of graces brought together for us by the Lord Jesus Christ himself against three evil deadly and original sins, which are the desire of the eyes, the desire of the flesh, and the pride of life.[45]

To read these two sermons on Christ's name together suggests that Rypon was giving audiences a choice of which numerical association to remember—the more difficult and incredibly numerologically productive figure of 888, with its various spiritual resonances, or the equally productive (but easier to calculate) number three, which also leads to a multiplicity of interpretations. Or, more likely, he may have been encouraging his audiences to consider both ways of valuing Jesus's name, for the resonances overlap. Rypon goes beyond the basic association of Jesus's name with the number three to dive deeply in the number of letters in Jesus's name in Latin, as well into the number of letters in Adam's name, in order to point to something fundamental about the nature of both Christ and humans. As Rypon explains, Jesus, "among the Latins," which is written with five letters, can be mystically understood according to the number five: "The number five in one way is composed from four and one, and in another way from three and two, and it is developed by the venerable Anselm on John, homily 7, on his wonderful work of praise of the cross."[46] Following Augustine in his Commentary on Psalm 96 (as well as other early writers), Rypon describes how the name Adam "is composed from four letters," which indicate "the four parts of the world, which are east and west, north and south, which are said in the barbaric language: 'Anathole disis archos mesembrios,'" with the first letter of each spelling "Adam."[47] These four letters of Adam's name, Rypon asserts, "signified that Adam himself was master over the four parts of the world in his beginning," and that with the fall, Adam's name signifies his separation from "his dominion" because of his sin.⁴⁸ Rypon then connects the four letter of Adam's name with all humankind: "In addition, a man is composed of four elements which at least in their parts are liable to corruption."⁴⁹ To this Rypon adds another reason the number four is so fitting for humankind and draws on some basic calculations of four as two squared as well as the sum of three plus one:

> The number four, therefore, agrees suitably with man then first because the name of the first man is composed of four letters, then secondly, because man (as was said) is composed of four elements. Then thirdly, since that number is composed of twice two, of which each is an equal number in an equal twin, it allows division, which division of numbers suitably agrees with man on account of two things. First, because through sin he was divided from his God; secondly, because he was divided in himself. Just as four is twice two, of which neither number is subordinate to the other, so also man was divided by sin from God because the lesser part after sin was not placed under [i.e., subordinated to] but was opposed to the superior part. Similar is the division of the number four (with regard to the argument), if he is said to be composed from three and one, for the wretched man was divided from the Trinity in divine things.⁵⁰

Having explored why the number four represents humankind so well, Rypon circles back to Jesus, who represents salvation with the number five, in a passage that moves from four plus one, to three plus two, then back to four plus one again: "But note how in the mystery of the number five comes salvation, that is, Jesus, to the number four, that is, man, God is joined in the unity of his combined nature, and if it is Jesus or the number three, namely to the Trinity of persons, two are united, namely body and soul, and thus the incorruptible is united to the corruptible, just as, according to the philosophers, the fifth incorruptible body is joined to the four elements."⁵¹ With this last statement, Rypon is referencing the fifth element as described by Aristotle and later understood to comprise the soul.⁵² In this impressive and detailed example, the fundamental properties of the numbers four (which is composed of two plus two or one plus three) and five (which is composed of one plus four or two plus three) contend. Five comes after four, of course, and what answers the problem of four (i.e., humankind) is five (i.e., Christ). Rypon continues, "Note as I said how in this name Jesus is understood not only the blessed Trinity, but also the incarnation of Jesus Christ, and aptly the entire faith. These four mentioned letters can also signify the cross of Christ stretched in four directions on which the incorruptible fifth hangs."[53] Jesus then becomes the image of the cross extended into the world of humankind, with his body, the fifth element, hanging upon it. Thus, Jesus becomes "one plus four" again, containing humankind within himself yet far exceeding it.

In these two sermons Rypon offers his audiences several remarkable numerological considerations of Jesus's spiritual value as seen through the letters of his name. Whether Jesus's name reveals the number three, five, or 888, all three numbers point to the role of Jesus as the redeemer of humankind. The sermonist shows himself to be a master of number symbolism and to be able to manipulate it easily. He is obviously drawing on learned sources here—Augustine and Bede, as well as other early theologians—and shows off his learned numerological interests. He is also comfortable working in different systems of number representation: the Greek system with its letters representing single digits, tens, and hundreds; the Roman system with its numerals that also employ letters; and the Hindu-Arabic system of numerals that utilize zero. Rypon, however, is equally comfortable using a nontraditional quantitative image to represent divine love. We shall now turn the most overt example of spiritual calculation offered in this entire study—a discussion in which Rypon wholeheartedly embraces the metaphor of accounting on a counting board or cloth, something we believe he would have been familiar with from daily practice. I believe that Rypon is aware of this idea of the "arithmetical mentality" underlying late medieval spiritual practices and is showing how even an act as mercantile as counting money can be employed for spiritual purposes. We have seen some minor examples of the counting of money and tithes in this study, but nothing we have seen can fully prepare us for Rypon's elaborate allegory.

PART 3: SPIRITUAL ACCOUNTING IN RYPON'S SERMON FOR THE NINTH SUNDAY AFTER TRINITY

In his sermon for the Ninth Sunday after Trinity, the theme is "Give an account of your stewardship" (Luke 16:2). Rypon elaborates on how to account for one's life, including a discussion of stewardship (with a note about proper tithing) as well as the spiritual and corporeal ways of accounting with acts of charity. In his example of money, Rypon takes on the very idea of the late medieval arithmetical mentality and imagines how accounting and monetary practices can be seen as a model for Christians who are accounting for their good works and their lives. In this sermon we see the culmination of all our examples of spiritual counting—Rypon shows how even mundane accounting can be a model for spiritual accounting.

As Johnson describes, Rypon had first-hand knowledge of accounting in his role as almoner at Durham Priory and prior at Finchale Priory.[54] Medieval almoners were charged with distributing money, food, and clothing to the poor and needy. In many religious houses, almoners were given a portion of the tithes to allocate.[55] It was thus a position that required good arithmetical skills. In this sermon Rypon draws on this experience in counting money, but also on the knowledge that his audience would understand the practice he was describing, no doubt because they had either engaged with money counting themselves or watched others. Because the theme of the sermon is giving an account of one's stewardship, Rypon urges his mixed lay and clerical audience, "Let us therefore here render the account for this life using the method of accounting," and describes specifically how to add twelve pence to reach one shilling, and twenty shillings to reach one pound, all of which he weaves into an elaborate spiritual allegory.[56] For this analogy, Rypon describes a medieval counting board (which could be made of cloth, leather, or wood), upon which a person used reckoning tokens or *jettons* to represent monetary units:

> It happens that, when accounting, pence are placed up to six, and then if they grow beyond six, one counter is placed above that six so that the counter transposed to a higher place by means of itself makes a shilling, namely twelve pence.[57] Morally to the point, the sixth number is the first perfect number, and it signifies all the time in which we live and work. Let us count that time well, first among ourselves in farthings and halfpennies, that is, in lesser deeds and greater ones, and those which are superfluous—namely, sins—let us clip, and let us insert into our calculation those which are true, namely, insofar as they are well paid out. Because in the counting of the first six pence stands, as it were, the foot of our calculation, on which are held the good works that we have done; let us place a counter above to stand for six pence, so that the one transposed will be valued at twelve pence, that is, one shilling. This shilling is faith; this faith together with good works is one and also unalloyed, indeed the foundation of every spiritual good, according to the Apostle.[58]

To appreciate fully Rypon's example, we must recognize how many of the number-related practices we have seen in the earlier chapters are being drawn into this discussion. His example of counting money relies on arithmetic (adding twelve pence to equal a shilling, adding twenty shillings to equal a pound, etc.), and further addition is implied by the references to halfpennies and farthings. Rypon also draws in basic number theory with his assertion that six is the first perfect number, although that of course also relies on numerological associations with the number six, as it signifies "the time in which we live and work"; a similar idea is expressed in *Dives and Pauper*, in the argument that seven comes after six, and therefore seven is the eternal rest after the work of our lives, which is best represented by the number six. Rypon elaborates on the spiritual meaning of the counting; six pence, "the foot of our calculation," equal a person's good works; two groups of six (the first represented by the counter that is placed above the six) equal a shilling, which stands for "faith," which is then quickly amended to "faith with good works." The pence or good works in this analogy are "the foot" of the calculation because on the medieval counting board (or cloth) the board is divided into units with the lowest denomination, the ones, at the bottom.[59]

Thus far the analogy, although detailed, is quite straightforward—a person counts pence to six, then replaces that six with a reckoning counter or jetton, and counts another six, to equal a shilling. One counts good works to reach "faith," which is then amended quickly to "faith and good works," no doubt because "good works" are thought to rest within the body of faith. Here Rypon continues with some crafty spiritually infused arithmetic, as he models how to calculate shillings (which together signify the articles of the faith) by five, which he equates with the five senses:

> When we now have this shilling, that is, faith with good works, let there be a further calculation, namely, of shillings—that is, of the articles of faith—by five, that is, the five senses; that is to say, the total reckoning of our calculation may be put in line by faith with good works, and then one counter may be substituted for the five on the right side and made equivalent with these five; that is, the five interior senses may be made equivalent with the five exterior senses in faith and the working of good works for the honor of God, who is at our right hand. And let them be passed over to the left side—to our neighbor—and then they make ten shillings, that is, the fulfillment of the Ten Commandments, so that the transferred counter makes a pound, which is composed from two equal things, namely, from ten and ten, and which aptly signifies the [two] parts of justice. [The first part is] that one should render to God what one owes from the goods of nature: the activity of the heart, [which is] love and faith; the activity of the mouth, by praising him and confessing

your sins; the activity of the body, by serving him and obeying his commandments.[60]

In the first passage, pence are added to reach a shilling; in this passage, Rypon describes how shillings can be added to reach a pound. Now shillings are added in sets of five rather than sets of six, because one pound can be divided into four sets of five. Rypon equates the five-shilling sets with the five senses, describing how a counter may be substituted for each set. As he reiterates, the basis of the calculation is faith with good works; when the counters are added together and replaced for each five, this indicates the five interior and exterior senses, which are brought into line with the "faith and the working of good works for the honor of God." Of particular note is how Rypon equates the special orientation of the counting board, and the movement that takes place on it, with either the "right" hand of God or the left, indicating one's neighbor. In this sense the sermonist is pressing the analogy as hard as he can—not only do the vertical movements have spiritual meaning (moving up from the foot of the calculation with pence), but also the two horizontal sides, left and right.

Rypon's linking of accounting with the five exterior and interior senses is also quite productive. Throughout his sermons, he explores the value and role of the five interior and exterior senses in understanding God and modeling Christian behavior.[61] For Rypon as for other medieval writers, the exterior senses can serve as a path to God, but they are also a way to sin; as we saw in the chapter on *Jacob's Well*, the senses are the floodgates that originally let in the sin that corrupted the water of the well and created the ooze of sin in the listener or reader's body and conscience. In Rypon's counting analogy, however, both the interior and the exterior senses are equitable because they are built on a foundation of faith and good works. In this case, the exterior senses are elevated to the status of the interior senses, something we rarely see in religious texts that compare the two kinds of senses.[62] Moreover, to use a monetary unit for each of the senses is to assume that they are all the same value. To add the exterior and interior senses, or two counters, is to make ten shillings, or the fulfillment of the Ten Commandments; to do this twice is to make a pound, "which is composed of two equal parts, the [two] parts of justice." Rypon then wraps the message back to what Christians must render to God: what is owed "from the goods of nature," "love and faith," "praising and confessing sins," and "obeying his commandments."

This elaborate discussion of counting sets out everything a Christian must do, including the need to obey and love God and his commandments, tithe correctly, and confess one's sins. In this remarkable example, Rypon equates actual currency with spiritual currency; he demonstrates how even the most mercantile act of counting can yield spiritual understanding, if one employs number in creative and flexible ways. In giving his example, the sermonist shows that he can even sanctify and spiritualize money. So much for the moneychangers in the temple whom Jesus throws out! Rather, Rypon offers his audience the example of the accurate tithe counter, almoner, or even tradesperson handling currency as the model of how a Christian ought to behave to please God.

As I have argued in this chapter, Rypon's engagement with number in his sermons not only reflects the attention given to number in the contemporary Middle English sermons explored in the first three chapters but also extends that discussion in new ways. Most striking is how Rypon can move between the older, learned numerological practice of assigning number values to letters and the numerological practice involved with an innovative analogy based on contemporary money-counting methods. Both of these numerological practices he employs to try to convince his audience of the value of the divine and the veneration God deserves. Rypon shows how the numerological can work within a learned, traditional past as well as practical medieval experience, all to demonstrate how the "arithmetic of salvation" can be pushed to its furthest limits.

In his 1983 essay "Arithmetic and the Mentality of Chaucer," Derek Brewer argued that, for late medieval writers, the "pleasure in numerology is totally different from, indeed at the opposite pole from, an interest in arithmetic." Whereas he associated the numerological with writers like the Pearl Poet, the arithmetical turn of Chaucer was a sign of "the leading edge of modern attitudes," which were drawn from commerce.[63] Brewer's statement was challenged quite early on by Thomas Shippey in his exploration of Chaucer's numerological interest in line counting in the *Book of the Duchess*, and certainly many scholars after would not draw such a strict line in the sand as did Brewer. All the sermonists and other authors I have discussed in this book do exactly what Brewer asserts they could not—they all mingle and meld arithmetical and numerological modes. Rypon offers a particularly strong example of someone who is both arithmetically minded and deeply invested in the numerological resonances of number. As Rypon demonstrates, late medieval sermonists can be focused on both the practicalities of counting and the spiritual resonances of those practices, to the point that they suggest one could even think of the act of making shillings from pence and pounds from shillings as an act that delights God.

Conclusion
Practical and Spiritual Numeracy in "The Book of Margery Kempe"

In this study I have argued that late medieval sermon writers in English as well as Latin invoked numbers, number theory, and various arithmetical operations as particularly useful ways to describe a Christian's relationship with God, including how best to venerate God as well as how best to understand his creation. I have argued that this kind of discussion of number, which is often combined with numerological or spiritual understandings, formed a kind of hybrid numerate practice that sermonists modeled in their sermons for audiences. Sermon writers engaged in this practice in order to invite their audiences to understand more fully Christian doctrine and Scripture, as well as to model how listeners and readers should conduct themselves morally in the world. I have raised the question of whether or not this kind of hybrid numerate practice traveled from the church out into the world—did medieval people leave this numerate practice at the church door when they exited the church after a sermon (or indeed, wherever they heard the sermon), or did this kind of spiritual calculation influence the activities in their daily lives?

In his treatise *On Acquiring a Trained Memory*, the fourteenth-century theologian, mathematician, and archbishop Thomas Bradwardine wrote that one could remember specific numbers by imagining a particular visual image for each number between one and ten. For example, Bradwardine suggests that for the number two, a person should picture either Moses with two horns or the two tablets with the Ten Commandments. For three, a person should picture the Trinity "as it is usually painted in churches"; for five, "Christ crucified with his five wounds"; and so forth.[1] Almost all the images he recommends are religious in nature. I have tried this method and can attest that it really does work on a small scale; I don't think I will ever have trouble remembering my license plate again. For those medieval people using this method to remember weights, numbers, and measures, the numbers' spiritual significance may well have influenced the way they thought of that number. (After all, thinking of my license plate now invokes a set of sophisticated religious associations that I would not otherwise have made.) But just because Bradwardine's method works does not necessarily mean that the typical medieval person used this particular method or something similar, for it is not clear if many people outside the university or reading treatises on memory would have known of it.

But we do know that the typical medieval person listened to sermons. Surely some people loved to listen to them, and others of course spent their sermon time doing other things, if priests' complaints about their audiences are anything to go by.[2] If we assume that the average medieval person listened to at least several sermons a year (and perhaps many more sermons than that) and was exposed to sermons that modeled spiritual calculation, did they then carry this hybrid numerate practice out into the world? When medieval sermon listeners counted to five, did they think of Christ's wounds or the circularity of five, which reminded them of the infinity of God?

What started me thinking about this question so intently was recalling an Easter sermon I heard about twenty years ago. As expected, the subject of the sermon was the resurrection of Christ. But when the preacher reached the part about rolling away the rock from Christ's tomb, he made an analogy to an unmade bed and announced to the congregation: "Now, whenever you see your unmade bed, you will think about the rock rolling away from the tomb." And in the twenty years since I heard that sermon, often when I look at my unmade bed in the morning (or the afternoon and evening) the memory comes to me of the sermon. I have spent much time trying to recall just what the specific association was that the preacher made between an unmade bed and the rock rolling away, but I do not remember, so I have tested out countless connections. I have also wondered frequently, if one is making the bed and contemplating the resurrection of Christ, does that make this chore an act of devotion? One might answer this by saying that whether or not it is an act of devotion would depend upon the person's intent and attitude while they were making the bed. To make the bed and be annoyed about the intrusive image (as I often am) would not be an act of devotion. In the same way, for a medieval person to count five of something (say, rabbits) and think of Christ's wounds and be frustrated by that connection would not be an act of devotion. However, if that same person counted five wine bottles and contemplated Christ's wounds, as well as how that wine represented Christ's blood, that could certainly be considered an act of devotion if the contemplation encouraged that person to be more pious or mindful of God.

Thus we return to the question, did medieval people who listened to spiritual interpretations of number and arithmetic and other mathematical operations in sermons draw on and incorporate those practices into their everyday acts of numeracy? Of course, this question is difficult to answer definitively without observing a medieval person's numerate practices and then asking that person to describe in detail what they were thinking and doing. Many modern numeracy studies do just this—they observe practices and interview informants. I will therefore conclude this book with a consideration of these pressing questions: How can we know that these discussions of number in sermons did not dead end with the priest as soon as the sermon ended? How can we tell if the sermons' reading and listening audiences responded to discussions of number and carried these practices into their everyday lives?

To attempt to answer these two questions, I will turn to the fifteenth-century *Book of Margery Kempe*, the combination spiritual memoir, autohagiography, and visionary text written by a lay merchant woman from Norfolk, England, who was trying to live a semireligious life (although unaffiliated with any order) in the world.[3] The combination of genres in her *Book* makes it a fascinatingly rich study for examining numbers, for the account records Kempe's lived experiences shaped through a religious lens. Kempe's *Book* includes over two hundred references to specific numbers, and I argue that a close examination of how she uses these numbers reveals that she is often thinking of numbers doing work on both practical and spiritual levels. Essentially, Kempe's *Book* demonstrates this hybrid pragmatic and spiritual numerate practice that late medieval sermons, as well as other religious texts, foster.

In this study I have demonstrated how concepts involving number and numeracy were developed in late medieval sermons, and I have gestured toward other religious literary genres that explore similar references. What underlies these discussions is the idea that basic numeracy played an important part in late medieval spiritual practices. Thomas Lentes has argued that number lay at the root of the "arithmetic of salvation": "Religious life was not merely marked by quantification and multiplication; rather, counting appeared as an essential component of the practice of piety."[4] For example, late medieval people counted prayers and indulgences; *The Stations of Rome* and other pilgrimage guides (both armchair and "real") list indulgences that may be earned or gathered by visiting places, and one could easily add them together to get specific numbers of years of pardon.⁵ In the late Middle Ages, the practice of counting prayers on the rosary also became quite common. As Anne Winston-Allen defines it, the rosary is "a literary text, a ritual and a social practice" all in one; we can add to that a numerate practice as well.⁶

This focus on numbers and enumeration is often equated with the rise of mercantilism, as new methods of accounting including double-digit bookkeeping developed. Several scholars have seen the attention to numbers in *The Book of Margery Kempe* in this context. As Sheila Delany, David Aers, Clarissa Atkinson, and others have argued, Kempe's religious expression is marked by the internalization of the late medieval mercantile understanding of accumulation and profit.⁷ For example, Aers asserts that "the market's permeation of religious consciousness" is clearly evident in her frequent desire to "purchase 'mor'" pardons,⁸ or in a passage like the following, when Kempe asks Christ to be the executor of her will and to bequeath her store of merit. She declares, "It is fully my wyl that thow yeve Maystyr N. halfyndel to encres of hys meryte, as yf he dede hem hys owyn self. And the other halvendel, Lord, sprede on thi frendys and thi enmyes, for I wyl have but thiself for my mede" (8.636–40) (It is fully my will that you give Master N. half for the increase of his merit, as if he did it for himself. And the other half, Lord, spread on your friends and your enemies, for I will have only yourself for my reward).⁹ Christ then replies that because of her great charity Kempe will have a double reward in heaven—that is, "God Himself as her ultimate reward," which is, as Brian Gastle suggests, quite a good return for an investment.¹⁰

It is hard *not* to see passages like these as reflective of a proto-capitalistic mentality. After all, Kempe remembers and records specific amounts such how much she is given by the bishop, both to distribute to the poor and to purchase her own clothing with: Kempe asserts that every day the bishop of Lincoln gives "to xiii powyr men xiii pens and xiii lovys" (15.1094–95) (to thirteen poor men, thirteen pence and thirteen loaves); the bishop then gives her "xxvi schelyngys and viii pens to byen hyr clothyng wyth and for to prey for hym" (15.1139–40) (twenty-six shillings and eight pence to buy her clothing with and to pray for him). However, in my 2013 essay "Numeracy and Number in *The Book of Margery Kempe*," I explored how, and what, and why Kempe counted, and I made the argument that, of the over 230 references to specific numbers in her *Book*, money accounts for only about one-fifth of the things she counted. I argued that in addition to remembering specific sums, Kempe actually reflected scriptural language as well as the language of other visionary texts in many of the numbers she recorded, as in the above example of the "double reward in heaven," or in the following episode when

Christ reassures Kempe that "many hundryd thowsand sowlys shal be savyd be thi prayers" (7.612–13) (many hundred thousand souls shall be saved by your prayers), and then later he repeats that "I have many tymys seyd to the that many thowsand sowlys shal be savyd thorw thi preyerys" (78.6249–50) (I have many times said to you that many thousand souls shall be saved through your prayers).[11] "Many hundred thousand" is the highest number referred to in the *Book* and no doubt indicates an enormous amount, more than could be counted. Kempe is clearly echoing biblical language here, for the Bible makes numerous references to "many thousands," "tens of thousands," and "hundreds of thousands." For example, Revelation reports the army of horsemen to number "twenty thousand times ten thousand," and in 2 Chronicles we find that "a hundred thousand valiant men" were hired "for a hundred talents of silver."[12]

In the years since I first wrote the article on Kempe's numeracy and began researching the use of numbers in a range of medieval religious texts, I discovered that sermons often engage in discussions of number even more deeply than other religious texts do. Thus, in light of what I have learned while working on this project, I would like to take up the question of Margery Kempe's attention to number yet again, this time to demonstrate how she internalized and demonstrated several of the number-related practices I have described in this study.

But why discuss Margery Kempe in a book on sermons? Basically, because Kempe is an avid sermon listener and also a preacher of sorts—there is a wealth of scholarly literature on Kempe both seeking out sermons and serving as preacher and teacher.[13] However, Kempe was not just a listener to (and occasional preacher of) sermons. She was also an avid consumer of pastoral, devotional, and visionary texts, as we learn in the *Book* when we are told that the priestly scribe read to her for seven years. She was also perhaps a watcher of biblical cycle plays when she went to York, and we can imagine she heard and consumed all sorts of other religious texts while on pilgrimage. Many of these religious texts also contain references to number, and we cannot use Kempe as an example of someone who heard only sermons and no other religious texts. I do, however, believe that Kempe did experience an intense discussion of numbers from sermons and that she would also have been exposed to this kind of treatment in other devotional and pastoral texts. Kempe's *Book* offers us a valuable and compelling example of what I have termed a hybrid numerate practice in which number functions on both a pragmatic and a spiritual level. Thus, rather than just being a mercantile counter, Kempe is a religious, spiritual counter as well.

For Kempe counts many things in her *Book* in addition to money. She counts the numerous times and ways that she falls away from Christ and draws near to him. For example, her illness after her first pregnancy lasts "half yer, viii wekys and odde days" (1.200–201) (half a year, eight weeks, and some days); afterward she is shriven twice or three times a day, and she rises at two in the morning for prayers and remains in the church until noon (3.368–73). Kempe is specific in her reporting of her ebb and flow with the Lord: she counts aids and witnesses to her religious devotions, as well as lengths of religious tests and practices. In doing so she relies on what rhetoricians refer to as the "rhetoric of precision."[14] Precise numbers are a good way to authenticate experiences for audiences and to assert authorial expertise.

The *Book* teems with examples of Kempe counting the duration of religious experiences, for her precisely recorded times emphasize the great extent of her spiritual practice. Naoë Kukita Yoshikawa has noted how the *Book* is structured around liturgical time; events are linked to specific calendar days, such as Epiphany, when Kempe has a vision of the infant Christ, and the Wednesday of Easter Week, when she convinces her husband not to have sex with her.[15] But Kempe's attention to duration of time is also striking. She counts the length of time for a certain soul in purgatory (thirty years) (19.1495), the number of years certain people have left to live (ten years or seven years) (23.1742), and the number of weeks she spends on pilgrimage: thirteen weeks in Venice (27.2130–31), three weeks in Jerusalem (29.2331), and two weeks in Compostela (45.3650). She records the length of time she waits to speak with the bishop of Lincoln, which is three weeks (15.1056), and how long she waits in Bristol to sail for Compostela, six weeks (44.3525). She measures periods of chastity, noting that her husband did not have sex with her for eight weeks (11.717–18; 724). She counts how long it takes to have a Pentecostal miracle of tongues in Rome (thirteen days) and the number of years she experiences the holy visitations of Christ (twenty-five years) (33.2687–703; 87.7230–31). And when she is in Beverly being questioned for Lollardy, she records that a clerk wants to imprison her for forty days (54.4493).

Many of the events and experiences that Kempe enumerates or quantifies reveal the influence of numerological significance. Because of the particular form of her spiritual autobiography, with its many passages recounting specific events of Kempe's life, it can be difficult to determine how often she intends numerological interpretations, and how often she is simply recording a lived experience of measurement. In other words, when is a measure of *three* just three units and not intended to suggest the Trinity? Moreover, in those cases where allegorical interpretations may not be intended, we must ask if Kempe was able to recall the precise measurements because the allegorical meanings of the numbers influenced her memory of the experiences.

The influence of numerology, however, is clear in several examples of Kempe's use of the number three. "Three" of course is suggestive of the Trinity, as we see in other religious texts and as is so often emphasized in sermons.[16] Kempe measures many religious events, practices, and trials in threes. She of course refers to the three persons of the Trinity on many occasions (e.g., 16.1251–61), and at one point she even recalls how she entered a chapel with a lady and priest "al thre togedyr" (19.1467) (all three together), suggesting her association of church with "threeness." She also recounts durations that occur in threes: her three years of great labor (3.380), and elsewhere her three years of temptation (4.416; 11.759); her three weeks spent waiting for the bishop of Lincoln (15.1056), and the three weeks she dwelled in Jerusalem (29.2331). In each of these examples the number three emphasizes either a religious trial or a devotional practice Kempe undertakes with difficulty and dedication. She endures three years of temptation in order to be closer to the Trinity; she spends three weeks waiting for the bishop in order to express her experiences with the Trinity; she travels in Jerusalem for three weeks, where she seeks important pilgrimage sites related to the Trinity.

Five, although not appearing frequently in the *Book*, is invoked at a specific moment that clearly signifies the wounds of Christ. The *Book* records that when Kempe's husband falls down the stairs and hurts his head, he has "v teyntys" (five linen plugs) in his head wounds (76.6012). Up until this moment, Kempe has wanted to devote all her attention to Christ, but Christ tells her she must care for her husband, and Kempe suffers both the slander of the community (who blame her for her husband's accident) and the difficulties of looking after her ill and incontinent husband. The five wounds suffered by her husband suggest how her caring for her husband is actually part of her devotion to Christ, to whose wounds she has an especially strong devotion.

The number seven also appears with some frequency in the *Book*, as does fourteen, its double. Of course, seven can have great spiritual significance: we need only think of the seven deadly sins, the seven virtues, and so on, whose spiritual significance was developed frequently in sermons. Kempe's *Book* also records many measures of seven, and the use of this number may reflect its popular allegorical significance. For example, a friend gives Kempe seven marks so that she can pray for her in Compostela (44.3501–3). Did Kempe recall this specific amount, seven marks, because of her mercantile nature, which would not let her forget a monetary amount? Or are we to interpret the seven marks as an apt sum for Kempe to pray on behalf of a friend who has no doubt engaged in some aspect of mortal sin? As Pauper in *Dives and Pauper* asserts, if a person commits one sin, they commit all seven; thus seven marks emphasize the need for prayer and repentance, as well as how efficacious Kempe's prayers are in helping the sinful. Moreover, Kempe's clerical scribe describes the seven years of reading they engage in, seven years in which he reads devotional, scriptural, and visionary texts that are helpful and sustaining for both Kempe and himself.[17] These seven years of reading might suggest the readers' focus on the seven virtues, to combat the seven deadly sins. Or the seven years could reflect the focus on spiritual bliss that comes after the six days (i.e., a lifetime) of spiritual works in the world.

The *Book* also demonstrates the medieval Christian fondness for the number twelve, which appears often in the Bible (the twelve tribes of Israel, the twelve apostles, etc.). Kempe envisions herself as the young Virgin Mary's servant until Mary reaches the age of twelve (6.550); Kempe then dwells with Saint Elizabeth and Mary for twelve weeks before Saint John is born, and she sees the infant Christ on the Twelfth Day (6.570, 7.590). This biblical focus on twelve is then translated into Kempe's own life. Later in the *Book*, when Kempe is praying in the church of Saint Margaret on Pentecost, she is hit on the back and head with a falling stone and beam, which weigh, in turn, three and six pounds; she records that she feels no pain for twelve weeks afterward (9.672–73). In this instance, the *three*-pound stone is then doubled as a *six*-pound beam, which is then doubled as *twelve* weeks; one could also add the three and six pounds to equal nine, which then makes the series three, six, nine, twelve, emphasizing the progression by steps of three, or the Trinity. I have argued elsewhere that in this scene Kempe is patterning a religious martyrdom; here she experiences the glory of potential martyrdom and a miracle of survival, all on a day in which twelve apostles experienced the gift of tongues.[18] In this case, Kempe adopts the number of the apostles and translates that into weeks without pain. At another point, when Kempe is tormented with visions of men showing their "bare members" to her, she is told she must suffer that pain for twelve days, signifying that she has lost God's grace for those days (59.4893, 4902, 4906); she is never further apart from Christ than she is during this time period.[19]

I could continue here with many other examples of numbers that I believe have spiritual resonances in the *Book*, but I will limit myself to just several more. Kempe cites the number forty far more frequently than thirty or fifty, which could suggest that the practice of counting by scores influenced Kempe's lived experience and/or memory. However, in certain instances the number forty has been included and/or remembered for its spiritual significance. For instance, when Kempe is accused of Lollardy in Beverly and a clerk threatens to imprison her for forty days (54.4493), this number has biblical and liturgical references; while it is the term imposed by a writ of "Significat" in church courts, for Kempe it is almost certainly reflective of Christ's forty days and nights of trial in the desert.[20] In this sense, Kempe sees her life as a kind of *imitatio Christi*, as she patterns and/or remembers the events she experiences as being reflective of Christ's life.

Kempe also refers to one hundred and one thousand frequently, which may invoke the discussions of those numbers as "perfect" numbers, both from number theory and from numerology. For example, Kempe asserts that she wishes she could be "slayn an hundryd sithys on a day, yff it wer possibyl" (77.6165–66) (slain one hundred times in a day, if it were possible) for the love of Christ, which would suggest one hundred is serving as an extremely high number that could be replaced by a nonspecific phrase like "a great many." But it also suggests that being slain for God's love, like a martyred saint, is such a perfect act of love that it can only be represented with a multiple of ten. In addition, Christ reassures Kempe that her silence is more pleasing to him than a thousand Paternosters (35.2920–22) and promises that he prefers "o yer of thynkyng in thi mende" (one year of thinking in your mind) over "an hundryd yer of preyng wyth thi mowth" (36.2934–36) (a hundred years of praying with your mouth), which suggests that even the perfection of one hundred years of Kempe's prayers and one thousand Paternosters said by Kempe are not equal to her inner love for Christ. Kempe reflects this same idea when she claims that she would not have lost the ring that Christ gave her for a thousand pounds (31.2545–46). Kempe would rather have Christ's wedding ring than a "perfect" and huge sum of money, ten times ten times ten pounds.

Medieval sermons offer many examples of spiritual calculation in the form of arithmetic as a way to appreciate God's love, to venerate him, and to live more Christian lives. Sermonists suggest that engaging in this math, whether it be addition, multiplication, factoring, and so on, especially when coupled with numerological overtones, reveals truths about Scripture and the world. We see evidence of several practices related to arithmetic in Kempe's *Book* that I believe reflect this focus on describing and venerating God. First is her frequent practice of doubling (or *duplation*) and halving (or *mediation*) of numbers, which seems to shape her memory of events; these were common arithmetical practices in the Middle Ages.[21] For example, Kempe relates how she tries to convince a man of "L wyntyr age" (fifty years old) to accompany her on pilgrimage, but he refuses, stating, "I wold not for an hundryd pownd" (30.2485, 2504) (I would not for a hundred pounds) lest she be harmed in some way while with him. This is a typical pattern of the *Book*. When Kempe travels to Compostela for fourteen days, she describes her entry into the city on the seventh day. When she has her fits of crying, she records that she cries fourteen times in one day, and seven on another (28.2237).[22] As mentioned, the stone that fell on her as she prayed in church weighed three pounds; the beam that also fell was doubled, at six pounds. On another occasion, she records how the pain in her side lessened from day to day, which is a process of halving: sometimes she had pain for eight hours, sometimes four, and sometimes two (56.4620–21).[23] In addition to a predilection for halving, these numbers also suggest spiritual factoring; for example, God lessens Kempe's pain by factors (eight hours become four and then two hours) as her devotion increases; God protects her from bodily harm and pain (from objects weighing three and six pounds) for twelve weeks because of her intense devotion.

We also see several instances of implied multiplication in the *Book*. Kempe sets up a basic multiplication problem when she relates how she is punished for not wanting to hear about the damned as well as the saved. She states that the Lord

> suffyrd hir to have as many evyl thowtys as sche had beforn of good thowtys. And this vexacyon enduryd xii days togedyr, and lyche as befortyme sche had iiii owrys of the fornoon in holy spechys and dalyawns wyth owr Lord, so had sche now as many owrys of fowle thowtys and fowle mendys of letchery and alle unclennes. (59.4853–57)

> suffered her to have as many evil thoughts as she had good thoughts before. And this vexation endured twelve days altogether, and just as before she had the four hours of the morning in holy speech and dalliance with the Lord, so now she had as many hours of foul thoughts and foul imaginings of lechery and all uncleanness.

Kempe sets up the equation: she has as many bad thoughts as she had good thoughts, lasting for twelve days, four hours a day. She then describes the range and kinds of abominable thoughts she has, leaving the reader to imagine how many terrible thoughts one could have in four hours times twelve days, or forty-eight hours. What if she had one bad thought a minute? Two?

And, if as readers we are asked to calculate the number of sinful thoughts, we are then by extension invited to imagine the tremendous number of good thoughts she must have had in forty-eight hours, let alone twenty-five years.

As I discussed in chapter 3 of this study, Kempe offers a complicated arithmetical problem when she describes the scourging of Christ. She sees "sextene men wyth sextene scorgys, and eche scorge had viii babelys of leed on the ende, and every babyl was ful of scharp prekelys, as it had ben the rowelys of a spor. And tho men wyth the scorgys madyn comenawnt that ich of hem schulde yevyn owr Lord xl strokys" (Sixteen men with sixteen scourges [i.e., each with a scourge] and each scourge had eight balls of lead on the end, and every ball was full of sharp prickles, as if it had been the wheels on a spur. And then the men with the scourges made a vow that each of them should give our Lord forty strokes) (80.6413–17). Kempe suggests that it is valuable to try to calculate the number of Christ's wounds, even if one is unable to arrive at the exact number because of the undefined "full of sharp prickles."[24]

Multiplication is also suggested in several of Christ's speeches to Kempe as he encourages her to appreciate how much he values her devotion. In chapter 84, he takes a number Kempe uses to assert her religious devotion and folds it into his arithmetical equation, turning it to her benefit once again. Christ commands Kempe to tell the wife of a very sick man that she [Kempe] should go to to the abbey of Denny in Cambridgeshire. When Kempe tells the wife, the wife replies, "I wolde not . . . that myn husband deyid whil ye were owt for xl schelyngys" (I wish not . . . that my husband die while you are out for forty shillings), to which Kempe answers, "Yyf ye wold yeve me an hundryd pownde, I wolde not abyden at hom" (If you would give me a hundred pounds, I would not abide at home) (84.6819–20). Later in the chapter, Christ reassures Kempe that she will have all the reward in heaven for "good wills and good desires" as if she had accomplished the actual deeds, and in doing so he invokes the one hundred pounds: "And also thu hast thowt that thu woldist, yyf thu haddist had good anow, a made many abbeys for my lofe, for religiows men and women to dwellyn in, and a yovyn iche of hem hundryd powndys be yer for to ben my servawntys" (84.6859–63) (And also you have thought that you would, if you had goods enough, made many abbeys for my love, for religious men and women to dwell in, and have given each of them one hundred pounds a year so that they can be my servants). Christ implies that, were we given specific measures, we could multiply number of abbeys by number of monks and nuns by one hundred pounds by number of years to arrive at a sum approximating Kempe's desired prayers. However, this arithmetical problem resists quantification because of the lack of specific measures. Moreover, in another chapter, Christ tells Kempe that he prefers her to suffer the verbal torment of others rather than martyrdom: "Dowtyr, it is mor plesyng unto me that thu suffyr despitys and scornys, schamys and reprevys, wrongys and disesys, than yif thin hed wer smet of thre tymes on the day, every day for sevyn yer" (54.4386–88) (Daughter, it is more pleasing to me that you suffer contempt and scorn, shame and reproofs, wrongs and discomforts, than if your head were smitten off three times in a day, every day for seven years), which would calculate to 7,665 beheadings, a number greater than the countable wounds from his passion. Once again, however, the arithmetical problem is set up but not multiplied out; the important point is not the actual result but rather the increased devotion experienced by Kempe and the reader during the process of contemplating calculation, or even resisting calculation. Rather than inviting specific answers, the problems are supposed to suggest significantly large amounts, often more than can be easily counted.

The *Book* sets up problems that ask readers and listeners to engage in arithmetical practices. Kempe does not calculate the answers herself but rather encourages her audience to reach a deeper level of spiritual understanding as they contemplate those problems. The text therefore both embraces and resists counting. Of course, resistance to counting can increase devotion, as when Julian likens the blood from Christ's head to the drops of water that fall from the eaves of a house "after a greate showre of reyne," drops "that fall so thick that no man may numbre them with bodily witte."[25]

As I also mentioned earlier in this study, Kempe directly invokes the concept of infinity by closing her *Book* with a prayer that attempts to add up objects in the natural world to approximate infinity. Kempe attempts to list all the minute, countable things in the world like blades of grass, grains of sand, individual hairs of beasts, and so on to demonstrate how much love and praise the Lord deserves. However, as Nicholas Watson has suggested, adding these up can never reach infinity. Kempe, therefore, is demonstrating that one can never quite know God through number, although trying to understand him quantitatively is perhaps the best way one has to approach knowing him as well as pleasing him.

What does a reconsideration of Kempe's attention to number allow us to understand about the *Book*? No doubt Kempe's mercantile background does shape her experience of numbers. However, it is important not to overlook how Kempe uses number for spiritual purposes. She uses it to express the duration and frequency of her religious experiences and practices, and at times she draws on popular numerological understanding, as well as offering quantitative ways of approaching God. Thus, in addition to her oft-commented-upon ways of experiencing the divine through the senses, a focus on number shows her engaging with other ways of knowing God. Medieval readers of Kempe's *Book* would have recognized and appreciated her use of number and arithmetical operations in ways that modern audiences and scholars have overlooked.

I believe that Kemp's attention to spiritual calculation comes from listening to devotional books being read, from spiritual conversation with others, from contemplating the role of numbers in Scripture, and especially from listening to sermons. This kind of attention to modeling discussions of number, number theory, arithmetic, and other mathematical operations shaped the way medieval audiences thought of number, if we can take Kempe's *Book* as an example of one woman's lived experience and memory of number. Of course, we must acknowledge that because the *Book* is a visionary text, it makes sense that Kempe would employ a spiritual sense of number. Perhaps if we had another text by Kempe (for example, a list of expenses for her failed businesses), those numbers could not be read symbolically at all. Kempe's use of number in her *Book* may reveal how she was trying to represent her life in a religious manner, and wanting to shape how others read it; spiritual calculation is one such persuasive method to accomplish these goals.

In this study, I have introduced evidence from a variety of genres that have these numerical discussions, not just sermons. We find references to number and mathematical operations in pastoral treatises, biblical cycle plays, saints' lives, devotional texts, and visionary works. These genres remain largely unexplored when it comes to discussions of number. I thus end this conclusion with a call for further research into the use of numbers and mathematical operations in a wider range of religious texts across languages, as well as how these are modeled in other genres that are not predominantly religious in nature. Only then will we be able to appreciate more fully the richness of medieval people's numeracy.

APPENDIX:
METHODS OF COUNTING AND CALCULATION
IN THE LATER MIDDLE AGES

For those who are interested in how medieval people counted and calculated, two sources will prove invaluable: Karl Menninger's *Number Words and Number Symbols: A Cultural History of Numbers* and Moritz Wedell's substantial entry on "Numbers" in the *Handbook of Medieval Culture*.[1] In this appendix I offer a brief discussion of some of the most important tools of numeracy as well as an overview of the kinds of sources we have available to understand the numeracy of the non-university-educated laity in the Middle Ages.

FINGER COUNTING

For many medieval people, it is surmised that day-to-day acts of counting, addition, and subtraction were often performed on the fingers.[2] The typical history of medieval finger counting in England is related as follows: Romans counted on their fingers and would have brought their finger counting to England in the early centuries CE. It then probably became something of a lost art after the German invasions of the fifth century, only to be revived by the monasteries that were founded beginning in the seventh century. Usually cited as primary evidence is Bede's finger-counting explanation from his early eighth-century cosmological text *De temporum ratione*. The first chapter of this text, Bede's *De computo vel loquela digitorum*, describes how numbers are formed with the fingers and hands; the left hand counted units and the right hand marked the tens, hundreds, and thousands. Several later medieval copies even include how to represent the numbers ten thousand to one million, which involved touching other parts of one's body.[3] Because medievalists have argued that monks slapping their bodies to indicate the larger numbers would have been quite humorous, it has been suggested that these larger numbers were not really intended for use. This raises the question, Would a monk have needed to know (or had use for) numbers above ten thousand? As numbers in the Bible can certainly be higher than ten thousand, it stands to reason that a monk might have wanted to be able to represent those numbers.

The description of finger counting in Bede, as well as several other descriptions of counting on the hands and fingers that appear in early manuscripts,[4] has led us to assume that many medieval people counted on their fingers. Of course, there are limitations to this evidence; we must question whether this was indeed an universal monastic tradition that continued throughout the centuries, as well as whether monastic finger counting inspired or was similar to lay people's finger counting. Finger counting may well have had different forms depending on the trade and location of the practitioner. Also, I have not found solid evidence supporting the assumption that finger counting ceased during the Germanic invasions of the early Middle Ages and was only reintroduced by monastic foundations a century or two later. Alexander Murray in *Reason and Society in the Middle Ages* cites an eleventh-century source that states that using one's hands and touching thumb tips was a rustic form of measurement.[5] Other practices of using body parts for counting might have been common; for example, the twelfth-century encyclopedia of European artistic practices *De diversis artibus* gives all sorts of modes of measuring, including measuring with nails, fingers, hands, and feet.[6] Further information may be provided by ethnomathematicians and anthropologists, who have explored how non–formally educated populations count. For example, it has been documented that the Oksapmin from Papua New Guinea "use a nonwritten 27-body-part counting system to represent number in traditional activities."[7]

Another piece of evidence suggests that finger counting was being practiced by merchants in the Mediterranean region around the beginning of the thirteenth century. Leonardo Pisano, otherwise known as Fibonacci, wrote in his *Liber abaci* (The Book of Calculation), an arithmetical text for educating merchants, that "those who wish to know the art of calculating, its subtleties and ingenuities, must know computing with hand figures, a most wise invention of antiquity."[8] Fibonacci's statement seems to indicate that late twelfth- and early thirteenth-century merchants used finger counting in their business transactions, although it may also suggest that finger counting had fallen out of practice in favor of other methods, and Fibonacci was suggesting a return to the practice.[9] We surmise that finger counting could potentially take several forms: the fingers could merely reflect mental arithmetic or mark intermediary steps in the mental process, or counting could actually be accomplished on the fingers. Moreover, finger counting may or may not have required the use of memorized tables or figures. Arithmetical treatises recommend memorizing multiplication and cube tables, and it is quite likely that people from a wide variety of occupations would have memorized certain common calculations that were needed on a frequent basis.

In general, it seems relatively safe to assume that at least a segment of the medieval population counted on their fingers, and that when the sermons I have explored in this study modeled and encouraged audiences to calculate, some of those listeners and/or readers could have accomplished this on their fingers, perhaps with the aid of memorized tables.

WRITING AND RECORDING NUMBERS

In the Middle Ages, the recording of numbers and calculations could involve a number of simple tools. The word "calculate" comes from the Latin *calculus*, or small stone; the verb "to calculate" was first introduced into English in the sixteenth century.[10] Even before this word, however, manipulatives could be used to add, subtract, multiply, or divide, as well as to measure lengths and volumes. Any small manipulative, such as a stone or stick, could potentially be used to aid mental calculation or to perform and/or record calculations. In Middle English, the word often used is "reckon," which has the sense of "to enumerate a list," "to count out for payment," as well as "to determine by counting" or "to calculate."[11] The early thirteenth-century *Ancrene Wisse*, for example, states of the makers of the figures of "augrim," "as þeose rikeneres doð þe habbeð muche to rikenen."[12]

When recorded, numbers could be written as strokes on a tally stick. A number of tally sticks from all sorts of ventures and practices of commerce are still extant.[13] In order to record a certain transaction on a tally stick, a person could choose the length or thickness of the stick to indicate a quantity; they could then make any number of small cuts on the stick to indicate specific numbers. When lending money for a debt, the lender marked the tally stick and then broke it in half; when the borrower repaid the debt, the sticks were joined and either thrown away or destroyed.[14] We have multiple references to their use by the laity in vernacular texts such as Chaucer's *Canterbury Tales,* Gower's *Confessio Amantis*, and Langland's *Piers Plowman*.[15]

Numbers could also be recorded in dirt, on slate, on parchment, or paper.[16] Numbers could appear as Roman numerals (with or without abbreviations) or as words; fractions could be written with an "s" for *semi* or "half."[17] We should note that, although Hindu-Arabic numerals had been introduced to Latin Europe in the late tenth century, reintroduced in the twelfth-century mathematical translations from the Arabic and promoted by Fibonacci in his early thirteenth-century *Liber Abaci*, they did not finally replace Roman numerals for the typical person until the seventeenth century. Moreover, "zero" did not gain prominence in vernacular texts until the sixteenth century.[18]

Counting and arithmetical operations such as adding, subtracting, multiplying, and dividing may also have been conducted on some kind of abacus or counting board. The early Middle Ages inherited the Roman style of abacus, which represented decimal place value. This model contained beads or stones for thousands, hundreds, tens, and single units. In the late tenth century, Gerbert of Aurillac (later Pope Sylvester II) introduced to monasteries an abacus using Arabic numerals, and there is evidence that by the thirteenth century the abacus had entered secular use.[19] In assessing its popularity in both religious and lay settings, however, we are hindered by the lack of physical evidence. Very few, if any, abaci from western Europe survive; it has been suggested that they were burnt for fuel or destroyed after they fell out of fashion in the early modern period.[20]

More common than the abacus were various forms of wooden counting or reckoning boards, which could also be made of cloth or leather. One popular in England featured a board drawn with lines with flat counters representing numbers; this design would give its name to the English Exchequer.[21] The simpler counting board became increasingly popular with merchants, who are thought to have used boards and abaci in conjunction with finger counting and rote memorization of multiplication tables.[22] Once again we are hindered by the lack of extant counting boards; being wooden, they were not preserved after they fell out of fashion. However, some of the metal counters or *jettons* have survived.[23]

Other objects could also be used in ways similar to counting boards and abaci; the rosary, for example, which was developed in the later Middle Ages, has been described as a kind of abacus, one that allowed users to count their prayers and record their merit. As Thomas Lentes writes, quoting Gisland Ritz, "Rather like an abacus, it was also used as an (ac)counting tool with which the faithful sought to 'oversee the prescribed or intended number of prayers to be said.'"[24] Thus, according to Ritz, medieval culture fostered a kind of "bookkeeping mentality," with the accumulation of prayer.

I do not include the discussion of tools in this section to suggest that medieval people listening to a sermon with calculation in it suddenly whipped out an abacus to begin calculating during the sermon. But it is useful to think of the wide scope of counting tools that a medieval person might have had access to, including the rosary. Modern studies indicate that if a person is proficient at using a particular counting tool, like an abacus, that practice can shape how they perform mental arithmetic. For example, someone who uses an abacus frequently may imagine manipulating an abacus in their mind (or gesturing on an imaginary abacus) as they calculate.[25] This insight into modern mental practice may help us imagine how a medieval person performed their own mental calculations.

VERNACULAR NUMERACY

Certainly the most helpful modern focus for uncovering medieval practices of lay numeracy is what was once called "street mathematics" or "informal mathematics" and is now termed "vernacular numeracy," or those practices that are acquired through informal learning.[26] A number of anthropological studies on vernacular numeracy from diverse cultures stretching back several decades challenge uninformed notions of what non–formally educated people are able to do. These studies demonstrate how people from a variety of cultures invent ways to allow them to count, record (at least temporarily), and reckon in sophisticated ways. They demonstrate how high people count, how they count, and when they count. For example, a study from 1967 conducted in Liberia detailed how non–formally educated adults used stones to solve problems up to thirty or forty,[27] and a study from 1979, also conducted in Liberia, examined how non–formally educated tailors used buttons for counting.[28] People appear quite resourceful when it comes to counting, and we can imagine that non–formally educated medieval laborers, tradespeople, and merchants were equally as inventive. Studies of vernacular numeracy also demonstrate how people acquire their numeracy skills—often from watching other people, from their parents and family, and from their coworkers, which we assume was also how many medieval people learned.

One particularly useful study for thinking about medieval numeracy is Geoffrey Saxe's 1988 article "The Mathematics of Child Street Vendors." Saxe studied ten- to twelve-year-old candy street vendors with little or no formal education in the northeast of Brazil. This was a particularly useful population to study because Brazilian inflation meant the children needed to perform currency calculations with very high numbers. As Saxe concluded, "most vendors ... had developed adequate strategies to solve arithmetical and ratio problems involving large numerical values."[29] He discovered that when adding numbers (such as 37 plus 24), the children would "often restructure the problem into 'convenient' values for which they already [knew] the sums, proceeding, in contrast to the formal algorithmic procedure, from 10s to unit values. Using such a procedure, 37 + 24 may become 30 + 20 and 7 + 4, which in turn may become 50 + 10 + 1, and in turn yields the sum 61."[30] According to Saxe, the development of such "alternative procedures ... [is] linked to the everyday practices in which individuals participate."[31] This practice of regrouping gives us some insight into how medieval people might have calculated and is modeled in several of the sermons that I have discussed. Other ethnomathematical studies reveal practices that we can see in the Middle English arithmetical treatises. One such study in 1998 revealed how street vendors "solve multiplication problems through repeated addition,"[32] or what is known as "duplation" in Middle English. Thus, to multiply eight times four, one might add eight plus eight to get sixteen; one could either double sixteen or add two more eights to reach thirty-two. We see this practice of duplation several times in *The Book of Margery Kempe*.

The field of ethnomathematics therefore is an emerging one that allows us to examine non–formally acquired numerate skills and their practice by members of diverse communities. We must therefore try to imagine the mathematical concepts and practices a medieval person must have invoked and employed on a daily basis, even if they have left little or no written record.

WRITTEN GUIDES

As I have argued in this book, extant sermons reveal much about how medieval people thought about numbers and calculation. In this section, I would like to address several other written primary sources that directly engage in number and arithmetic. There are several arithmetical treatises extant in English from the fifteenth century, such as *The Crafte of Nombrynge*, that may give us a good idea of the state of arithmetical knowledge available in the vernacular at the end of the Middle Ages. These treatises feature basic number theory (including squares and cubes) derived from Boethius, as well as demonstrations of addition, subtraction, multiplication, and division of numbers in the tens and hundreds of thousands, using Hindu-Arabic numerals.[33] *The Crafte of Nombrynge* contains sections modeling duplation and mediation, as well as instructions on how to perform arithmetic without writing down the figures.[34] This idea of mental computation is especially important, for we imagine that although merchants and tradespeople may have had some form of slate, abacus, or dust board to calculate on, much of the calculation process, if not all, was probably performed in the mind.

We could also turn to other genres of Middle English texts to uncover what general expectations for numeracy were. For example, the late fifteenth-century printed text *Guide for Pilgrims unto the Holy Land*, published by Wynkyn de Worde and based in part on the *Itineraries* of William Wey, teems with numbers and assumes a range of numerate abilities in its audience. The opening pages list the distances between towns on various pilgrimage routes, suggesting the addition of measures; this is followed by a complicated list of currency exchange rates, which assumes an ability to add, divide, and multiply whole numbers as well as fractions. Moreover, the text includes short foreign-language word lists in Greek, Arabic, and Turkish; in these lists the words for numbers are the first translated (and the Turkish list consists only of numbers), suggesting that numbers form the basis of practical communication between different languages and cultures.[35] De Worde's text, therefore, expects its audience has a familiarity with distances, weights, monetary exchange, and so on, and this must have been a significant selling feature (it appeared in two subsequent editions, in 1515 and 1524).

A number of scholarly studies also address the numerical engagements of English merchants and tradespeople; for example, we might turn to the discussions of the national and international cloth trade, lead trade, or wine trade in Jennifer Kermode's *Medieval Merchants: York, Beverley, Hull in the Later Middle Ages*[36] and Lisa Jefferson's *The Medieval Account Books of the Mercers of London*, which give insight into the mercers' mathematical practices; Jefferson examines accounts from 1344–1464, including itemized lists of debts, amounts received, and rents, as well as incidental expenses such as hiring workmen to brush the snow from the roof.[37] Based on studies such as these, medieval merchants and tradespeople comfortably engaged in complex calculations including adding, subtracting, multiplying, dividing, fractions, and so forth.

Perhaps the most studied medieval and early modern people for their numeracy are Italian merchants. Much is known about Italian merchant education, thanks to extant documents. Italian merchants often learned their trades through apprenticeships,[38] and during the thirteenth century in Italy merchants developed "abacus schools," which taught a "syllabus of commercial arithmetic."[39] An example of how popular these merchant schools were in Italy can be found in the Florentine banker Giovanni Villani's *Nuova Chronica*; Villani records that in Florence in 1338 there were one thousand to twelve hundred boys learning at six abacus schools.[40]

At the abacus schools arithmetic was taught with Hindu-Arabic (rather than Roman) numerals, and other subjects included geometry, vernacular reading, and bookkeeping, essentially everything a budding merchant would need to know to succeed in his profession. The central text of the abacus school was Leonardo of Pisa's (aka Fibonacci's) *Liber Abacus*, which specifically addressed the fundamentals of merchants' calculations, including measures, currency conversions, weights, simple and compound interest, calculating profits, discounts, and so on.[41] The descriptions are quite thorough and the text detailed; for example, a description of how to divide 13,976 by 23 and to check the answer takes several paragraphs.[42]

Another text that is useful for displaying the kinds of numerate practices an Italian merchant would have possessed at this time is the *Zibaldone da Canal*, an early fourteenth-century Venetian merchant's compilation. The notebook begins with mathematical exercises, the kind the compiler would have learned at a school (11).[43] His mathematical problems involve fractions and ratios, the price of gold and silver "in varying degrees of purity," "simple geometric calculations of area and volume," as well as squaring the circle, and "calculations for entertainment," or math puzzles without a specific or practical" purpose (13), such as the puzzle about a cat that climbs up one-fourth of the distance of the tower every day, but then slips back one-fifth of the distance he climbed every night; on the top of the tower is a mouse that descends one third of the way during the day and at night returns back one-fourth of the distance he had traveled. The text then asks, "In how many days will the cat and the mouse meet?" (54). The inclusion of such puzzles in the *Zibaldone da Canal* suggests that merchants may have enjoyed exercising their mathematical abilities.

Many of the examples in the *Zibaldone da Canal* might sound familiar to modern-day students. What follows is an example that reads much like a modern story-problem about trains: "Make me this calculation: from Venice to Ancona is 200 miles. A ship is at Ancona and wants to go to Venice, and it goes in 30 days, and at Venice there is another ship that is going to Ancona, and it goes in 40 days. I ask you, if they both leave at the same time, each to go on its voyage, in how many days will these ships come together?" (61). The text then performs the arithmetic, arriving at the answer that "when the one from Venice has made 66 2/3 miles and the one from Anacona has made 133 1/3 miles, they will meet" (61). The answer, however, does not answer the original question of how many days it would take them to meet.[44] A more difficult question is as follows:

> Make me this calculation: there were three partners who had a ship built. This ship cost, all together, £9848 to build. One of them invested from his capital £2721. The other of them invested from his capital £5849, and the third of them invested from his capital £1278.
>
> This ship went to Constantinople and returned, and profited £2000. I ask you: how much is coming to each of them in proportion to his share? (55)

The text then describes how to calculate the problem by identifying £9848 as the divisor: "If you want to know how much is coming to each, say thus: for him who invested £2721 we ought to say 2000 times 2721 makes 5442000, which one ought to divide by 9848, from which comes £552 5904/9848." The remaining two calculations are performed, with slight discrepancies in the fractions, as the editor notes.[45] This is not the original copy of the notebook; was it scribal error or originally a "close" but not exact answer? Or did the author engage in some approximation while calculating the amounts? Whichever the answer, the problem works out to the nearest pound. These word problems, particularly the currency questions, demonstrate how comfortable a merchant would need to be with multiplying, dividing, and adding numbers into the hundreds of thousands or even millions, as well as how comfortable he would need to be with ratios and fractions. The answers could serve as models for figuring out other problems involving similar situations, such as how to calculate profit for investors.

England, unfortunately, provides no such arithmetical books such as the *Zibaldone da Canal* or the *Liber Abaci* of Leonardo Pisano. England also did not have any abacus schools per se, but there were schools where merchants could be educated. In his study on medieval schools, Nicholas Orme describes a number of tradespeople (including a grocer and goldsmith) and merchants who founded grammar schools in the fifteenth century. In addition, "town corporations began to be recorded defending or improving their local schools."[46] Moreover, we must imagine that medieval English merchants were exposed to Italian calculation practices, as numerate practices did not stop at national borders. It is highly likely that English merchants modeled their own calculation practices on those of Mediterranean traders.

This appendix, of course, has offered just a brief excursion into the wide field of medieval numeracy studies, and I encourage readers to continue the journey by exploring the many recent studies that examine how an individual person's (or a culture's) numeracy is shaped by social forces, as well as the long-reaching ramifications of that shaping. Searching for the terms "adult numeracy," for example, in the search engines Scopus and Web of Science will pull up hundreds of essays and books on unequal educational practices related to socioeconomic status, how (in)numeracy can affect people's health care, and the intersections between numeracy and disability, just to name a few. These studies remind us that numeracy, like literacy, is intimately connected to issues of social justice.

NOTES

INTRODUCTION

1. Johnson, "Introduction," 1:1. For the quotation from the Wife of Bath, see Chaucer, "The Wife of Bath's Prologue," in *Riverside Chaucer*, 112, lines 551–52.
2. Murray, *Reason and Society*, 203.
3. Ibid., 189, 191.
4. See, for example, Brewer, "Arithmetic"; Shippey, "Chaucer's Arithmetical Mentality"; and Acker, "Emergence of an Arithmetical Mentality."
5. Boyer and Merzbach, *History of Mathematics*. See also, for example, Gullberg, *Mathematics*.
6. Folkerts, "Euclid in Medieval Europe."
7. See, for example, Folkerts, *Development of Mathematics*; *Algebra of Abū Kāmil*.
8. Meyer and Suntrup, *Lexikon der mittelalterlichen Zahlenbedeutungen*.
9. The *Oxford English Dictionary* defines numerology as "divination by numbers; the study of the occult or hidden meanings of numbers." In this study, I use the term "numerology" to indicate assigning or recognizing scriptural or other religious associations with particular numbers. For this use of "numerology" to indicate the spiritual sense of number, see Wallis, "'Number Mystique.'" Terms used in other modern texts include "arithmology," or the spiritual or mystical meaning of numbers, and "arithmancy," or the assigning of a number value to a word or phrase (and made popular by J. K. Rowling's Harry Potter series). For a succinct definition of these two terms in a popular work, see Greer, *Secrets of the Lost Symbol*. In my study, I prefer to use the general term "numerology."
10. Wallis, "'Number Mystique,'" 183.
11. Lentes, "Counting Piety," 55. Other important studies include Angenendt et al., "Counting Piety," and R. Reynolds, "'At Sixes and Sevens.'"
12. Wedell, "Numbers."
13. Tavormina, "Mathematical Conjectures."
14. Watson, "Making of *The Book of Margery Kempe*," esp. 418–24; Rust, "*Arma Christi*"; Fulton, "Praying by Numbers"; Connolly, "Preaching by Numbers"; Connolly, "Practical Reading."
15. For a discussion of the meaning of *literacy*, see Stock, *Implications of Literacy*, 3–11. For the introduction of the word "numeracy," see the Crowther Report: "In schools where the conditions we have described in the last paragraph prevail, little is done to make science specialists more 'literate' than they were when they left the Fifth Form and nothing to make arts specialists more 'numerate,' if we may coin a word to represent the mirror image of literacy."
16. See the Cockcroft Report, "Mathematics Counts."
17. Sellars, *Numeracy in Authentic Contexts*, 144; see also White et al., "Critical Numeracy and Abstraction: Percentages."
18. Crump, *Anthropology of Numbers*.
19. Earlier studies include, for example, Carraher, Carraher, and Schliemann, "Mathematics in the Streets and in Schools," and Nunes, Schliemann, and Carraher, *Street Mathematics*. Journals dedicated to numeracy studies include *Numeracy*, published by the University of South Florida, and *Literacy and Numeracy Studies*, published by the University of Technology Sydney.
20. To define devotion, I turn to Cécile de Morrée, in "Singing Together Alone," who asserts, "Devotion . . . can be characterized as

the realization of religious beliefs, ideas, and traditions into a certain attitude to life. Devotion, then, consists of two basic elements: on the one hand the theoretical element consisting of, for example, written guidelines or explanatory texts regarding devotional practice, and on the other hand devotional practice itself. This practice, in turn, consists of an inner experience and an outward, perceptible practice" (86). For an extended discussion of the nature of devotion, see also Brantley, *Reading in the Wilderness*.

21. Scholarship on English sermons includes Owst, *Literature and Pulpit*, and Owst, *Preaching*. For a discussion of Owst's work, see Pearsall, "G. R. Owst." For more on English sermons, see also Waldron, "Susan Powell," xiii–xv; Spencer, *English Preaching*; and Wenzel, *Preaching in the Age of Chaucer*.

22. For the concept of "knowing thyself" in relation to *Jacob's Well*, see Fitzgibbons, "*Jacob's Well* and Penitential Pedagogy."

CHAPTER 1

1. Bracciolini, *Facetiae*, 2:156, no. 228.
2. Throughout the book, I use the term "sermonist" frequently when referring to either a sermon writer or preacher (see *Oxford English Dictionary*, s.v. "sermonist," def. 1). Modern usage also employs "sermonist" to refer to a scholar who studies sermons.
3. Steenbrugge, *Drama and Sermon*, x–xi, from Spencer, *English Preaching*, 203.
4. Connolly, "Preaching by Numbers," 83. See also Connolly, "Practical Reading," for her discussion of enumeration in a variety of miscellanies featuring medical, devotional, and astrological texts, esp. 156–57.
5. Martí de Barcelona, "*L'Ars Praedicatandi* de Fransesc Eiximenes," 323, quoted in Wenzel, *Medieval Artes Praedicandi*, 82–83.
6. Many studies address the division of sermons. See, for example, Wenzel, *Medieval Artes Praedicandi*; Murphy, *Rhetoric in the Middle Ages*; Higden, *Ars Componendi Sermones*. As Mary Carruthers has argued, this labeling of parts with numbers stems from the practice of using a memory grid; she gives several excellent examples of how number is used to construct memory, from Hugh of St. Victor and from Thomas Wayles (Carruthers, *Book of Memory*, 130–31). For number as a way to construct memory, see Hugh of St. Victor, in Carruthers, *Book of Memory*, 340.

7. For the ancient and modern sermon distinctions, see, for example, Wenzel, *Medieval Artes Praedicandi*, 44 on; Johnson, "Introduction"; Andersson, *Constructing the Medieval Sermon*.

8. Adams and Hanska, *Jewish-Christian Encounter*, 2.

9. As Eyal Poleg explains, "Whereas the pericope was comprised of several verses commonly constituting an identifiable narrative unit, the thema retained only a fragment of the pericope." Poleg, "'Ladder Set Up on Earth,'" 209–10.

10. Scheepsma, *Limburg Sermons*, 27.

11. Wenzel, *Medieval Artes Praedicandi*, 65–66.

12. Ibid., 74.

13. Ibid., 54.

14. Ibid., 71, 74. For Martin de Cordoba, See Rubio Álvarez, "*Ars Praedicandi*," 342–43; Thomas de Tuderto, *Ars sermoncinandi ac collationes faciendi*, edited by June Babcock in "Ars sermocinandi."

15. Wenzel, *Medieval Artes Praedicandi*, 80, from the unedited Valencia, Cathedral Library, MS 184, fol. 24.

16. Ibid., 66–67, from Valencia, Cathedral Library, MS 184, fol. 19v–20.

17. Ibid., 67. The *Ars copia* adds this distinction: the thema can be divided via *distinctio* ("concerned with an individual word") or *divisio* (concerned with "an entire clause or sentence"). Ibid., 70, from Valencia, Cathedral Library, MS 184, fol. 19v.

18. Ibid., 67; see also Hazel, "Translation, with Commentary."

19. Wenzel, *Medieval Artes Praedicandi*, 70, from "Nota pro arte faciendi collaciones et sermones," from the unedited manuscript Lincoln, Cathedral Library, MS 227.

20. M. Carruthers, *Book of Memory*, 131.

21. Ibid., 131, from Charland, *Artes Praedicandi*, 370.

22. As Carruthers argues, "Of special interest in this advice is the assumption on Thomas Waleys's part that both preacher and auditor relied on the numerical system for retaining discourse, for the key both to successful dilation and to retention is orderly division by number." M. Carruthers, *Book of Memory*, 131.

23. O'Mara and Paul, *Repertorium*, Cambridge, Corpus Christi College, 392, Palm Sunday, 1:64–65. The *Repertorium* contains both *implicits* and *explicits* of sermons in Middle English, as well as a summary (and occasional direct translation) of the contents of the sermons. Whenever possible, I have further consulted editions of individual sermons. Unless otherwise indicated, the modern English translations are my own.

24. O'Mara and Paul, *Repertorium*, Cambridge, Corpus Christi College, 392, Palm Sunday, 1:64–65.

25. O'Mara and Paul, *Repertorium*, Cambridge, Pembroke College, 285, St. Nicholas, 1:78.

26. Summary/translation from O'Mara and Paul, *Repertorium*, Cambridge Pembroke College, 285, St. Nicholas, 1:77–78.

27. Summary/translation from O'Mara and Paul, *Repertorium*, Hatfield House Cecil Papers 280, First Sunday in Advent, 1:318.

28. Summary/translation from O'Mara and Paul, *Repertorium*, Hatfield House Cecil Papers 280, First Sunday in Lent, 1:323. Note how the sermonist addresses "contemplation and resisting temptation" together, in order to emphasize the number three.

29. Summary/translation from O'Mara and Paul, *Repertorium*, London, British Library, Harley 2247, Ascension Day, 2:1148–49. For a discussion of this manuscript, see Hill, "Regendering the *Festial*."

30. Fletcher, *Late Medieval Popular Preaching*, 118–19. A schema of the sermon "Alleluia" demonstrates how the sermon "escape[s] the gravitational structural pull of the 'modern' sermon form," although it relies on *distinciones* "before getting airborne" (121). Another wonderful example of sermon division can be found in Fletcher's edition and discussion of "Pentienciam agite," which details the four things that move Christians to penitence: Reason, Treason, Dread, and Meed. Reason is then subdivided into four parts, as are treason and dread; meed is not subdivided at all. Fletcher includes a helpful chart that clearly shows how the division and subdivisions work.

31. Ibid., 212.

32. For the term "allegorical numerology," see Wallis, "'Number Mystique,'" 181. Wallis defines "allegorical numerology" as "where numbers derive their meanings from correspondence to Biblical events or theological concepts" (ibid.).

33. Note that some modern texts prefer the term "arithmology" for this practice.

34. For twentieth- and twenty-first-century divination practices, see, for example, Jordan, *Numerology*; Bell, *Love and Sex*; Christie, *Numerology*.

35. Lucas, *Astrology and Numerology*, 47–48. See also Hopper, *Medieval Number Symbolism*.

36. Lucas, *Astrology and Numerology*, 48. Note that early Christians recognized that other cultures practiced forms of numerology. As Saint Ambrose writes in his "Letter to Horontianus," in commenting on the days of creation, "The number seven is good, but we do not explain it after the doctrine of Pythagoras and the other philosophers, but rather according to the manifestation and the grace of the Spirit." See Herbert, *Catholic Encyclopedia*, 11:151, s.v. "Use of Numbers."

37. Meyer and Suntrup, *Lexikon der mittelalterlichen Zahlenbedeutungen*; Bullinger, *Number in Scripture*. See also John Davis, *Biblical Numerology*.

38. Modern readers may be less familiar with the medieval idea of the number eight signifying baptism. See Jensen, *Living Water*, especially chapter 6.

39. Summary/translation from O'Mara and Paul, *Repertorium*, Cambridge St. John's College, G. 22, Seventh Sunday after Trinity,

1:111. For the sermon in Middle English, see *English Wycliffite Sermons*, 5:346–47.

40. Summary/translation from O'Mara and Paul, *Repertorium*, Lincoln Cathedral Library 133, unidentified occasion, 1:346.

41. Hudson, *English Wyclifitte Sermons*, Sermo 37, 1:379; O'Mara and Paul, *Repertorium*, London, British Library, Additional 40672, Septuagesima, 1:514.

42. Summary/translation from O'Mara and Paul, *Repertorium*, Oxford, Bodleian Library, Bodley 806, Twenty-Fourth Sunday after Trinity, 3:1805–1806. For the full Middle English passage, see "Sermon 24," in *English Wycliffite Sermons*, 1:318–19.

43. Summary/translation from O'Mara and Paul, *Repertorium*, Dublin, Trinity College 241, Easter Day, 1:256.

44. Ibid., 1:257.

45. "The Fasts of the Four Times," in *Speculum Sacerdotale*, 90. For a discussion of the three powers of the soul, see Bonaventure, "Conscience and Synderesis," 188.

46. O'Mara and Paul, *Repertorium*, London, British Library, Additional 36791, unidentified occasion, 1:388; for the Middle English, see "The Fasts of the Four Times," 90–93. For the popularity of these tetrads, see Sears, *Ages of Man*.

47. Summary/translation from O'Mara and Paul, *Repertorium*, Dublin, Trinity College 241, Circumcision of Christ, 1:275.

48. Note that the numbering of this biblical verse is Wisdom 11:20 or 11:21, depending on whether the numbering of the Greek Septuagint or Latin Vulgate is used.

49. For a helpful overview of number theory in medieval English texts, see Acker, "Emergence of an Arithmetical Mentality," which offers a clear discussion of the difference between "algorism" and "arithmetic." See also Acker, "*Crafte of Nombrynge*."

50. For an English translation of *De institutione arithmetica*, see Boethius, *Boethian Number Theory*. For the influence of Boethius, see also Evans, "Introductions to Boethius's 'Arithmetica.'" For the medieval history of number theory, see, for example, Ore, *Number Theory and Its History* and others. Discussions of proportion, which can be traced to Pythagoras, also find their way into other vernacular texts. *The Pilgrimage of the Soul*, for example, includes a discussion of "the fair diapente, the sweet diapason . . . the lusti diatesseron," which relate to musical tones (5.2.89b), and suggest that vernacular audiences would have been at least somewhat familiar with these ideas. *Middle English Pilgrimage of the Soul*, quotation from the *MED* entry for "diapente." See also Agmon, "Proto-Tonal Theory."

51. Mattéi, "Nicholas of Gerasa and the Arithmetic Scale of the Divine." For a brief discussion of Pythagoras's conception of number, see "The Pythagorean-Platonic Period," in Koetsier and Bergmans, "Introduction," 13–15. See also Wedell, "Numbers" (specifically "number theory," 1243–54). According to Wallis, Nicomachus was in the "Neo-Pythagorean and Neo-Platonic tradition of number metaphysics" ("'Number Mystique,'" 181). For a brief introduction to Neo-Pythagoreanism and Neo-Plantonism, see Koetsier and Bergmans, "Introduction," 15–18.

52. Guillaumin, "Boethius's *De Institutione Arithemetica*," 161.

53. See also Peck in "Number as Cosmic Language," for discussion of what was taught in schools. James Weisheipl argues that in the early fourteenth century students at Oxford were required to study arithmetic for three weeks at Oxford. Weishepl, "Curriculum," and Weisheipl, "Developments." See also Tavormina, "Mathematical Conjectures," 281.

54. Boethius, *Boethian Number Theory*, 96–97.

55. For a helpful overview of Boethius's work on numbers, see Guillaumin, "Boethius's *De Institutione Arithmetica*."

56. Cassiodorus, *Institutiones divinarum et saecularium litterarum*, 1208–16. See also Wedell, "Numbers," 1249–50.

57. See Folkerts, "Euclid in Medieval Europe" and Zhang, "Euclid's Number-Theoretical Work."

58. See the entry for "algebra" in Glick, Livesey, and Wallis, *Medieval Science*, 29, as well as Leonardo Pisano, *Fibonacci's Liber Abaci*.

59. Note that most *quadrivium* offerings did not include these later books of Euclid. See Folkerts, *Euclid in Medieval Europe*.

60. For Isidore, see Guillaumin, "Boethius's *De institutione arithemtica*," 153–57, and book 3, "Mathematics," in Isidore, *Etymologies*, 89–107. According to Wallis, "Christian numerology, as conveyed in handbooks for Bible study like Isidore of Seville's *Liber de numeris*, or in the commentaries of patristic and early medieval exegetes, is the fusion of this exegetical tradition with a Christianized version of the cosmological and contemplative philosophical tradition" (Wallis, "'Number Mystique,'" 182).

61. See Dederich, "Trevisa's Translation."

62. Wallis, "'Number Mystique,'" 181.

63. *On the Properties of Things*, 2.1357.

64. Augustine, *Literal Meaning of Genesis*, 1:104, 4.2.2; 1:106, 4.2.6. According to Koetsier and Bergmans, "The existence of eternal truth in mathematics implies the idea of Eternal Truth, which is an important ingredient of St. Augustine's proof of the existence of God and the immortality of the soul" ("Introduction," 19). For Wallis, Augustine's discussion of the meaning of the number six demonstrates a fusion of this philosophical and allegorical numerology. Wallis, "'Number Mystique,'" 181.

65. See O'Brien, *Bede's Temple*; Bede, *On the Tabernacle*; and Morrison, "Bede's *De Tabernaculo* and *De Templo*."

66. Mandziuk, "Drawn to Scale," 86–88.

67. Medieval measurement charms include details about the measurements of Christ or Mary. For "devotions that developed around the 'measure' or people or objects," see Bury, "Measure of the Virgin's Foot," 129–30.

68. Boethius, *Boethian Number Theory*, 165.

69. Hugh of St. Victor, *Exegetica de scripturis et scriptoribus sacris* 15, in Migne, Patrologia Latina 175:22–23, in Peck, "Number as Cosmic Language," 59.

70. Bede, *On the Tabernacle*, 96 and 96n5; Bede, *Reckoning of Time*, "Calculating or Speaking with the Fingers," 9–13 and 254–63. See his finger counting as well in the appendix to this book. Note that in explaining the circularity of the O made by the fingers in the hand, Bede is not referring to zero. In the early ninth century a Persian mathematician, al-Khwārizmī, wrote a book that explored Hindu numerals, as well as zero. This treatise was then translated into Latin in the twelfth century. For the history of al-Khwārizmī, see Rashed, *Al-Khwārizmī*.

71. Bede, *On the Tabernacle*, 96.

72. *On the Property of Things*, 2.1359.

73. *Three Prose Versions of the Secreta Secretorum*, 1:214, lines 21–23.

74. For a discussion of this, see Sears, *Ages of Man*, 11.

75. Catherine of Siena, *Orcherd of Syon*, 398–99, lines 10–16.

76. *Middle English "Mirror,"* 326; O'Mara and Paul, *Repertorium*, Oxford, Bodleian, Holkham misc. 40, Ninth Sunday after Trinity, 3:2115. For a discussion of this manuscript, see Somerset, *Feeling Like Saints*, esp. 210–15. See also *Middle English "Mirror"*; Duncan and Connolly, *Middle English Mirror*.

77. *Middle English "Mirror,"* 151–52; O'Mara and Paul, *Repertorium*, Oxford, Bodleian, Holkham misc. 40, Fourth Sunday in Lent, 3:2079.

78. Summary/translation from O'Mara and Paul, *Repertorium*, Dublin, Trinity College 241, Fourth Sunday in Lent, 1:252.

79. Rand, "Syon Pardon Sermon," 342. The translation is mine. Note that some pardon passages provide more challenging addition problems. Rand offers another version of the Syon pardon, in London, British Library, Harley 2321, that is particularly difficult: "On Estron day is foryefnes of þat .iij. parte of alle synnes and .iij. m^i.vij. C .iiij^{xx}. and .viij. yerre and als many lentes and .iij. howndred dayes. And yche day within þe

vtas of Estron is remission of þe .iij. parte of alle synnes, and in m^i .iiij.^{xx} and xiij yere. And .iij. m^i .iij. ^{xx} and .xiij. lentes and .vj. C dayes" (319).

80. Summary/translation from O'Mara and Paul, *Repertorium*, Oxford, Bodleian Library, MS Douce 53, Twenty-Fifth Sunday after Trinity, 3:1815.

> as it semeþ to seint Austyn . . . þat þe day of doome is uppon us, where seynt Austyn seiþ þat, as in þe sixte day God made man and in þe sevenþe day he restide from all his werkis, so in þe sixte þousand of ȝeeris God bouȝte man, and in þe seuenþe þousand of ȝeeris þe world shal cece. And bi þe cronyclis of þe world þer ben passid of þe seuenþe þousand sixe hundred and fyue. And up hap, as Crist bood not vnto þe eende of þe sixte þousand for to bigge man, but bouȝte man in þe eende of þe secunde hundrid of þe sixte þousand, so liȝtly shal he not abide into þe eende of þe sevenþe þousand for to deeme þe world. (*Two Wycliffite Texts*, 22)

81. Summary/translation from O'Mara and Paul, *Repertorium*, London, British Library, Harley 2276, First Sunday in Lent, 2:1258. See also *Lenten Sermons*.

82. Mirk, *John Mirk's Festial*, 1:66–67; O'Mara and Paul, *Repertorium*, London, British Library, Cotton Claudius A.ii, Sexagesima, 2:952.

83. This practice, of course, has a long history. In *On the Temple*, Bede explains why the temple was sixty cubits long, twenty cubits wide, and thirty cubits high: "So six has to do with the perfection of the work, two with the love of God and neighbor, and three with the hope of the vision of God. Each number is rightly multiplied by ten because it is only through faith and the obsersvance of the decalogue of the law that our patience gets salutary exercise or our charity burns profitably or our hope is rapt aloft to yearn for the things of eternity" (23).

84. Summary/translation from O'Mara and Paul, *Repertorium*, London, British Library, Additional 36791, First Sunday in Lent, 1:381. "The Quadragesime was ordeynede for typynge of dayes of the yere. Ther ben in the yere ccclxv, of the whiche the x. parte is xxxvi. dayes. But for we owe to be good Cristen men and devowt we moste in our fastynge put to hem iiii. dayes whiche ben clepid clensyng dayes." *Speculum Sacerdotale*, 56.

85. Summary/translation from O'Mara and Paul, *Repertorium*, London, British Library, Royal 18.B.xxiii, Epiphany, 2:1453. "It was also þe lasse merveil of þer hasty commynge in xiij daies from so farre countre, for as Austyn, Ierom, and Fulgencius seyn, þei reden vppon beestes þat men callen dromedus, dromodi . . . wiche, as Ysodre seithe . . . þei ben beestes of so gret swyftnes þat on of hem will esely bere a man an 100 myle on a daye." *Middle English Sermons*, 227.

86. Summary/translation from O'Mara and Paul, *Repertorium*, London, British Library, Additional 36791, All Souls, 1:445.

> And the vii.^{the} day and the xxx.^{ti} day toke begynnynge of the Olde Testament, for as the children of Israel wepte by vii. dayes and Moyses xxx., so doþ holy chirche office and nedes of hire dede bodies. And þerfore by vii. dayes we do office vnto oure dedes that they may come the rather to reste or ellis for þe septenarie of the body and sowle. For the sowle hath thre strengþes: *scilicet*, racionabilite, concupiscibilite, and irascibilite. And the body is i-made of iiii. elamentis, and þerfore for that the synnes may be i-waschid a-way by vii., [we celebrate the septenarie.] Þries x. makeþ xxx., and by the ternary, *scilicet*, the iii. x., is signyfied the trinite, and be the x. is betokened the x. commaundmentis. And þerfore we make a tertenarie, *scilicet*, the space of xxx. dayes in offices and nedes of the dede, for þat that may be foryeuen to hem that they haue trespasid in obseruaunce of the x. commaundementis a-ȝeynste the trinite. Neuertheles som doþ it by iii. dayes in representacion of the thre dayes of Cristes sepulcre and for intent

þat the dede my3t haue for3eueness of that the whiche he trespasid in in si3t, werke, and worde. And som takeþ space of ix. dayes þrou3 custom and consideracion that the sowles mowe be delyuered fro peynes and ioyned to the ix. ordres of aungelis. (*Speculum Sacerdotale*, 231–32)
For more on why Masses were said seven and thirty days after death, see Saltamacchia, "Funeral Procession from Venice to Milan," 205. See also Gittings, "Urban Funerals," 171–73.

87. Lentes, "Counting Piety," 57–58.

88. Summary/translation from O'Mara and Paul, *Repertorium*, London, British Library, Harley 2276, Seventh Sunday after Trinity 2:1296.

89. Translation/summary from O'Mara and Paul, *Repertorium*, London, Westminster Abbey Library 34/20, Lent, 2:1590.

90. Summary/translation from O'Mara and Paul, *Repertorium*, Oxford, Bodleian, Holkham misc. 40, unidentified occasion, 3:2164. This sermon is not included in the *Middle English "Mirror."*

91. For another example of a ratio, see William Taylor's sermon for the Twenty-Fifth Sunday after Trinity: "It is sufficient for people to live forty years, yet a thousand years is like a single day to God" (O'Mara and Paul, *Repertorium*, Oxford, Bodleian Library, Douce 53, Twenty-Fifth Sunday after Trinity, 3:1815.). See also the sermon "On the Dead": "The righteous will be seven times brighter that the sun but the unbelieving, who do not forsake sin, will become so black and horrible in the fire that they will be a hundred times darker than night" (O'Mara and Paul, *Repertorium*, Cambridge, Trinity College, B.14.52, 1:183).

92. Acker, "Emergence of an Arithmetical Mentality," 296: quoting Steele in *Earliest Arithmetics in English* (xv), Acker writes, "algoristic reckoning was first carried out using 'a board [covered] with fine sand,' similar, apparently, to the Greek sand tray described by Martianus Capella and Trevisa. Such a board may be the intended referent in a remarkably early (?a 1200) and unlikely context, the *Ancrene Wisse*" (296). As William G. Marx suggests, "See the 'Towneley Last Judgment Play' wherein Tutivillus carries a Ragroll of his running tally of souls bound for hell. Also, this writing in ashes reminds of the scene of Jesus writing in the dirt in the 'N-Town Woman Taken in Adultery Play' wherein he lists the individual sins of the Pharisee, Accuser, and Scribe" (private email).

93. *Early South-English Legendary*, 438, lines 232–36. William G. Marx has suggested that the casting of numbers in the dust could also suggest "playing at dice, too, as the soldiers gambled for Jesus's robe in the Crucifixion plays." This episode is also discussed in Acker, "Emergence of an Arithmetical Mentality," 296.

94. *Early South-English Legendary*, 438, lines 238–44.

95. *Early South-English Legendary*, 438, lines 238–44.

96. Acker, "Emergence of an Arithmetical Mentality," 301n36. See "Trinity Sunday," in Mirk, *John Mirk's Festial*, 153–54.

97. Fletcher, "Magnus predicator et deuotus." See also Wenzel's discussion of Felton in his *Latin Sermon Collections*, 54–57.

98. John Felton, Easter or Corpus Christi Sermon, 137.

99. Quoted in Smith, *Ten Commandments*, 50, from Grosseteste, *On the Six Days of Creation*, 7.14.18, 219.

100. For the *Glossa Ordinaria*, see *Bibliorum Sacrorum cum Glossa Ordinaria*, with links available online from the Lollard Society: Religion, Language, Literature, http://lollardsociety.org/?page_id=409.

101. The five loaves are most frequently associated with the five books of Moses or the old law. See, for example, O'Mara and Paul, *Repertorium*, Dublin, Trinity College 241, Twenty-Fifth Sunday after Trinity, 1:222.

102. Summary/translation from O'Mara and Paul, *Repertorium*, Cambridge, Sidney Sussex College 74, sermon on the Fourth

Sunday in Lent or the Twenty-Fifth Sunday after Trinity, 1:92–93.

103. Summary/translation from O'Mara and Paul, *Repertorium*, Cambridge St. John's College, G. 22, 1:112.

104. Summary/translation from O'Mara and Paul, *Repertorium*, Dublin, Trinity College 241, Twenty-Fifth Sunday after Trinity, 1:222.

105. Summary/translation from O'Mara and Paul, *Repertorium*, London, British Library, Additional 40672, Twenty-Fifth Sunday after Trinity, 1:497. For the sermon in Middle English, see *English Wycliffite Sermons*, 1:322–25, at 324: "Þese two fyschis ben two bookys of wysdam and of prophetis."

106. Summary/translation from O'Mara and Paul, *Repertorium*, Oxford, Bodleian Library, Bodley 806, Twenty-Fifth Sunday after Trinity, 3:1808.

107. Summary/translation from O'Mara and Paul, *Repertorium*, Dublin, Trinity College 241, Fourth Sunday in Lent, 1:251–52.

108. Summary/translation from O'Mara and Paul, *Repertorium*, Dublin, Trinity College 241, Twenty-Fifth Sunday after Trinity, 1:222.

109. Summary/translation from O'Mara and Paul, *Repertorium*, London, British Library, Additional 40672, Twenty-Fifth Sunday after Trinity, 1:497. See also *English Wycliffite Sermons*, Twenty-Fifth Sunday after Trinity, 1.323: "And hit ys seyd comunly þat, as þe nowmbre of two is þe furste þat comeþ from onheede of nowmbres, so þese two feestis bytoknen þat men for þer synne ben fallen in þis neede to be fed þus"; Seventh Sunday after Trinity, 1.249: "And of greet wit weren þere two, as seyntes beren witnesse, for two is þe furste noumbre þat comeþ aftur onhede; and þerefore nowmbre þat patreþ from vnite."

CHAPTER 2

1. All quotations from *Dives and Pauper* in this chapter are from Priscilla Heath Barnum's edition and cited in text by volume, part, and page number. Modern English translations are my own unless otherwise indicated. For a discussion of the author of *Dives and Pauper* and the Longleat 4 sermons, see Hudson and Spencer, "Old Author, New Work." The sermons contain a number of references to the treatise on the Ten Commandments. For example, sermon 19 in Longleat 4 (O'Mara and Paul, *Repertorium*, 4:2521). For the identification as a Franciscan working on behalf of a wealthy English person, see Hudson and Spencer, "Old Author, New Work," esp. 227–28, 233.

2. Hudson and Spencer, "Old Author, New Work," 220.

3. The manuscript may be viewed at the Longleat House library, or a microfiche may be rented from the library. Willmott, "Edition of Selected Sermons," also contains editions of selected sermons.

4. In this chapter, I quote from both O'Mara and Paul's *Repertorium* as well as from the manuscript itself. All citations for the *Repertorium* are listed by volume and page number; whenever possible I have included Middle English quotations from the manuscript Longleat 4, which I indicate by folio number. I indicate when Modern English translations of passages are not my own.

5. According to Wogan-Browne et al., the sermon cycle "outspokenly opposes the recent imposition of Arundel's *Constitutions* of 1409, insisting on the continuing duty of all knowledgeable Christians to preach and teach God's law." Wogan-Browne et al., *Idea of the Vernacular*, 249, citing Hudson and Spencer, "Old Author, New Work," n.p. For other scholarly discussions of the texts, see French, *People of the Parish*; Wood, *Medieval Economic Thought*; Harper, "'A Tokene and a Book'"; Schirmer, "Representing Reading"; Watson, "Conceptions of the Word"; Simpson, "Orthodoxy's Image Trouble."

6. Flannery and Walker, "'Vttirli Onknowe'?"; see also Gillespie, "1412–1534." For a discussion of Longleat 4 and *Dives and Pauper* together, see Boffey, "Some Middle English Sermon Verse."

7. Tavormina, "Mathematical Conjectures."

8. Gillespie, "1412–1534," 165.

9. Wogan-Browne, *Idea of the Vernacular*, 249, from Hudson and Spencer, "Old Author, New Work." Hudson and Spencer give the date of *Dives and Pauper* as ca. 1405–10 (222).

10. Wogan-Brown, *Idea of the Vernacular*, 249.

11. For the printed editions, see Early English Books Online: *Diues [and] pauper* (London: printed by Richard Pynson, 1493), STC 2nd ed. 19212; *Diues [et] pauper* (Westminster: printed by Wynkyn de worde, 1496), STC 2nd ed. 19213; *Diues and pauper* (London: printed by T. Berthelet, 1536), STC 2nd ed. 19214.

12. For a lengthy discussion of this and following passages, see Tavormina, "Mathematical Conjectures."

13. *Dives and Pauper*, 1.1.284.

14. For discussion of the number six and the "hexameral tradition," see Meyer and Suntrup, *Lexikon*, 442–50, s.v. "sechs."

15. Voigt, "Perfect Numbers."

16. Bede, *On the Tabernacle*, 33. In *On the Temple*, Bede writes, "For the number six whereby the world was made, conventionally denotes the perfection of good works" (22).

17. Bede, *On the Tabernacle*, 51.

18. Tavormina, "Mathematical Conjectures," 272.

19. Ibid., 274–75 and 281. See also Weisheipl, "Curriculum," and Weisheipl, "Developments."

20. James Davis, *Medieval Market Morality*, 64.

21. As Jeremy Catto explains, "Books of moral guidance such as *Dives and Pauper*... were, it seems, more likely to be found in the hands of pastors and confessors, and their contents administered in confession, or in sermons; their objective, however, was the refinement by examination of conscience of the individual" (Catto, "1349–1412," 115).

22. Wogan-Brown, *Idea of the Vernacular*, 142; Hudson and Spencer, "Old Author, New Work," 220.

23. See O'Mara and Paul, *Repertorium*, for the prefatory material and description manuscript of contents, 4:2484. The Longleat 4 sermons are described in volume four of this continuously paged four-volume collection; incipits and explicits are included in Middle English.

24. O'Mara and Paul, *Repertorium*, 4:2484, citing Willmott, "Edition of Selected Sermons," 63–65.

25. Scholars imagine either a listening or reading audience for these sermons—they may be a collection of postils instead of sermons, which some scholars take to mean that they were biblical interpretations intended for a reading audience instead of a listening audience. Other scholars, however, emphasize how, in the fourteenth and fifteenth centuries, postils "developed as a new and popular type of sermon transmission." See Schiewer, "*Sub Iudaica Infirmitate*," 70. For a discussion of the postil form and its use in preaching, see Thayer, "Support for Preaching," in which she argues that the postil "provided a basic level of preaching in the later Middles Ages" (130).

26. Quotation from O'Mara and Paul, *Repertorium*, sermon 2, Second Sunday in Advent, 4:2487. "But jerom... seyn þat fyftene dayys aforn þe doom schul fallin fyftene wonderful tokeyns" (Longleat 4, 3v).

27. See O'Mara and Paul, *Repertorium*, sermon 2, Second Sunday in Advent, 4:2488, for a summary of this sermon.

> I sey ȝow for soþe seyþ crist þat þis generacon schal nat pasin tyl alle þese þinges be don. Were dyn of foure maner generacion þe fyrste was of þe erþe withouten man and womman as adam. The secunde was of man withouten womman as eue of adam. The þrydde was of womman withouten man as crist of marie. Þe ferþe is of man and womman as we ben alle. The fyrste generacion and þe secunde and þe þrydde ben pasid and neuer schul be don eft. Þe ferþe generacion lestiþ ȝet and schal lestin tyl alle þese þinges þat crist spak of in þe gospel ben don.

Thanne schal þis generacion cesin and pasin from deyȝing to alwey lyvynge þe wyckede in þyne þe goode in blisse. (Longleat 4, 4v)

28. See O'Mara and Paul, *Repertorium*, sermon 41, Tenth Sunday after Trinity, 4:2562, for a summary of this sermon. "We fyndyn þat crist wepte fyue tymys. Fyrst he wepte in his ȝougþe. and þerfore he seyde. myn fyrste voys þat I ȝaf in myn byrþe was wepinge. for þanne he wepte as oþer chyldryn don.... Also crist wepte for rewþe and compassion.... Also crist wepte whene he reysid lazar from deth to lyue.... Also crist wepte for þe fallinge of judas.... Also crist wepte on þe cros" (Longleat 4, 85r).

29. See O'Mara and Paul, *Repertorium*, sermon 19, Fourth Sunday in Lent, 4:2521, for a summary of this sermon "Be þe two fyschys ben undyrstondyn þe prophetys and þe psalmys whyche temperedyn and aslakdeyn þe betyrnesse of þe olde lawe" (Longeat 4, 41v).

30. See O'Mara and Paul, *Repertorium*, sermon 36, Fifth Sunday after Trinity, 4:2553, for a summary of this sermon.

> Be þe fyrste fychynge is understondin þe couersion of peplis to þe feyth of holy churche for boþin gode and wyckyd turned in to þe feyth and manye of hem be heresye retyn þe net of goddys word and wentyn doun to helle for false oppinyounys and herrouris þat þey heldin aȝens þe feyth and þanne þe entredin so manye wyckyd synerys in to þe schyp of holy chyrche þat holy chyrche was þanne and ȝet is in poynt to perishen for þe multitude of schrewys þat wern þanne and ȝet be in holy churche and leuyn as holy chyrche leuith.... Be þe fysching aftyr crists passion is understondin þe gaderinge to geder in to heuene of hem þat schul ben sauyd. (Longleat 4, 75v–76r)

31. Quotation from O'Mara and Paul, *Repertorium*, sermon 19, Fourth Sunday in Lent, 4:2521.

> Fyve louys ben undyrstondyn soriwe of herte schryfte of mouthe almesse preyere and fastynge whych alþou it ben scharp and nout sauori ȝet it ben nedful to mannys soule and be grace of wyt it turnyn to synful soulis al to lykynge and to þe joye and blisse for it bryngyn hem to endeles plente and to endeles blisse. Also be þese fyve louys ben undyrstondyn sorwe for leuynge of gode dedis shame of oure mysdedis dred of þe doom dred of helle pyne and dred of þe offens of god. Also be þese fyue louys ben understondyn mende of oure deth oftyn þyngkyng of þe myschef of þis world mende of oure tyme that is past and lost and mysspent in synne penance suffrynge and knowynge of our frelete. (Longleat 4, 41v)

32. Quotation from O'Mara and Paul, *Repertorium*, sermon 56, Twenty-Fifth Sunday after Trinity, 4:2594.

> In heuene schal ben endeles fulsomnesse of alle gode for þat man schal ben feld in alle hys fyue witts whyche tedings ben understondin be þe fyue louys for þat þe syȝte of man and womman schal ben fyld in þe syȝte of crist.... And þat þe smelling of man and womman schal ben fild and fed in þe swete odour of crist and þerfore alle seynts þanne schul seyn þat is writyn in þe book of loue.... Also oure tastinge schal ben fild in þe tastinge of þe swetnesse of crist.... The touchinge and felinge of man and womman schal ben fild and fed in þe touchinge of crist oure beste frend and meste belouyd.... Also þe heringe of man and womman schal ben fild in heringe of þe voys of crist whiche is so swete so mere and so likinge þat euery seynt in heuene seyth þus to crist as we findin in þe book of loue. (Longleat 4, 119v)

33. Quotation from O'Mara and Paul, *Repertorium*, sermon 33, Second Sunday after Trinity, 4:2547.

> I haue bouȝt fyue ȝockys of oxsin and I goo to asayyn ys. Al þe besinesse of þe coueþtous man ys abowtyn erþely þings and þerfore hys besinesse and his

travayle ys lyknyd to þe travayle of oxsin þat travaylin mest in heryynge and brekynge of þe lond and of þe erthe. He bouȝte fyue ȝockys of oxsin in tokene þat alle þe fyue wytts of þe couetous man ben al bent doun to þe erþe be þe ȝok of coueytyse whyche berith doun mannys herte hys þouȝt and hys loue to þe erþe as þe ȝok berith doun þe oxsis hefed to þe erþe so þat þe coueyteous man many nout lyftyn up hys herte and hys eyȝe to god. (Longleat 4, 68v)

34. See O'Mara and Paul, *Repertorium*, sermon 57, Annunciation, 4.2595, for a summary of the sermon.

> And þerfore crist þe sexte day and in þe sexte houre of þe day and in þe sexte monyth and in þe sexte age of þe world and in þe sexte þousand of ȝers be cam man and deyde for mankende for þe same day and þe same houre þre and þritti ȝer afryr oure ladi seynte marie saw here dere sone hangyng on þe tre in whyche day and in whyche houre sche conceyuyd hym of þe holi gost at þe gretynge of gabriel. God made þe world for mankende in þe numbre of sexe dayes and he made mankende in þe sexte day in tokene þat alle his werkis weren gode and perfyȝt and þat man was mest perfiȝt creature for whom he made alle oþer creaturis. (Longleat 4, 120v)

Note how the sermonist calls six the "perfect number": "In þis perfyȝt numbre god made þe world and man kende and reformyd aȝen mankende in tokene þat alle his dedis wern perfyȝt and gode and þat he made noþing omys" (Longleat 4, 120v).

35. See O'Mara and Paul, *Repertorium*, sermon 46, Fifteenth Sunday after Trinity, 4:2573, for a summary of this sermon. "Also þe lylye flour hath sexe leuys borwid aȝen dounward. for seynts han þe sexe deedis of mercy boþ in gostly and bodily toward bere euene cristene and oþer dedis of perfeccion. for sexe is a perfyȝt noumbre and betokeneth dedis of perfeccion" (Longleat 4, 97v).

36. Quotation from O'Mara and Paul, *Repertorium*, sermon 9, Second Sunday after the Octave of Epiphany, 4:2501. "The sexte water potts of at þis weddinge ben sexse sacraments þat ȝeuyn grace whyche ben bapteme confirmacion penance þe sacrament of þe auȝteer holy ordre and þe laste anoyntynge" (18v); "Þe sexse potts of ston ben sexse ags of þe world in whyche al mankende ran as water to helle" (Longleat 4, 18v). "In þis weddinge be nedful sexse potts of water to wasche soulis defilyd with synne. These potts ben sexse causis of sorwe for synne" (Longleat 4, 19v).

37. See O'Mara and Paul, *Repertorium*, sermon 15, Quinguagesima, 4:2513, for a summary of this sermon. "And tak heed þat as þe world was mad in sexse dayes. so mankende was reformyd and maad aȝen be sexse werkis of oure redempcion" (Longleat 4, 31r).

38. Quotation from O'Mara and Paul, *Repertorium*, sermon 21, Palm Sunday, 4:2525.

> Cryst deyde þe sexte day þat is fryday to reformyn mankende aȝen whych was maad þe sexte day and unmaad be synne. The sexte our of þe day adam eet of þe tre aȝens þe byddyng of god and þerfore þe sexte our of þe day wente up on þe tre and was don on þe cros to makyn asseth for adammys synne.... The neynþe our of þe day adam for his synne was tachyd out of paradys and þe ȝatys of paradys þan weryn schet aȝens mankende and þerfore cryst deyde þe neynþe our of þe day and þorw his deth made assyth for adammys synne and openyd þe ȝatys of paradys to þe þef and to mankende and in tokene þat of he suffayd his syde to ben openyd þe same our. (Longleat 4, 48r)

39. Quotation from O'Mara and Paul, *Repertorium*, sermon 38, Seventh Sunday after Trinity, 4:2556–57. The sermonist mentions different kinds of people who reject Christ and asserts that the deeper people are in sin the farther they are from Christ, ending with heathens:

heþene peple þat haddin non knowynge of goddys lawe and turnedin hem to crist þey comyn to hym from fer. The synner goth sexe dayys jorne from god. The fyrste dayys jorne is myslykinge whyche endyth in consent to synne. The secunde dayys jorne is consent to synne whyche endyth in the dede doynge. The þrydde dayys jorne is þe synful dede doynge whyche endyth in custum of synne. The ferthe dayys jorne from god is custom of synne whyche endyth in nede to synnen. for custom of synne makith a man so able and so inclynyd to synne þat he may nout withstondin withouten greet dyffycalte. The fyueþe dayys jorne is nede of custum to sennyn and it endyth in dyspysinge of god . . . and takith non heed to god and nout dredith god ne helle. . . . The sexte dayys jorne from god is fixyth dyspysing of god and it endith often in þe ny3t of dysperacion þat is þe neste in þe laste jorne to helle. (Longleat 4, 79r)

40. See O'Mara and Paul, *Repertorium*, sermon 27, Fifth Sunday after Easter, 4:2536, for a summary of this sermon. "And in tokene of þese þre þe holy gost apperede in þre lyknessis. In þe lyknesse of a sky3e þat pourith water doun o þe erþe . . . Also he apperyd in þe lyknesse of a dowe þat ys abryd who iten galle. . . . Also he apperid in þe lyknesse of fyr þat goth alwey upward" (Longleat 4, 57r).

41. See O'Mara and Paul, *Repertorium*, sermon 18, Third Sunday in Lent, 4:2519, for a summary of this sermon. "Gostly to spekyn be þis fend þat made þe man dowm is undirstondyn dedly synne wych mankyth man and woman down a fore god. . . . And þre synnys ben lechery coueytyse and pride" (Longleat 4, 38r).

42. Quotation from O'Mara and Paul, *Repertorium*, sermon 39, Eighth Sunday after Trinity, 4:2559. "Ghostly to spekin ben þre false prophets of whyche we muste ben waar. þo ben þe feend. þe world. and þe flesch" (Longleat 4, 81v).

43. Quotation from O'Mara and Paul, *Repertorium*, sermon 45, Fourteenth Sunday after Trinity, 4:2570. "Gostly to spekin be þese ten meselsis ben understondin alle þat synnyn a3enis þe ten comaundementes for as seynt jon seyth . . . earþely synne or it is coueytyse of þe flesch and þat is letchere. or it is coueytyse of þe ey3e and þat is wordly coueytyse. or it is pride of lyuynge" (Longleat 4, 94v).

44. See O'Mara and Paul, *Repertorium*, sermon 15, Quinquagesima, 4.2513, for a summary of this sermon. "For þis numbre is foure sithis þre in tokene þat he he ches hem princepali to berin a bou3tin and to prechin þe fey3t of þe holy trinyte be four partyys of þe world. est. and west. south. and north" (Longleat 4, 30v).

45. Quotation from O'Mara and Paul, *Repertorium*, sermon 8, First Sunday after the Octave of Epiphany, 4:2499. "At twelve 3er age he began to schewin hys wisdom and techings of oure feyth. in tokene þat þe feyth stant princepaly in twelue articles and þe twelue apostolis it schulde princepaly ben multiplyid al aboutin þe world and as twelue comyth of thre and foure be multiplicacion. So schulde þe feyth of þe holy trinyte be prechinge and techinge of þe foure gospels been multyplyid in knowing al a bou3tyn þe world" (Longleat 4, 15v).

46. Quotation from O'Mara and Paul, *Repertorium*, sermon 14, Sexagesima, 4:2511.
In somme it bringith forth fru3t an hundrid fold as in maydeins martyris and pchouris. In somme sexty fold as in widuys. In somme þritty fold as in weddyd folk. For in wedlak ben þre gode þings. Þo ben fru3t and brynging forth of chyldrin and þe sacrament of matrymonie whiche þre multiplyyd by þe keping of þe ten commaundementes ben worþi mechil mede. Sexty longith to wyduys for to ben princepaly it longith to mutiplyin the sexse dedis of mercy be keping of þe ten commandementes. . . . An hundrid longith to maydenys for it comith of ten multiplyyd be hem self. For an hundrid is ten sithys ten. and so medful maydenhod sekith non multiplicacion fleschly of oþer but only to multiplyin

hem self in oþer gostly in virtue and gode dedis be kepig of þe ten commandements and offrin hem self to god be chaste. (Longleat 4, 28v)

47. Quotation from O'Mara and Paul, *Repertorium*, sermon 34, Third Sunday after Trinity, 4:2549. "Thanne Crist sone rey schepperde of reasonable creaturys lefte neynty and neyne ["schep," added in margin] in desert þo ben þe neyne ordrys of aungelys whyche pasingly kepin þe ten comaundements of god" (Longleat 4, 71r).

48. Middle English quotation from O'Mara and Paul, *Repertorium*, sermon 16, First Sunday in Lent, 4:2514–15.

49. Quotation from ibid., 4:2515. "i.ii. iiii.v.viii.x.x.x. been partyys inclusynge vl. and þese to gedere makyn evene .l. allso it is foure sythys .x. and be x. arn undyrstondyn þe .x. commaundementis befoure þe foure gospelys and foure genial [cardinal] vertuys þo ben ry3tfulnesse strengþe sleyþe and temperance and þerfore we fastyn vl dayys to makyn assyth for þe trespas þat we han don a3ens þe x. comaundementes and a3ens þe foure gospelys and a3ens þe foure genial virtuys" (Longleat 4, 35v).

50. Quotation from O'Mara and Paul, *Repertorium*, sermon 56, Twenty-Fifth Sunday after Trinity, 4:2593.

> And for þat þis gospel makith so opin menede of crists comynge and of þe fyue louys and of þe fyue þousand of men þat wern fedde with þo louys þerfore þis gospel is red þe fifthe sonday aforn þe comynge of crist amongs mankende in tokene þat after þe fyue agis of þe world and after fyue þousand 3eer from þe begynynge of þe world crist came fyrst bodili amongst mankende. . . . Also holi churche makith menede of crists comynge þis sonday whiche is þe laste sonday of þe 3eer for as þe cercule of þe 3eer is performyd and þe sonne comtyh a3en to þe same poynt in þe fyrmament þat it gan þe 3eer. So is þe cercule of alle offis of þe 3eer is performyd þis sonday and þis woke, and as þe offis of holi cherche began at þe avent þat is to seye in englisch at þe comyng of crist so al þe offis of þe 3eer endith in þe comynge of crist. And þerfore skilfulli þe offis endith þe fyuethe sonday aforn cristemesse in tokene þat þe cercule of þe offis is perfomyd. For þe numbre of fyue is clepid a cercule in numbris. Forwhy multiplye fyve be fyue or be ony odde numbre and it schal comyn a3en to fyue and endyn in fyue and multiplie fyve be an euen numbre and it schal makin a perfy3t cercule of numbris forwhi fyue sithis fyue is fyue and twenty. And þryys fyue is fyuetene and twyys fyue is ten and foure siþis fyue is twenty and þerfore skilfulli þe cercule of goddis offis endyth in þe fyue and twentithe sonday aftyr þe trynite and þe fyuethe sonday aforn cristemesse. (Longleat 4, 118r)

51. Middle English quotation from O'Mara and Paul, *Repertorium*, sermon 56, Twenty-Fifth Sunday after Trinity, 4:2593.

52. Boethius, *Boethian Number Theory*, 153.

53. *On the Properties of Things*, 2.1364. Similarly, Isidore of Seville writes, "The circular number, when it is multiplied by itself, beginning with itself, ends with itself." Brehaut, *Encyclopedist of the Dark Ages*, 130.

54. For a summary of this sermon, see O'Mara and Paul, *Repertorium*, London, British Library, Additional 40672, sermon 85, "Common of a Virgin not a Martyr," 1:589. The Middle English quotation is from *English Wycliffite Sermons*, 2:173–74.

55. See, for example, Powell, "Untying the Knot," 59–60; Labbie, *Lacan's Medievalism*, 195.

56. Geraldine Heng argues that this symbol of perfection is undercut by the instability of his identity. See Heng, "Feminine Knots," 504.

57. Quotation from O'Mara and Paul, *Repertorium*, sermon 38, Seventh Sunday after Trinity, 4:2557.

> In þe fyrste feste wern fed fyue þousand of men. in tokene þat it was more leeful to þe jews in þe elde lawe to folwyn the lusts of here fyue witts þan it is to

cristene peple in þe newe lawe. And þefore þe numbre of peple fed at þis feste was foure þousand of men. For cristene peple shulde be gouernyd and fed be þe teching of þe foure gospellis whych is more perfy3t lore þan was þe elde lawe and also cristene peple shulde be gouernyd and fed wiþ þe foure cardynal virtuys.... Foure is a numbre of stabylte. For what þing is foure square it is stable and nout ly3tly turnyth. So cristene peple shulde ben stable in þe feyth and in charite of god. for þey ben groundyd on a stable square ston. þat is crist. Fyue is clepyd a round numbre. for multiplye fyue be fyue as oftyn as þu wylt and thu schalt alwey comyn a3en to fyue. as a cercle begynnyth at a poynt and turnyth a3en to þe same poynt. And þerfore þe numbre of fyue is lykenyd to a round þing and it sygnefyyth unstabylte of þe peple in þe elde lawe and also it signefyith unstabylte of þe elde lawe, for boþin wern meuable and wol unstable. (Longleat 4, 79r)

58. McCluskey, "Boethius's Astronomy and Cosmology," 63.

59. "Quadrate schap and square is most stedefast and stable, and bitokneþ þerfore most þe stablenesse of al holy chirche and stedefastnesse of a Cristene soule in vertues and sciens and lore þat he knowiþ wiþ alle seintes, what is lengþe and brede, highnesse and depnes." *On the Property of Things*, 2.1358. See also Dederich, "Trevisa's Translation." In his discussion of the triangle, Trevisa also writes that the quadrangle "is most solid and stedefaste among figures and numbers, and is square and presenteþ þe lore of the gospel, þat haþ stedefastnesse in þe foure parties of þe world, as Beda seiþ super Genesim." *On the Property of Things*, 2.1371.

60. Quotation from O'Mara and Paul, *Repertorium*, sermon 38, Seventh Sunday after Trinity, 4:2557. "Wommen and chyldryn ben nout tolde in þis numbre of foure. But þey ben outakin as we redin in þe gospel of seynt mathu. xv for be kende wommen and chyldryn ben unstable and freele. but be grace þey ben often more stable þan ben men" (Longleat 4, 79r).

61. As Boethius writes, "There are those substances which grow from equal numbers, such as squares, or those which unity forms, that is the odd numbers.... So it is that every number which comes from these figures.... One is a stable and the other an unstable variation; the first has the strength of an immobile substance, the other is a changing mobility." Boethius, *Boethian Number Theory*, 155.

62. Quotation from O'Mara and Paul, *Repertorium*, sermon 6, Circumcision of Christ, 4:2495. "for ey3te ys þe fyrste sad numbre" (Longleat 4, 11v); "For þis numbre ey3te is a sad square numbre as seyn þese clerkys for it is twyys twyys two and it hath þre euene metyngs for it is euene in heyethe and brede and þiknesse as a dee wych is but oon dee and hath heyithe brede and þicknesse alle þre euene whyche þre arn but oon dee and non of hem is oþer and so it betokenyth þe feyth of þe holy trynyte whych is oon god andþre formys al euene in my3t" (Longleat 4, 11v).

63. See *Middle English Dictionary*, s.v. "sad," defs. 2 and 3.

64. Dan Michel, *Dan Michel's Ayenbite of Inwyt*, 234.

65. Boethius, *Boethian Number Theory*, 96.

66. Voigt, "Perfect Numbers." See also Dickson, *History of the Theory of Numbers*, 1:4; citation from *Bibliotheca Rerum Germanicarum, Tomus Sextus, Monumenta Alcuiniana* (Berlin, 1873), epistolae 259, pp. 818–21.

67. Quotation from O'Mara and Paul, *Repertorium*, sermon 55, Twenty-Fourth Sunday after Trinity, 4:2591.

68. Note that the words "superaboundaunt" and "superaboundance" appear in the *Middle English Dictionary*, but not in the sense in which they are used in number theory.

69. See Stephen Wailes, "Hrotsvit's Plays," 135–36.

70. Hrotsvit of Gandersheim, *Florilegia*, 84–85.

71. "Praise be thereof to the supreme wisdom of the Creator / and to the marvelous science of this world's Maker, / who not only created the world in the beginning out of nothing and ordered everything according to number, measure and weight, / but also in the seasons and in the ages of men gave us the ability to grasp the wondrous science of the arts." Hrotsvit of Gandersheim, *Florilegia*, 86.

72. Sticca, "Sacred Drama," 156. For a reference to how Sapientia ("as a foreign woman") and her daughters make Hadrian look foolish in part through their mathematical conversation, see Brown, "Hrotsvit's Sapientia," 166–67. Wilson writes, "Hadrian, who is called a fool, is apparently ignorant of arithmetical properties. Yet this Emperor is particularly reputed to have been well educated, especially in mathematics." Hrotsvit of Gandersheim, *Florilegia*, 84.

73. Quotation from O'Mara and Paul, *Repertorium*, sermon 8, First Sunday after the Octave of Epiphany, 4:2499. "At twelue ȝer age he began to schewin hys wysdom and techings of our feyth. in tokene þat þe feyth stant princepaly in twelue articulis and be twelue apostolis it schulde princepaly ben multiplyid al abouȝtin þe world and as twelue comyth of þre and foure be multyplicacion. So schulde þe feyth of þe holy trinyte be preching and teching of þe foure gospels ben multyplyid in knowing al abouȝtyn þe world" (Longleat 4, 15v). For discussions of the number twelve in medieval religious texts, see Meyer and Suntrup, *Lexikon*, s.v. "zwölf," 619–46.

74. Quotation from O'Mara and Paul, *Repertorium*, sermon 15, Quinquagesima, 4:2513.

> For þis numbre is foure sithis þre in tokene þat he ches hem princepali to berin a bouȝtin and to prechin þe feyȝt of þe holy trynite be foure partyys of þe world. est. and west. south. and north. Also for þis numbre in kende is fyrst plente uous and fructuous and tokene

þat þey schulde bringin forth fruȝt of salvacion of mannis soule al abouȝtin þe world"; "The gospel hath þre partys: the fyrst is aforn warnynge of crists passion and of hys endinge. The second party makith mende of mercifyl myracle doynge. The þrydde party makith mende of akendely þankinge. (Longleat 4, 30v)

75. Note that the earliest reference to the York Christi plays is from 1377; see Steenbrugge, *Drama and Sermon*, ix. For a discussion of the questions surrounding the text of the plays and if the text represents a fourteenth-, fifteenth-, or sixteenth-century version, see Steenbrugge, *Drama and Sermon*, xiv. Pamela King explores both York's Corpus Christi Pentecost Play and Chester's Whitsun Play in "Playing Pentecost"; see her discussion of the Potters, 61–62.

76. Play 43, *Pentecost*, in *York Corpus Christi Plays*, lines 1–11. See https://d.lib.rochester.edu/teams/text/Davidson-play-43-pentecost. Note that I have employed Davidson's glosses and notes in the translation.

77. Quoted in Shippey, "Chaucer's Arithmetical Mentality," 192, from Augustine, *City of God*, 534–35, 4.15. See also Augustine, *Tractates on the Gospel of John 11–27*, 284–86, tractate 27:10. The Chester cycle begins with the choosing of the twelfth apostle, or the election of Matthew to the apostles.

78. Play 43, *Pentecost*, in *York Corpus Christi Plays*, lines 1–11. See https://d.lib.rochester.edu/teams/text/Davidson-play-43-pentecost.

79. Boethius, *De institutione arithmetica*, 89.

80. For example, according to Peter Darby, "In *Expositio Actuum Apostolorum*, Bede suggests that the elevation of a twelfth apostle to replace Judas is an allegory for the eschatological fate of the Jews. Matthias restored the apostles to a state of perfection, which is symbolised by the number 12, just as the conversion of the Jews is expected to

restore the Church to the perfect state at the end of the world." Darby, *Bede and the End of Time*, 108.

81. See Hugh of St. Victor, *De scripturis et scriptoribus sacris* 15, in Migne, Patrologia Latina 175:22–23, in Peck, "Number as Cosmic Language," 58.

82. See *Piers Plowman* 3.174: "Þow hast honged on my Nekke . Enleue tymes." In Langland, *Parallel Extracts*, ed Skeat. See Lattin, "Some Aspects of Medieval Number Symbolism in Langland's *Piers Plowman*,"; see also Versluis, "*Piers Plowman*" for a discussion of alphanumerical patterns in the poem.

83. Williams, *Deformed Discourse*, 226.

84. See *Middle English Dictionary*, s.v. "stabli," 1a and 1b.

85. Quotation from O'Mara and Paul, *Repertorium*, sermon 40, Ninth Sunday after Trinity, 4:2560.

> But for þat in dyuers cuntries ben diuers mesuris and dyuers namys of mesuris þerfore it is hard to seyn it kendely in englysch. But soth it is þat he forȝaf more whene he forȝaf twenty cors of whete þan he dede whene he forȝaf fyuety barelys of olee. Als ȝyf I forȝeue þee twenty pens I forȝeue þee more þan ȝyf I forȝeue þee but fyuety ferþings. So whene þe dette or þe trespas is gret or grieuous forȝeuenesse of a lytyl part of penaunce þat longyth þerto may ben more þan forȝeuenesse of half penaunce þat longyth to smale trespas or smale detts. (Longleat 4, 83v)

CHAPTER 3

1. The manuscript itself dates from the mid-fifteenth century, and the sermons were probably "composed in the first quarter of the fifteenth century." *Jacob's Well*, ed. Brandeis, xiii; for a discussion of dating, see L. Carruthers, "Richard Lavynham," 17, and L. Carruthers, "Where Did *Jacob's Well* Come From?"

2. Carruthers concludes, "While the nature of the text, the subjects treated, and the more frequent forms of direct address used, all suggest a lay audience listening in church, a certain number of passages indicate a possible clerical audience." "'Know Thyself,'" 221. See also L. Carruthers, "*Great Curse*," 45. For a discussion of sources that reveal the focus of the *Well* author, see, for example, Gregg, "Exempla of 'Jacob's Well.'"

3. Fitzgibbons, "*Jacob's Well* and Penitential Pedagogy," 225, 228. The modern English translation is mine.

4. Ibid., 229.

5. Ibid., 231, 226, 231.

6. L. Carruthers, "Liturgical Setting of *Jacob's Well*," 18–21. See also Atchley, "'Wose' of *Jacob's Well*," 40–66, and Fitzgibbons, "*Jacob's Well* and Penitential Pedagogy," 217.

7. The first fifty sermons of *Jacob's Well* have been edited by Arthur Brandeis in *Jacob's Well*. The remaining forty-five sermons have been edited by Clinton P. E. Atchley and are available only in his dissertation, "'Wose' of Jacob's Well." These are the editions used in this chapter, which I cite by editor and page number.

8. *Jacob's Well*, ed. Brandeis, vi. The first sermon of the cycle (pp. 1–4) gives an overview of the entire cycle.

9. Spencer, *English Preaching in the Late Middle Ages*, 369–70n35. See also Katherine R. Cooper, who describes *Jacob's Well* as a "sapience manual," or a "volume of spiritual wisdom primarily written for clerics." Cooper, "'My Cruel Conscience,'" 14.

10. "The preacher's congregation, in short, is larged composed of that pious middle class found in England at the end of the fourteenth and beginning of the fifteenth centuries, a class to which Chaucer himself belonged." L. Carruthers, "'Know Thyself,'" 240. See also L. Carruthers, "Where Did *Jacob's Well* Come From?," 339; L. Carruthers, "Liturgical Setting of *Jacob's Well*," esp. 12–16.

11. Atchley, "Audience of *Jacob's Well*," n.p. For further discussion of *Jacob's Well*'s audience, see Phillips, *Transforming Talk*, 18–31, Fitzgibbons, "*Jacob's Well* and Penitential Pedagogy," 220–23; Beattie, *Medieval Single Women*, 42–43.

12. Fitzgibbons, "Poverty, Dignity, and Lay Spirituality," 229, 231.

13. Ibid., 230. See also Fitzgibbons, "*Jacob's Well* and Penitential Pedagogy."

14. All modern English translations from *Jacob's Well* are my own.

15. *Jacob's Well*, 24, referencing "alle þo þat . . . ȝeuyn þe xj. scheef for þe tythe."

16. For more on the practice of tithing, see Dodds, "Managing Tithes."

17. Note the Douay-Rheims, "Why was not this ointment sold for three hundred pence, and given to the poor?" (John 12:5).

18. According to the *Middle English Dictionary*, "wemo" is an expression of impatience or astonishment. See *MED*, s.v. "wemai."

19. *Towneley Plays*, 14–15, lines 192–210.

20. This translation of this line is from Bevington, *Medieval Drama*, 281.

21. Ibid., 15.

22. Davidson, "Cain in the Mysteries," 209.

23. *Towneley Plays*, 15, lines 218–21.

24. Ibid., 15, lines 223–24.

25. As William G. Marx observes, "Cain is the incompetent, jealous, vengeful brother. He has run out of fingers to count on and must guess what numbers come next, which opens him to Abel's criticism. Cain senses mocking—just like him to transfer what he would think and say to what he imagines his brother is thinking. More cause for resentment and revenge. The Wakefield Master seems to have a hand in writing this play, and he was not above using comedy for dramatic purposes. Especially if most of the audience, say, could out-count Cain. . . . Cain's lines seem to say that he's not willing to part with any of his crop, especially when it will amount to a tenth of it. How about parting with only a twelfth of it (who'll know, his eyes are closed?) or a fifteenth part, or a sixteenth part? And that sacrificed part being the worst of the harvest? In the end, it will all count against him, so to speak." (Private email)

26. *Middle English Dictionary*, s.v. "threve."

27. Robert Sturges draws strong parallels between Cain and fifteenth-century Yorkshire agricultural laborers, "suggesting further possibilities for audience identification." Sturges, *Circulation of Power*, 98. For the festive qualities of the play that would have made Cain appeal more to audiences, see Edminster, *Preaching Fox*, 55–71. For Cain as evil, see Davidson, "Cain in the Mysteries."

28. For a discussion of the sources of the ladder in *Jacob's Well*, see L. Carruthers, "Allegory and Bible Interpretation," 8–9 and 11–13.

29. The translation of this passage comes from O'Mara and Paul, *Repertorium*, Salisbury Cathedral Library 103, sermon 91, 4.2445.

30. See, for example, Atchley, "'Wose' of *Jacob's Well*," 199.

31. The idea of "stability" is also invoked in the following passage from a discussion of "Equitate and veritate": "Taketh þise iiij. vertuys forseyd and makyth þerwyth ȝoure welle iiij. sqware. and þanne schalle it dure & stande & abyde. & noȝt falle in. ne fayle." Ibid., 220.

32. Lentes, "Counting Piety," 57–58.

33. Kempe, *Book of Margery Kempe*, 80.6413–17.

34. Kempe's sum is close to the oft-calculated figures of 5460, 5475, 5490, and 6666; see Bynum, *Wonderful Blood*, 264n16. See also Breeze, "Number of Christ's Wounds."

35. Watson, "Making of *The Book of Margery Kempe*," 418–19.

36. Susan Phillips discusses this exemplum in her *Transforming Talk*; she explores how the sermon writer has adapted the typical version of the exemplum, in which it is not clear at first who is tallying the hermit's steps (29–30).

37. Kempe, *Book of Margery Kempe* (ed. Windeatt), lines 8472–95, p. 426. The translation is from Windeatt, *Book of Margery Kempe* (trans. Windeatt), 296.

38. Watson, "Making of *The Book of Margery Kempe*," 419. I would like to thank

Steven Rozenski for first drawing my attention to this passage, as well as to the length of the sentence. See also Cooper-Rompato, "Number and Numeracy."

39. Watson, "Making of *The Book of Margery Kempe*," 419–20.

40. Ibid., 421.

41. See the *Middle English Dictionary*, s.v. "mesure (n.)," defs. 1 and 7. For a discussion of medieval measurements, see "Measuring," in Wedell, "Numbers," 1223–33.

42. John Lydgate, "A Song of Just Mesure," in *Minor Poems of John Lydgate*, 2:773, lines 17–21.

43. William G. Marx, private email. See *Mankind*, lines 237–44, in *Three Late Medieval Morality Plays*, 16. I would like to extend my thanks to William G. Marx for drawing my attention to this passage.

44. "Play 35, Crucifixio Christi," in *York Corpus Christi Plays*, line 107. See also Rogerson, *York Mystery Plays*, 178.

45. "Play 35, Crucifixio Christi," lines 111–12. The Fourth Soldier later declares, "Owe, this werke is all unmeete. / This borning muste all be amende" (127–28).

46. Ibid., lines 229–30.

47. Ibid., 253–60, italics added.

48. From William G. Marx, personal correspondence.

49. For example, he writes, "þe iiij. foot of sobyrnesses is mesure in heryng." Atchley, "'Wose' of *Jacob's Well*," 108.

50. "Whanne a lytel poudyr of erthe is cast on ȝou in ȝoure graue, ȝe schul be lesse dred þan þe leste persone, and lest of pryce of all the world!" Ibid., 4, ed. Brandeis.

51. John Felton, Easter Sermon, in Wenzel, *Preaching in the Age of Chaucer*, 137, and 137n10. Wenzel states that he translates this sermon from Oxford, Bodleian Library, MS Bodley 187, fols. 47r–49r, collated with Cambridge, Jesus College, MS 13, part 5, fols. 126v–128. For Euclid on the circle, see book 1 of *Euclid's Elements of Geometry*. For more about the circle in medieval geometry, see, for example, Katz et al., *Sourcebook*; Clagett, "Impact of Archimedes on Medieval Science." For more on the textual tradition of medieval geometry, see, for example, Zaitsev, "Meaning of Early Medieval Geometry." Those interested in medieval geometrical texts might also consult Victor, *Practical Geometry*.

52. According to the *Oxford English Dictionary*, a "fathom" was the length of a forearm until the fifteenth century (3a), when it was more commonly defined as "the length covered by the outstretched arms, including the hands to the tip of the longest finger; hence, a definite measure of 6 feet" (3b). According to the *Middle English Dictionary*, "fadme" is defined as "a measure of length, equivalent to six feet or thereabouts" (def. 1a).

53. Quotation from O'Mara and Paul, *Repertorium*, London, British Library, Additional 40672, Sixteenth Sunday after Trinity, 1:870.

54. *Bible Moralisée*, in Codex Vindobonensis 2554, fol. IV.

55. Celeyrette, "Mathematics and Theology," 162, from Nicholas of Cusa, *On Learned Ignorance*, 1:23, 38–39.

56. *Elements* 11, definition 13, from *Euclid's Elements of Geometry*, 424.

57. The first recorded use of the word "prism" (from the Latin *prisma*) in English is sixteenth century. OED, s.v. "*prism*." Plato believed that five basic shapes (aka Platonic solids) made the universe: tetrahedron, cube, octahedron, dodecahedron, and icosahedron. The calculation of volumes of irregular shape was done by Archimedes. See Clagett, "Impact of Archimedes." Euclid treated the prism and pyramid and Archimedes the round bodies (the sphere, cone, cylinder). For more on medieval geometry, see Victor, *Practical Geometry*.

58. The *Middle English Dictionary* defines "square" as the shape of a square and also the side of a square or equilateral triangle. See s.v. "square" (n.) defs. 1 and 2.

59. For example, in his discussion of Gluttony, the writer elaborates on the tree of evil tongue with its many branches, which then branch into leaves. *Jacob's Well*, ed. Brandeis, 153.

60. As Katherine Cooper argues, "In spite of the text's attempt to define contrition as a measurable (though seven-part) process, completion of the sacrament becomes ever harder to obtain because of the increasing complexity and rigor of each separate step. This increasing arduousness poses questions for the ability of any penitent to actually complete the sacrament at all." Cooper, "'My Cruel Conscience,'" 16.

CHAPTER 4

1. Volume 1 of the two-volume collection, *Selected Sermons*, was published in 2019, and the second volume is in preparation..

2. Wenzel, *Latin Sermon Collections*, 66; also quoted in Johnson, "Robert Rypon," 38.

3. Johnson, "Robert Rypon," 39. Wenzel writes of Rypon's "originality"; see Wenzel, *Latin Sermon Collections*, 73.

4. Wenzel notes Rypon's attention to the seven deadly sins in Wenzel, *Latin Sermon Collections*, 71–72.

5. Johnson has argued how Rypon "internalizes images and the lexicon he derives from authorities to the extent that image and lexicon become part of his own imaginative landscape." Johnson, "Imaginative Landscape," 178.

6. Johnson, "Robert Rypon," 41, and Johnson, "Introduction," in *Selected Sermons*, 41.

7. Johnson, "Robert Rypon," 40.

8. Ibid., 41, from Harvey, *Lay Religious Life*, 125. See also Johnson, "Introduction," in *Selected Sermons*, 6.

9. Johnson, "Imaginative Landscape," 180.

10. See, for example, Adams and Hanska, *Jewish-Christian Encounter*, 3, and Scheepsma, *Limburg Sermons*, 33.

11. An example defining a monastic identity would include an address like *fratres carissimi*; *carissimi* could refer to either or both lay and monastic audiences. For a fuller discussion of audience, see "audience" in Wenzel, *Latin Sermon Collections*, 9–10, and Muessig, *Preacher, Sermon and Audience*.

12. Here the work of Carolyn Muessig is especially helpful. See Muessig, *Medieval Monastic Preaching*, esp. 13–14, as well as the essay in Muessig's collection by Horner, "Benedictines and Preaching"; see also Wright, "Vercelli Homilies XI–XIII."

13. Wenzel, *Latin Sermon Collections*, 66n1.

14. Ibid., 67.

15. For a discussion of Hindu-Arabic (more commonly known as Arabic) numerals in England, see the appendix to this book as well as Steele, *Earliest Arithmetics in English*, xvi–xvii and 3–4.

16. Rypon, *Selected Sermons*, 1:85, 87. All Latin quotations and English translations from volume 1 are cited by Johnson's volume and page number. Quotations from volume 2, which is currently in preparation by Johnson, are cited by volume and working draft page number. I would like to thank Holly Johnson, Sara Johnson, and Sherri Olson for their expertise and guidance on the translations from volume 2. Holly Johnson kindly provided initial working drafts of her translations that will appear, revised, in volume 2 of Robert Rypon's sermons from the Dallas Medieval Texts and Translations series. I then worked on these drafts in consultation with Sara Johnson and Sherri Olson. All errors, of course, are my own, and readers are encouraged to consult the translations by Holly Johnson when her edition appears in print.

> Pro processu collacionis, sicut de notificacione ita de populo et virtute, tripliciter reperio in scriptura. Est enim notificacio per signa, per verba, per facta: per signa expressiua intrinsece perfeccionis, per verba persuasiua scientifice predicacionis, per facta ostensiua saluifice accionis. Est insuper trifarius, videlicet populus perfectus, populus subiectus, et populus ex vtrisque collectus. Populus perfectus est populus clericalis, populus subiectus est populus laicalis, populus ex vtrisque

collectus est populus generalis. Est postrema virtus phisica seu naturalis, virtus ethica seu moralis, virtus theologica seu supernaturalis. (1:84, 86)

17. Ibid., 1:101. "Et ad notificandum istas virtutes sicut et virtutes theologicas, que sunt fides, spes, et caritas, sunt 4 regule in natura. Prima est ista: solum bonum amandum est. Secunda est hec: Omne malum est fugiendum. Tercia est ista negatiua: Non omne bonum est equaliter diligendum. Quarta est ista similiter negatiua: Non omne malum equaliter est odiendum set quodlibet secundum gradum sue malicie" (1:100).

18. Wenzel, *Latin Sermon Collections*, 68.

19. Rypon, *Selected Sermons*, 1:151. "Spinosa sepes auaricie"; "profunda fouea gule vel luxurie quibus annexa est accidia" (1:150).

20. Ibid., 1:307. "Istis vii gradibus humilitatis debent omnes Christiani ascendere vsque ad eminenciam sante vite, que est octauus gradus attingens vsque ad solarium, scilicet celum, id est beatitudinem" (1:306).

21. Ibid., 1:309. "Vnde gradus per quos milites ascendant ad celum sunt isti" (1:308).

22. Ibid., 1:313. "Isti ergo sunt gradus per quos agricultores et ciues ascendent ad celum" (1:312).

23. Ibid., 1:219. "Quod quilibet Christianus debet indui fortitudine et decore virtuali" (1:218).

24. Ibid., 1:221. "Sampson fortissimus audiens fraudulencem vocem Dalide mer[e]tricis perdidit totam fortitudinem suam que consistebat in 7 crinibus" (1:220).

25. Ibid., 1:223. "Et spoliat Sampson 7 crinibus, id est 7 donis Spiritus Sancti in quibus includuntur omnes virtutes necessarie ad salutem" (1:220, 222).

26. Ibid., 1:223. "Et traditur Philisteis qui interpretantur cadentes vel ruina. Traditur (inquam) potestati diabolorum qui ceciderunt de celo in precipitis viciorum, et post hanc vitam nisi resipuerit in inferni profundum" (1.222).

27. Ibid., 1:223. "Immo sicut Sampson recrescentibus crinibus creuit in fortitudine et tandem se ipsum cum maxima multitudine Philistiorum interfecit, sic reuera talis qui claudiens in stulticia huius mundi cecidit in malicia peccatorum, recrescentibus in ipso 7 pilos, id est 7 peccatis mortalibus tandem seipsum cum multis prauis Philisteis, videlicet cum ipsis qui per ipsum in maliciam ceciderunt, spiritualiter punit et occidit" (1:222).

28. For Augustine on Samson, see Webb, "Abraham, Samson," esp. 224–30.

29. Rypon, *Selected Sermons*, 2:n.p, forthcoming. I would like to thank Holly Johnson for sharing her volume in preparation. Without her work, I could not have undertaken this chapter. "Et recitat ibidem Apostolus que sunt opera carnis et qui sunt fructus spiritus. Opera autem carnis recitat Apostolus in numero septendenario qui componitur ex 7 et 10 fructuum in singum quod 10 opera carnis sunt contra 10 precepta, et numerus septenarius operum carnis conuenit 7 peccatis mortalibus que sunt contraria 7 donis Spiritus Sancti vel virtuti 7 sacramentorum ecclesie."

30. Luke 14:31–32, New Revised Standard Version.

31. Rypon, *Selected Sermons*, 1:297. "Moraliter quilibet predicator verbi Dei, immo quilibet homo, dicitur rex qui regnum sue anime debet regere. Alius rex cui occurrit est Deus qui est Rex regum. Predicator committit bellum cum Deo et occurrit ei cum decem milibus quando predicando decem mandata Domini presumit ex sua predicacione conuertere populum. Eciam homo occurrit Deo cum decem milibus quando ex sola implecione decem mandatorum credit se mereri celum. Set certe Deus occurrit tam predicatori quam auditori quam cuicumque alteri homini cum viginti milibus quia vere potest nobis dicere, quecumque bona pro me feceris feci in duplo plura pro te" (1:296).

32. Ibid., 1:297. "Immo Deus occurret nobis obiciens omnia peccata que fecimus corde, ore, et opere, que indubie in duplo plura sunt quam omnia bona opera que fecimus" (1:296).

33. Ibid., 1:121. "Omnia ista prefigurata in historia antedicta iam verificantur in primo paschate in ecclesia celebrato in quo, vt constat, ecclesia de immolacione, occisione, sanguinis effusione, et vera commestione agni immaculati, scilicet Iesu Christi, de baptismo, de penitencia fecit celebrem mencionem et in quo realiter verus populus transit spiritualiter de Egipto" (1:118, 120).

34. Ibid., 1:121. "In cuius signum filii Israel transeuntes de Egipto non leguntur ad illam redisse; sic peccator transiens, vt premittitur, de peccato non debet ad illud redire, set dietam suam per 40 annos cum filiis Israel in deserto, scilicet totam vitam suam deserendo peccatum continuare. Et bene notatur cursus vite humane per numerum quadragenarium quia in illo numero consecramus tempus penitencie pro peccato in qua penitencia quia cotidie peccamus debemus transcurrere vitam nostrum" (1:120).

35. Ibid., 1.123. "Insuper in isto paschate habemus veram euidenciam implendi decalogum in iusticia diuina. . . . Set constat quod in 40 sunt quatuor 10 per que 10 notatur decalogus qui debet multiplicari per 4 quia debet impleri per 4 partes anni per quas currit vita humana et in 4 complexionibus corporis in quibus consistunt vires corporales in signum quod decalogus debet continue et cum omnibus viribus adimplere" (1:122).

36. Ibid., 1:125. "Sicut enim Christus post 40 dies resurreccionis ascendit in celum, sic et nos pertransito cursu vite qui in hoc festo notatur, vt premissum est, pertransito (inquam) ad verum exemplar huius festi, ad celum finaliter ascendemus" (1:124).

37. Ibid., 2:n.p. "Pro quibus notandum quod in Sacra Scriptura reperiuntur xi nomina demonum, et si forsan sint plura, possunt tamen reduci ad ista. Numerus itaque vndenarius congrue pertinet ad demonum nomina, quia secundum beatum Gregorium cum decalogus sit in numero denario, decalogi transgresso in qua includitur omne peccatum apte per numerum vndenarium demonum designatur. Quorum nomina sunt hec: Demon, Diabolus, Sathan vel Sathanas, Belial, Bemoth, Baal, Beel, Belphegor, Belzebub, Asmodeus, Leuiathan" (2:n.p.).

38. Quod videtur quasi impossibile pro hac via puro homini cuicumque cum nullus sciat nec scire possit naturam vnius atthomi. Cuius racio est quia atthomus est corpus dimensionatum potens recipere circa se circulum. In circulo autem continentur omnes figure recte linee et ita infinita subiecta et consequenter infinite passiones ac infinite conclusiones, et sic infinita scibilia sunt in eo. Et hinc est quod dixit quidam philosophus: hoc vnum scio me nichil scire. Quinimmo vanitas est de aliquo instabili superbire quia scilicet illud quod est instabile de facili est casurum. Set sciencia, presertim mundana, est instabilissimam in obliuionem caduca per aliquem morbum subitaneum corporalem. Perinde dicit quidam philosophus quod due tele cerebrum hominis circumcingunt, quarum vna est propinquior cerebro, et vocatur pia mater, et alia remocior, et vocatur dura et facit ipsum omnia scita imperpetuum obliuisci. (2:n.p.)

For a discussion of medieval atomism, see, for example, Grellard and Robert, *Atomism*.

39. Secundo quantum ad nominis Iesu denominacionem dicit beatus Bernardus, super Cantica, sermone 19, sicut notatur infra in sermone in dominica palmarum super illo themate: Quid faciam de Iesu [Matt. 27:22] in antethemate eiusdem. Tercio quoad signacionem huius nominis Iesus notandum quod apud Grecos scribitur 6 litteris, videlicet iota, eta, sigma, o, y, sigma. Que littere sonant apud Latinos: I, E, S, O Y, diptongus pro quibus Latini ponunt hanc litteram V, et sima. Ceterum secundum morem Latinorum scribitur cum tribus litteris Grecis, scilicet iota, etha, sima, titulo supraposito seu adiecto. Que tres littere possunt moraliter designare Trinitatem

in diuinis, cuius persone secunde titulus adicitur, scilicet humanitas incarnati. Que scriptura trium litterarum sonat apud nos Iesus. (Rypon, *Selected Sermons*, 2:n.p.)

40. Note that this appears to be an error; the second column should contain letters signifying numbers in the tens, and the third column numbers in the hundreds. Rypon calculates the number signified by Jesus's name correctly according to the Greek system.

41. Quantum ad scripturam huius nominis benedicti, quoad 6 litteras, dicit venerabilis Beda super illo Luce secundo 2[:21], Vocatum est nomen eius Iesus, quod numerus litterarum huius nominis perpetua salutis nostre misteria redolet. Nam quelibet littera huius nominis numerum certum notat nostre salutis misterium denotantem. Pro quo notandum quod secundum aliquos sunt in alphabeto Greco 24 littere et tres figure superaddite, ita quod littere cum figuris sunt ter nouem. Vnde in primo nouenario quelibet littera signat numerum digitum secundum litterarum et numerii ordinem vsque nouem. In secundo nonenario computatur quelibet figura pro suo multiplicato numero centenario secundum ordinem algorismi. Prima itaque littera huius nominis Iesus, scilicet iota, id est I, notat 10 quia iota est prima littera in secundo nonenario alphabeti Greci. In secundo littera etha, hoc est e, notat 8. Tercia littera est sima que est secunda in tercio nonenario et designat in numero 200. Quarta littera est o breuis et septima in secundo nonenario, et notat 70. Y est quarta littera in tercio nonenario, et signat 400. Sigma, vt predictum est, notat 200. Vnde omnes isti numeri coaddiucti, scilicet 10, 8, 200, 70, 400, et 200, et reddunt 888, qui numerus per o reductus figure diuinice resurrectionis concordat. Nam dominus octauo die, scilicet in crastino sabbati, resurrexit. Sic et nos post septem etates, id est post sabbatum animarum, in octaua quasi etate resurgemus. (Rypon, *Selected Sermons*, 2:n.p.)

42. Eight hundred eighty-eight is traditionally the number of Jesus, stemming from Irenaeus, *Against Heresies* 1.8.5, 12; see also 2.34.4. See Hopper, *Medieval Number Symbolism*, 63; Fideler, *Jesus Christ, Sun of God*, 30, 266.

43. Vel aliter dici potest quod nomen saluatoris, scilicet Iesus, simpliciter 8 contineat quia siue 8 multiplicentur per 10 siue per 100 resultat numerus octonarius. Nam multiplicatus 8 per 10 resultant 80, et multiplicatus 8 per 100 resultant 800. Vnde ex multiplicacione 8 per 100 intelligitur nostra resurreccio sicut prius, et in multiplicacione 8 per 10, vnde resultant 80, notatur quod per decalogi impleccionem deueniemus ad perfectum beatitudinem. Tandem 8 per 100 ductis cum numerus centenarius in scriptura significet premium perfectorum notatur quod per 8, scilicet Iesum, peruenimus ad premium sempiternum. In cuius signum primum filium promissionis, scilicet Ysaac, qui interpretatur risus vel gaudium Abraham centenarius generabat. Ex quibus omnibus patet satis quod in huius nominis Iesus interpretacione, nominacione, et signacione est pium remedium et iuuamen. Et hoc est quod scribitur Actuum 4[:12]: Nec enim aliud nomen est sub celo datum hominibus in quo oporteat nos saluos fieri, nisi in hoc nomem. (Rypon, *Selected Sermons*, 2:n.p.)

44. Quoted in Schimmel, *Mystery of Numbers*, 110; see also M. Reynolds, "Octagon in Leonardo's Drawings," 57.

45. Rypon, *Selected Sermons*, 2:n.p. Quod notatur in hoc nomine Iesu, primo per euis scripturam, secundo per eius interpretacionem, tercio per eius significacionem. Scribitur enim,

secundum Grecos, tribus figuris que sunt iota, etha, sigma. Iotha interpretatur perfeccio Domini; etha robustus mens; sima exaudabilis. Vnde totum simul, Iesus, id est perfeccio Domini mei robusti exaudibilis. Primo per scripturam quod scribitur tribus litteris vel figuris monstrat nobis fidem Trinitatis vel trium naturarum in Christo, scilicet deitatis et humanitatis in qua sunt due substancie vel nature, scilicet corpus et anima. Vel scribitur tribus figuris per trinitatem graciarum nobis collatarum per ipsum dominum Iesum Christum contra tria mala capitalia et originalia que concupiscencia oculorum, concupiscencia carnis, et superbia vite [Ioh. 2:16]. (Rypon, *Selected Sermons*, 2:n.p.)

46. "Ceterum hoc nomen Iesus apud Latinos, scribitur quinque litteris, que scriptura mistice intellecta secundum proprietates numerum quinarii docet satis: *quid faciam*, etc. Numerus quinarius vno modo componitur ex 4 et vno et alio modo ex tribus et duobus, et est processus venerabilis Anselmi super Iohannem, omelia 7, super opere suo mirabili *De laude crucis*" (2:n.p.).

47. "Nomen itaque nostri primi parentis, scilicet Adam, componitur ex 4 litteris que sunt inicia 4 nominum signancium 4 partes mundi, que sunt oriens et occidens, boreas et auster, que dicuntur lingua barbara: anachole, disis, archos, mesembrios. Vnde versus anachole dedit a, disis d, contulit, archos a, mesembrios m, congrue fiet Adam" (2:n.p.).

48. "Iste 4 littere significabant ipsum Adam dominari quatuor partibus mundi in suo principio. Set quid? Certe diuisio ipsarum litterarum a suis integris vere signat separacionem Adam a suo dominio per peccatum" (2:n.p.).

49. "Insuper homo componitur ex 4 elementis que inter se saltem in suis partibus corrupcioni sunt obnoxia" (2:n.p.).

50. Numerus igitur quaternarius congrue competit homini tum primo quia nomen primi hominis compositur ex 4 litteris, tum secundo quia homo, vt dictum est, componitur ex 4 elementis, tum tercio quia ille numerus componitur ex bis duobus quorum vterque est numerus par inequa gemina diuisionem admittit, que numerorum diuisio bene competit homini propter duo. Primo quia per peccatum diuidebatur a Deo suo; secundo quia in se diuidebatur. Sicut 4 in bis duo quorum neuter numerus alteri subicitur, sic et homo diuidebatur per peccatum <...> quod pars inferior post peccatum non subiciebatur set aduersabatur parti superiori. Consimilis est diuisio numeri quaternarii ad propositum si dicatur componi ex tribus et vno. Nam miser homo diuisus fuerat a Trinitate in diuinis. (2:n.p.)

51. "Set ecce quomodo in misterio numeri quinarii venit salus, id est Iesus: ad numerum quaternarium, id est hominem, coniunctus est Deus in vnitatem suppositi, et si sit Iesus vel ad numerum ternarium, scilicet ad Trinitatem personarum, vnita sunt duo, scilicet corpus et anima, et sic corruptibili vnitur incorruptibile sicut corpus in quantum, secundum philosophos, incorruptibile coniungitur 4 elementis" (2:n.p.).

52. See Bos, "The Fifth Element as the Substance of the Soul," chap. 14 in *Soul and Its Instrumental Body*, 258–303.

53. "Ecce, vt predixi, quomodo in hoc nomine Iesu intelligitur nedum Trinitas benedicta, veram eciam incarnacio Iesu Christi et per conueniens tota fides. Hee eciam 4 littere predicte signare possunt crucem Christi distentam in 4 partes in qua quintus incorruptibile pependit" (Rypon, *Selected Sermons*, 2:n.p.).

54. Johnson also notes that "account rolls written in Rypon's hand are extant at the Durham University Library." See ibid., 1:342n23.

55. Lawrence, *Medieval Monasticism*, 118.

56. Johnson asserts that this sermon is for a mixed audience comprised of both the laity and clergy. See Johnson, "Imaginative Landscape," 186.

57. Johnson refers readers to Menninger, *Number Words and Number Symbols*, which "includes a drawing in a manuscript of a checkered counting board and a brief explanation of how it works (348). He notes that dummy coins were necessary in computation because there were no pound or shilling coins; these were only 'computational units, not actual monetary values' (343). Counting money in England was made more complex because the 'English coinage system was built not upon the number 10, but upon the inconvenient numbers 4, 12, and 20' (343), a reality Rypon exploits in the connections he draws between the placing of coins and counters and living a Christian life." Rypon, *Selected Sermons*, 1:342n25.

58. Rypon, *Selected Sermons*, 1:193, 195.
Reddamus igitur hic racionem pro vita ista capientes formam de modo computandi. Constat quod computando ponuntur denarii vsque ad sex, et tunc si super excrescent vltra sex, ponitur vnum computatorium supra illa sex quod computatorium per se translatum ad superiorum locum efficit solidum, scilicet xii denarii. Moraliter ad propositum. Numerus senarius est numerus primus perfectus et signat totum tempus in quo viuimus et operamur. Computemus bene illud tempus primo apud nosmet ipsos in quadrantibus et obulis, id est in minoribus factis et maioribus, et illa que sunt superflua, puta peccata, resecemus, et ea que sunt vera nostro compoto inseramus, scilicet dumtaxat bene expensa. Quia in computacione primorum sex denariorum stat quasi pes compoti nostri quibus operibus bonis habitis; superponamus vnum computatorium, scilicet pro vi denariis, quod translatum valebit 12 denariis, id est solido. Qui solidus est fides que fides cum bonis operibus vna est et solida, immo omnium bonorum spiritualium fundamentum secundum Apostolum. (1:192, 194)

59. For the medieval counting board and jettons, see Barnard, *Casting-Counter*; Berry, *Medieval English Jettons*.

60. Rypon, *Selected Sermons*, 1:195.
Iam solido habito, scilicet fide cum bonis operibus, fiat vlterior compotus, scilicet solidorum, id est articulorum fidei, per 5, scicilet per 5 sensus, id est per fidem cum bonis operibus, tota racio nostri compoti continuetur, et tunc supponatur vnum computatorium illis 5 a parte dextra et equiparat illis 5; hoc est, equiparentur 5 sensus interiores ad 5 sensus exteriores in fide et operacione bonorum operum ad honorem Dei in quo est nostra dextra. Et transferantur ad sinistram, scilicet ad proximum, et tunc efficiunt x solidi, scilicet implecionem x preceptorum, quod computatorium translatum facit libram que compositor ex duobus equalibet, scilicet ex x et x, et congrue signat partes iusticie, scilicet quod reddat Deo que debet de bonis nature: actum corporis, dileccionem et fidem; actum oris ipsum laudando et peccata tua confitendo; actum corporis ipsi seruiendo et preceptis eius obediendo. (1:194).

61. See Johnson's discussion of the interior and exterior senses in Rypon's elaborate description of "the court of memory." "Imaginative Landscape," esp. 183 on.

62. The interior senses were often considered to be superior to the exterior senses. There is an extensive literature on senses in medieval culture; see, for example, Guvrilyuk and Coakley, *Spiritual Senses*.

63. Brewer, "Arithmetic," 162, 164.

CONCLUSION

An earlier version of this chapter appeared in Cooper-Rompato, "Numeracy and Number."

1. Bradwardine, *On Acquiring a Trained Memory* [*De memoria articificaile adquirenda*], in M. Carruthers, *Book of Memory*, 287. See also M. Carruthers, "Thomas Bradwardine."

2. See, for example, the complaints of Stephan von Landskron, including audience members sleeping during a sermon in Bast, *Honor Your Fathers*, 113. See also Bernhard of Clairvaux's observation on the boredom of the audience in Pranger, "Killing Time," 320.

3. I have chosen to describe Kempe as living a "semireligious life" in the world, although she is unaffiliated with any order, because recently a medievalist challenged me on the use of "lay" with Kempe, suggesting that Kempe is better described as "semireligious." In reflection on this correction, I agree that "lay" is not the best term to describe what Kempe saw as a religious and devotional calling. For a discussion of the influence of Walter Hilton's *Treatise on the Mixed Life* on Kempe, see Yoshikawa, *Margery Kempe's Meditations*, chapter 5.

4. Lentes, "Counting Piety," 55.

5. For an engaging discussion of pardons in the Middle English *Stacions of Rome*, see Benson, *Imagined Romes*, esp. 18–20.

6. Winston-Allen, *Stories of the Rose*, xii.

7. See, for example, Aers, *Community, Gender, and Individual Identity*; Delany, "Sexual Economics"; Fienberg, "Thematics of Value"; Ladd, "Margery Kempe"; Ashley, "Historicizing Margery."

8. Aers, *Community, Gender, and Individual Identity*, 80.

9. 8.636–40. All quotations from Kempe's *Book* are from Kempe, *Book of Margery Kempe*, and are cited by chapter and line number in the following paragraphs.

10. Gastle, "Breaking the Stained Glass Ceiling," 141. For a much more recent discussion of Margery Kempe and the language of credit, see the forthcoming dissertation from Nancy Haijing Jiang (Northwestern University) titled "The Trade of Penance: Confession and Commerce in Late Medieval Literature," which explores how the language of mercantile bargaining (as well as accounting, credit, and risk) are used to encourage lay penitential engagement.

11. Moreover, when Christ says that Kempe shall weep and mourn for his presence for fifteen years, she replies, "A, Lord, I schal thynkyn many thowsend yerys" (74.5910–12).

12. Revelation 9:16; 2 Chronicles 25:6; quotations are taken from the Douay-Rheims version of the Bible.

13. Barr, "he is bothyn modyr, brothyr, & syster"; Voaden, "Wolf in Sheep's Clothing"; Minnis, "Religious Roles"; Kerby-Fulton, "When Women Preached"; I. Davis, "Men and Margery: Negotiating Medieval Patriarchy," 47–50. See also Claire Waters, who explores how medieval women could "speak like a preacher" by creating an "alibi" or "elsewhere" space for themselves. Waters, *Angels and Earthly Creatures*, 122; Rebecca Krug references Waters when she writes that Kempe's "dislocation [to Rome] made it possible to teach" (*Margery Kempe and the Lonely Reader*, 187n36).

14. For the uses of precision, particularly in measurements, from the eighteenth century on, see Wise, *Values of Precision*.

15. Yoshikawa, *Margery Kempe's Meditations*.

16. See, for example, Watson, "Trinitarian Hermeneutic," and "Drei," in Meyer and Suntrup, *Lexikon der mittelalterlichen Zahlenbedeutungen*, 214–331.

17. The *Book* refers twice to the number of years the priest read to Kempe: "abowte vii yer" (60.4976–77) (about seven years) and "vii yer er viii yer" (58.4826) (seven or eight years).

18. Cooper-Rompato, "Decapitation, Martyrdom."

19. At another point, we are told that a particular series of events foretold by Christ was fulfilled twelve years later (18.1458).

20. For the "Significat," see "Court Christien," in Foster and Carey, *Chaucer's Church*, 31.

21. For duplation and mediation, see *Earliest Arithmetics in English*, esp. 14–20.

22. Kempe also states, "for sche was sumtyme so bareyn fro terrys a day, er sumtyme half a day" (82.6717).

23. On another occasion, Kempe reports that her "crying enduryd the terme of x yer.... And every Good Friday in alle the forseyd yerys sche was wepyng and sobbyng v er vi owrys togedyr" (57.4719–21).

24. For the inability of Kempe's quantitative reckoning to bridge the gap between human and heaven/the divine, see Watson, "Making of *The Book of Margery Kempe*," esp. 418–20.

25. Julian of Norwich, *"Shewings" of Julian of Norwich*, chap. 7, lines 248–50. For a discussion of "the productive power of one and zero" in Julian's text, see Robertson, "Julian of Norwich." Robertson argues that "Her far-ranging use of these numbers can help us appreciate how zero and one are far from the definitive numbers they are normally understood to be in the digital realm." https://www.archivejournal.net/essays/julian-of-norwich-and-the-digital.

APPENDIX

1. Menninger, *Number Words*, and Wedell, "Numbers." For those interested in measurement in the Middle Ages, see Heinz, "History of Medieval Metrology."

2. Williams and Williams, "Finger Numbers."

3. Menninger, *Number Words*, 207. For how Bede used numerical finger counting to express verbal messages, see Contreni, "Counting, Calendars, and Cosmology," 50–51. See also Bede, "Calculating or Speaking with the Fingers," in *Reckoning of Time*, 9–13 and 254–63.

4. This includes a way of dividing the hand and fingers into nineteen areas to aid monks in their calculation of Easter. For example, Bruce, *Silence and Sign Language*, and O'Daly, "Talk to the Hand."

5. Murray, *Reason and Society*, 176.

6. Ibid.

7. Saxe, "Mathematics of Child Street Vendors," 1416. See also Saxe, "Developing Forms of Arithmetical Thought," and Saxe, *Cultural Development of Mathematical Ideals*. Readers may also be interested in Nishiyama, "Counting with the Fingers," in which the author discusses modern cultural differences in finger counting and also muses on the (un)bendable pinky finger Romans and Bede used in counting. There are many recent studies exploring finger counting from psychological and cognitive science perspectives; see, for example, Morrissey et al., "Finger Counting Habits," and Barrocas et al., "Embodied Numerical Representations."

8. Leonardo Pisano, *Fibonacci's Liber Abaci*, 20.

9. For further discussion of medieval finger counting, see Menninger, *Number Words*, esp. 212–17.

10. *Oxford English Dictionary*, "Calculate, verb," def. 1a, http://www.oed.com.

11. *Oxford English Dictionary*, "Reckon, verb," def. 2a, http://www.oed.com.

12. *Ancrene Wisse*, ed. Millett. Robert Hasenfratz in his TEAMS edition of the *Ancrene Wisse* translates the sentence as follows: "The covetous [person] is his hearth-tender (lit., ash-stirrer ...), [who] lives (lit., fares) amidst ashes and busily bestirs himself to heap together many and huge piles; [he] blows into them (lit., therein) and blinds himself, pokes them and makes figures of calculations (i.e., scratchings which look like calculations ...) in them, as these account-keepers (lit., reckoners) do who have much to reckon (or, calculate)." *Ancrene Wisse*, ed. Hasenfratz, part 4, notes to 438–41.

13. For an image of a tally stick, see "Medieval Tally Sticks" at the Jewish Musuem, London, http://www.jewishmuseum.org.uk/50-ojbects/JM-653-JM-653-a.

14. See "Tally Sticks," in Menninger, *Number Words*, 223–48.

15. *Middle English Dictionary*, "Taille," def. 3.a ("Taille stich"). John Gower, *Confessio Amantis*, "Thoffice of the Chancellerie / Or of the kinges Tresorie / Ne for the writ ne for the taille / To warant mai noght thanne

availe" (5.1921–24), in Gower, *Confessio Amantis*, available online at http://name.umdl.umich.edu/confessio. See also *Piers Plowman*, B-Text, 4.57–58: "and bereth awey my whete / And taketh me but a taile for ten quarteres of otes." In Langland, *The Vision of William Concerning Piers the Plowman*, online at https://quod.lib.umich.edu/c/cme/AJT8124.0001.001/1:1.

16. Menninger, *Number Words*, 223–48.

17. See Preston, "Playing with Numbers."

18. For the history of Hindu-Arabic numerals in Europe, one could consult a detailed history of mathematics text such as Boyer and Merzbach, *History of Mathematics*, or a handbook entry such as Wedell, "Numbers." These texts also address the history of zero, and for those interested in reading further I recommend Robertson, "Julian of Norwich"; Seife, *Zero*; and Kaplan, *Nothing That Is*.

19. Pullan, *History of the Abacus*. For Gerbert of Aurillac, see Mahoney, "Mathematics," 149, and Bianchini and Senatore, "Gerbert of Aurillac." According to Menninger in *Number Words*, "The earliest evidence for the secular use of the abacus is indirect: it consists of French counters dating from the thirteenth century" (332).

20. See also Evans, "Schools and Scholars."

21. The oldest preserved medieval reckoning table is from the end of the fifteenth century; however, "Counting boards are very frequently mentioned in household inventories and wills." Menninger, *Number Words*, 333. The medieval Exchequer used a checkered counting cloth or table to calculate financial transactions. See Barnard, *Casting-Counter*. According to the OED, s.v. "exchequer" (def. 2), "The name originally referred to the table covered with a cloth divided into squares," which resembled a chess board. See also Jones, "Origins of Medieval Exchequer Accounting."

22. Evans, "From Abacus to Algorism." For a detailed discussion of these tools, see also Menninger, *Number Words*, 332–45, 362–74.

23. Berry, *Medieval English Jetons*.

24. Ritz, *Die christliche Gebetszählschnur*, n.p., quoted in Lentes, "Counting Piety," 63.

25. See, for example, Brookes et al., "Role of Gesture."

26. See Nunes, Schliemann, and Carraher, *Street Mathematics*. For the term "vernacular numeracy," see Broderick, *Vernacular Numeracy Practices*.

27. Nunes, Schliemann, and Carraher, *Street Mathematics*, 3; Gay and Cole, *New Mathematics*.

28. Nunes, Schliemann, and Carraher, *Street Mathematics*, 3–4; Reed and Lave, "Arithmetic as a Tool." For other studies, see Owens, "Diversifying Our Perspectives"; Francois and Pinxten, "Ethnomathematics"; Garii and Silverman, "Beyond the Classroom Walls"; Costa Goncalves, "From Work to Myths"; Were, "Objects of Learning."

29. Saxe, "Mathematics of Child Street Vendors," 1415.

30. Ibid., 1415–16.

31. Ibid., 1416.

32. Schliemann et al., "Use of Multiplicative Commutativity."

33. *Earliest Arithmetics in English*.

34. See Acker, "*Crafte of Nombrynge*," wherein Acker provides "A Checklist of Middle English Arithmetical Texts," including treatises and "brief notes on numeration" (75–78); Keiser, "Works of Science," 3637–40 and 3808–11.

35. Wynkyn de Worde, *Information for Pilgrims*, lists the date of the first edition as 1500; Hellinga argues for an earlier date of 1496 in "Tradition and Renewal," in Jensen, *Incunabula and Their Readers*, 13–30 and 207–9. See 14082 and 14083 for the 1515 and 1524 editions, titled *The Way to the Holy Lande*. For a discussion of de Worde's *Information* and Wey's *Itineraries*, as well as an exploration of the numbers included in the phrase books, see Cooper-Rompato, "Traveling Tongues."

36. Kermode, *Medieval Merchants*, 173–75.

37. Jefferson, *Medieval Account Books*, 1:508 and 2:904.

38. *Merchant Culture in Fourteenth Century Venice*, 25.

39. Black, "Education," 22–23.

40. Boys began at the age of eleven and attended for at least two years. Pin, "Contribution of Luca Pacioli," 168.

41. Ibid.

42. Leonardo Pisano, *Fibonacci's Liber Abaci*, 60–63.

43. References to the *Zibaldone da Canal* are drawn from *Merchant Culture in Fourteenth Century Venice*; page numbers appear parenthetically in the following paragraphs.

44. My thanks to John Morris for pointing this out to me. John E. Dotson, the translator of the modern edition of the *Zibaldone da Canal*, notes that Øystein Ore states "the calculation of time is correct, but the distances ought to be 114 2/7 and 85 5/7" (61n64). See Ore, "I problemi," lxxv.

45. "Again, say 2000 times 5849 makes 11698000 to divide by 9848, which comes to £1187 and 8460/9848 [8424/9848]. Again, we ought to say, 1278 times 2000 makes 2556000 to divide by 9848, which comes to £25 5064/9848 [5368/9848]." *Merchant Culture in Fourteenth Century Venice*, 55.

46. Orme, *Medieval Schools*, 242.

BIBLIOGRAPHY

MANUSCRIPTS

Cambridge
Corpus Christi College, MS 392
Pembroke College, MS 285
Sidney Sussex College, MS 74
St. John's College, MS G.22
Trinity College, MS B.14.52

Dublin
Trinity College, MS 241

Hatfield
Hatfield House, Cecil Papers 280

Lincoln
Lincoln Cathedral Library, MS 133

London
British Library
MS Additional 36791
MS Additional 40672
MS Cotton Claudius A.ii
MS Harley 2247
MS Harley 2276
MS Harley 4012
MS Harley 4894
MS Royal 18.B.xxiii
Westminster Abbey Library, MS 34/20

Oxford
Bodleian Library
MS Bodley 806
MS Douce 53
MS Holkham misc. 40

Salisbury
Salisbury Cathedral Library, MS 103

Warminster
Longleat House, MS 4

PRINTED PRIMARY SOURCES

The Algebra of Abū Kāmil: Kitāb fī al-Jabr wa'l-muqābala in a Commentary by Mordecai Finzi. Edited by Martin Levey. Madison: University of Wisconsin Press, 1966.

Ancrene Wisse. Edited by Robert Hasenfratz. Middle English Texts Series. Kalamazoo, MI: Medieval Institute Publications, 2000.

Ancrene Wisse. Edited by Bella Millett. Early English Text Society, o.s., 325–26. Oxford: Oxford University Press, 2005–6.

Atchley, Clinton P. E. "The 'Wose' of *Jacob's Well*: Text and Context." PhD diss., University of Washington, 1998.

Augustine. *The City of God Against the Pagans*. Edited and translated by Philip Levine. Cambridge: Harvard University Press, 1966.

———. *The Literal Meaning of Genesis*. Translated by John Hammond Taylor. Vol. 1. Mahwah, NJ: Paulist Press, 1982.

———. *Tractates on the Gospel of John 11–27*. Translated by John W. Rettig. The Fathers of the Church: A New Translation 79. Washington, DC: Catholic University of America Press, 1988.

Babcock, June. "Ars Sermocinandi ac Etiam Collationes Faciendi of Thomas of Todi, MS Paris, Bibl. Nat. 15965." Master's thesis, Cornell University, 1941.

Bede. *On Genesis*. Translated by Calvin Kendall. Translated Texts for Historians 48. Liverpool: Liverpool University Press, 2008.

———. *On the Tabernacle*. Translated by Arthur G. Holder. Translated Texts for Historians 18. Liverpool: Liverpool University Press, 1994.

———. *On the Temple*. Translated by Seán Connolly. Translated Texts for Historians 21. Liverpool: Liverpool University Press, 1996.

———. *The Reckoning of Time*. Translated by Faith Wallis. Translated Texts for Historians 29. Liverpool: Liverpool University Press, 1999.

Bibliorum Sacrorum cum Glossa Ordinaria. 6 vols. Venice, 1603.

Boethius. *Boethian Number Theory: A Translation of the "De Institutione Arithmetica" (with Introduction and Notes)*. Translated and edited by Michael Masi. Studies in Classical Antiquity 6. Amsterdam: Rodopi, 2006.

———. *De institutione arithmetica*. Edited by Godofredus Friedlein. Bibliotheca scriptorium Graecorum et Romanorum Teubneriana. Leipzig: Teubner, 1867. Reprint, Frankfurt am Main: Minerva, 1966.

Bonaventure. "Conscience and Synderesis." In *The Cambridge Translations of Medieval Philosophical Texts*, vol. 2, *Ethics and Political Philosophy*, edited by Arthur Stephen McGrade, John Kilcullen, and Matthew Kempshall, 169–99. Cambridge: Cambridge University Press, 2000.

Bracciolini, Poggio. *The Facetiae, or Jocose Tales of Poggio*. 2 vols. Paris: Liseux, 1879.

Bradwardine, Thomas. "De memoria artificiale." In M. Carruthers, *Book of Memory*, appendix C, 281–88.

Cassiodorus, *Institutiones divinarum et saecularium litterarum* [*De artibus ac disciplinis liberalium litterarum*]. In Migne, Patrologia Latina 70:1149–1220. Paris, 1879.

Catherine of Siena. *The Orcherd of Syon*. Edited by Phyllis Hodgson and Gabriel M. Liegey. Early English Text Society, o.s., 258. London: Oxford University Press, 1966.

Chaucer, Geoffrey. *The Riverside Chaucer*. Edited by Larry D. Benson. 3rd ed. Boston: Houghton Mifflin, 1987.

Clubb, Merrel D., Jr. "The Middle English *Pilgrimage of the Soul*: An Edition of MS. Egerton 615." PhD diss., University of Michigan, 1953.

The Crowther Report: 15–18. A Report of the Central Advisory Council for Education (England). London: Her Majesty's Stationery Office, 1959. Online at "Education in England: The History of Our Schools," http://www.educationengland.org.uk/documents/crowther/crowther1959-1.html.

Dederich, Robert M. "Trevisa's Translation of the Mathematical Section of Bartholomew's *De proprietatibus rerum*, Edited, with a glossary and notes, from the British Museum MS. Additional 27944." Master's thesis, University of Arizona, 1941. http://arizona.openrepository.com/arizona/bitstream/10150/553553/1/AZU_TD_BOX343_E9791_1941_19.pdf.

Dives and Pauper. Edited by Priscilla Heath Barnum. 2 vols. Early English Text Society, o.s., 275 and 280. London: Oxford University Press, 1976–80.

The Earliest Arithmetics in English. Edited by Robert Steele. Early English Text Society, e.s., 118. London: Oxford University Press, 1922. Reprinted 2001.

The Early South-English Legendary; Or, Lives of Saints. I. Ms. Laud, 108, in the Bodleian Library. Edited by Carl Horstmann. Early English Text Society, o.s., 87. London: Trübner, 1887.

English Wycliffite Sermons. Edited by Pamela Gradon and Anne Hudson. 5 vols. Oxford Texts Series. Oxford: Clarendon, 1983–96.

Euclid's Elements of Geometry. Edited and translated by Robert Fitzpatrick, from the Greek text of J. L. Heiberg. N.p., 2007.

Felton, John. "Easter or Corpus Christi Sermon." In Wenzel, *Preaching in the Age of Chaucer*, 133–43.

Fletcher, Alan John. *Late Medieval Popular Preaching in Britain and Ireland: Texts, Studies, and Interpretations*. Sermo 5. Turnhout: Brepols, 2009.

Gower, John. *Confessio Amantis*. In *The Complete Works of John Gower*, edited by G. C. Macaulay, vols. 2 and 3. Oxford: Clarendon, 1901–2.

Grosseteste, Robert. *On the Six Days of Creation: A Translation of the Hexaëmeron*. Translated by C. F. J. Martin. Auctores Britannici Medii Aevi 7. Oxford: Oxford University Press, 1999.

Hazel, Harry C., Jr. "A Translation, with Commentary, of the Bonaventuran *Ars concionandi*." PhD diss., Washington State University, 1972.

Higden, Ranulfus. *Ars Componendi Sermones*. Edited and translated by Margaret Jennings and Sally A. Wilson. Dallas Medieval Texts and Translations 2. Louvain: Peeters, 2003.

Hrotsvit of Gandersheim. *Hrotsvit of Gandersheim: A Florilegium of Her Works*. Edited by Katharina M. Wilson. 2 vols. Cambridge: D. S. Brewer, 1998–2000.

Hugh of St. Victor. *De scripturis et scriptoribus sacris*. In Migne, Patrologia Latina 175:9–28. Paris, 1879.

Isidore of Seville. *The Etymologies*. Translated by Stephen A. Barney, W. J. Lewis, J. A. Beach, and Oliver Berghof. Cambridge: Cambridge University Press, 2006.

———. *On the Nature of Things*. Edited and translated by Calvin B. Kendall and Faith Wallis. Translated Texts for Historians 66. Liverpool: Liverpool University Press, 2016.

Jacob's Well, an English Treatise on the Cleansing of Man's Conscience. Edited by Arthur Brandeis. Early English Text Society, o.s., 115. London: Paul, Trench and Trübner, 1900. Reprinted 1977.

Julian of Norwich. *The "Shewings" of Julian of Norwich*. Edited by Georgia Ronan Crampton. Middle English Texts. Kalamazoo, MI: Medieval Institute Publications, 2004.

Katz, Victor J., Menso Folkerts, Barnabas Hughes, Roi Wagner, and J. Lennart Berggren. *Sourcebook in the Mathematics of Medieval Europe and North Africa*. Princeton: Princeton University Press, 2016.

Kempe, Margery. *The Book of Margery Kempe*. Translated by Barry Windeatt. London: Penguin, 1985.

———. *The Book of Margery Kempe*. Edited by Barry Windeatt. Cambridge: D. S. Brewer, 2004.

Langland, William. *Parallel Extracts from Twenty-Nine Manuscripts of Piers Plowman*. Edited by Walter W. Skeat. Early English Text Society. London: Trübner, 1866.

———. *The Vision of William Concerning Piers the Plowman, Together with Vita de Dowel, Dobet, et Dobest*. Edited by Walter W. Skeat. 4 parts in 3 vols. Early English Text Society. Trübner, 1867–85. Reprint, London: Oxford University Press, 1968.

Lenten Sermons: Middle English Filius Matris Sermon Cycle as Contained in MS Harley 2276 in the British Library. Edited by C. Carpenter. Oxford: Oxford Texts Archive, 1983.

Leonardo Pisano. *Fibonacci's Liber Abaci: A Translation into Modern English of Leonardo Pisano's Book of Calculation*. Translated by Lawrence Sigler. Sources and Studies in the History of Mathematics and Physical Sciences. New York: Springer, 2002.

Lydgate, John. *The Minor Poems of John Lydgate*. Edited by Henry Noble MacCracken. 2 vols. Early English Text Society, o.s., 107 and 192. London: Oxford University Press, 1961–62.

Martí de Barcelona, P. "*L'Ars Praedicatandi de Fransesc Eiximenes.*" In *Homentage a Antoni Rubió i Lluch: Miscellània d'estudis literaris històrics i lingüístics*, edited by Jean Sarrailh and Vittore Rubiu, 2:301–40. Barcelona: Institut d'estudis Catalans, 1936.

"Mathematics Counts." In *The Cockcroft Report: Report of the Committee of Inquiry into the Teaching of Mathematics in Schools under the Chairmanship of Dr WH Cockcroft*. London: Her Majesty's Stationery Office, 1982. Online at "Education in England: The History of Our Schools," http://www.educationengland.org.uk/documents/cockcroft/cockcroft1982.html.

The Medieval Account Books of the Mercers of London. Edited and translated by Lisa Jefferson. 2 vols. London: Routledge, 2009.

Merchant Culture in Fourteenth Century Venice: The Zibaldone da Canal. Translated by John E. Dotson. Medieval and Renaissance Texts and Studies 98. Binghamton: Medieval and Renaissance Texts and Studies, 1994.

Michel, Dan. *Dan Michel's Ayenbite of Inwyt, or, Remorse of Conscience*. Edited by Richard Morris. Early English Text Society, o.s., 23. London: Trübner, 1866. Rev. ed., revised by Pamela Gradon. Oxford: Oxford University Press, 1965.

The Middle English "Mirror": An Edition Based on Bodleian Library MS Holkham misc. 40. Edited by Kathleen M. Blumreich. Medieval and Renaissance Texts and Studies 182. Tempe: Arizona Center for Medieval and Renaissance Studies, 2002.

The Middle English Mirror: Sermons from Advent to Sexegesima. Edited by Thomas G. Duncan and Margaret Connolly. Middle English Texts 24. Heidelberg: Universitätsverlag, Winter, 2003.

Middle English Sermons, Edited from British Museum MS. Royal 18 B. xxiii. Edited by Woodburn O. Ross. Early English Text Society, o.s., 209. Reprint, London: Oxford University Press, 1998.

Mirk, John. *John Mirk's Festial: Edited from British Library MS Cotton Claudius A.II*. Edited by Susan Powell. Early English Text Society, o.s., 334–35. Oxford: Oxford University Press, 2009–11.

———. *Mirk's Festial: A Collection of Homilies by Johannes Mirkus*. Edited by Theodore Erbe. Early English Text Society, e.s., 96. London: Kegan Paul, Trench and Trübner, 1905.

Nicholas of Cusa. *On Learned Ignorance*. Translated by Jasper Hopkins. Minneapolis: Arthur J. Banning Press, 1990.

O'Mara, Veronica, and Suzanne Paul. *A Repertorium of Middle English Prose Sermons*. 4 vols. Turnhout: Brepols, 2007.

On the Properties of Things: John Trevisa's Translation of Bartholomaeus Anglicus De Proprietatibus Rerum; A Critical Text. Edited by M. C. Seymour. 3 vols. Oxford: Clarendon, 1975–88.

Prik of Conscience. Edited by James H. Morey. Middle English Texts Series. Kalamazoo, MI: Medieval Institute Publications, 2012.

Rubio Álvarez, Fernando, ed. "*Ars Praedicandi* de Fray Martín de Córdoba." *La Ciudad de Dios* 172 (1959): 327–48.

Rypon, Robert. *Selected Sermons: Feast Days and Saints' Days*. Edited and translated by Holly Johnson. Dallas Medieval Texts and Translations 24, no. 1. Louvain: Peeters, 2019.

———. *Selected Sermons: Lenten Sermons*. Edited and translated by Holly Johnson. Dallas Medieval Texts and Translations 24, no. 2. Louvain: Peeters, in preparation.

South English Legendary. Edited by Charlotte D'Evelyn and Anna Mill.

Early English Text Society, 3 vols. London: Oxford University Press, 1956.
Speculum Sacerdotale: Edited from British Museum MS. Additional 36791. Edited by Edward H. Weatherly. London: Humphrey Milford, for the Early English Text Society, 1936.
Three Late Medieval Morality Plays: Mankind, Everyman, Mundus et Infans. Edited by G. A. Lester. London: Methuen Drama, 2014.
Three Prose Versions of the Secreta Secretorum. Edited by Robert Steele. London: Kegan Paul, Trench and Trübner, 1898; Woodbridge, Suffolk: Boydell & Brewer, for the Early English Text Society, 1996.
The Towneley Plays: Re-edited from the Unique Ms. Edited by George England and A. W. Pollard. Early English Text Society, e.s., 71. London: K. Paul, Trench and Trübner, 1907.
Two Wycliffite Texts: The Sermon of William Taylor 1406, The Testimony of William Thorpe 1407. Edited by Anne Hudson. Early English Text Society, o.s., 301. Oxford: Oxford University Press, 1993.
Victor, S. K., ed. and trans. *Practical Geometry in the High Middle Ages: "Artis cuius libet comsummatio" and the "Pratike de geometrie."* Memoirs of the American Philosophical Society 134. Philadelphia: American Philosophical Society, 1979.
Wynkyn de Worde. *Information for Pilgrims unto the Holy Land.* Edited by Edward Gordon Duff. London: University of Oxford, 1893.
The York Corpus Christi Plays. Edited by Clifford Davidson. Middle English Texts Series. Kalamazoo, MI: Medieval Institute Publications, 2011.

SECONDARY SOURCES

Acker, Paul. "*The Crafte of Nombrynge* in Columbia University Library, Plimpton MS 259." *Manuscripta* 37 (1993): 71–83.

———. "The Emergence of an Arithmetical Mentality in Middle English Literature." *Chaucer Review* 28, no. 3 (1994): 293–302.

Adams, Jonathan, and Jussi Hanska, eds. *The Jewish-Christian Encounter in Medieval Preaching.* New York: Routledge, 2014.

Aers, David. *Community, Gender, and Individual Identity: English Writing, 1360–1430.* London: Routledge, 1988.

Agmon, Eytan. "Proto-Tonal Theory: Tapping into 9th-Century Insights." *Music Theory Spectrum* 35, no. 1 (2013): 103–10.

Andersson, Roger, ed. *Constructing the Medieval Sermon.* Sermo 6. Turnhout: Brepols, 2008.

Angenendt, Arnold, Thomas Braucks, Rolf Busch, and Hubertus Lutterbach. "Counting Piety in the Early and High Middle Ages." In Jussen, *Ordering Medieval Society*, 15–54.

Ashley, Kathleen. "Historicizing Margery: *The Book of Margery Kempe* as Social Text." *Journal of Medieval and Early Modern Studies* 28 (1998): 371–88.

Atchley, Clinton P. E. "The Audience of *Jacob's Well*: Problems of Interpretation." Arkadelphia, AR: Henderson State University, 2001, updated 2002. https://www.hsu.edu/uploads/pages/2001-2afthe_audience_of_jacob.pdf.

Barnard, Francis Pierrepont. *The Casting-Counter and the Counting Board: A Chapter in the History of Numismatics and Early Arithmetic.* Oxford: Clarendon, 1917. Reprint, Castle Cary: Fox, 1981.

Barr, Beth Allison. "he is bothyn modyr, brothyr, & syster vn-to-me": Women and the Bible in Late Medieval and Early Modern Sermons." *Church History and Religious Culture* 94, no. 3 (2014): 297–315.

Barrocas, R., S. Roesch, V. Dresen, K. Moeller, and S. Pixner. "Embodied

Numerical Representations and Their Association with Multi-Digit Arithmetic Performance." *Cognitive Processing* 21, no. 1 (2020): 95–103.

Bast, Robert James. *Honor Your Fathers: Catechisms and the Emergence of a Patriarchal Ideology in Germany, 1400–1600*. Studies in Medieval and Reformation Thought 63. Leiden: Brill, 1997.

Beattie, Cordelia. *Medieval Single Women: The Politics of Social Classification in Late Medieval England*. Oxford: Oxford University Press, 2007.

Bell, Pam. *Love and Sex by the Numbers: A Numerology Guide to Romance*. New York: Quill, 2000.

Benson, C. David. *Imagined Romes: The Ancient City and Its Stories in Middle English Poetry*. University Park: Penn State University Press, 2019.

Berry, George. *Medieval English Jetons*. London: Spink, 1974.

Bevington, David, ed. *Medieval Drama*. Indianapolis: Hackett, 2012.

Bianchini, C., and L. J. Senatore. "Gerbert of Aurillac (c. 940–1003)." In *Distinguished Figures in Descriptive Geometry and Its Applications for Mechanism Science: From the Middle Ages to the 17th Century*, edited by Michela Cigola, 33–51. History of Mechanism and Machine Science 30. Cham: Springer, 2016.

Black, Robert. "Education and the Emergence of a Literate Society." In *Italy in the Age of the Renaissance: 1300–1550*, edited by John M. Najemy, 18–36. New York: Oxford University Press, 2004.

Boffey, Julia. "Some Middle English Sermon Verse and Its Transmission in Manuscript and Print." In Driver and O'Mara, *Preaching the Word*, 259–75.

Bos, A. P. *The Soul and Its Instrumental Body: A Reinterpretation of Aristotle's Philosophy of Living Nature*. Brill's Studies in Intellectual History 112. Leiden: Brill, 2003.

Boyer, Carl B., and Uta C. Merzbach. *A History of Mathematics*. 3rd ed. Hoboken, NJ: Wiley, 2011.

Brantley, Jessica. *Reading in the Wilderness: Private Devotion and Public Performance in Late Medieval England*. Chicago: University of Chicago Press, 2007.

Breeze, Andrew. "The Number of Christ's Wounds." *Bulletin of the Board of Celtic Studies* 32 (1985): 84–91.

Brehaut, Ernest. *An Encyclopedist of the Dark Ages: Isidore of Seville*. New York: Longmans, 1912.

Brewer, Derek. "Arithmetic and the Mentality of Chaucer." In *Literature in Fourteenth-Century England*, edited by Piero Boitani and Anna Torti, 155–64. Tübingen: G. Narr Verlag, 1983.

Broderick, Nuala. "Vernacular Numeracy Practices: An Exploration of the Numeracy Resources Young People Bring to Their Learning." PhD diss., University of Manchester, 2018.

Brookes, Neon B., Susan Goldin-Meadow, David Barner, and Michael Frank. "The Role of Gesture in Supporting Mental Representations: The Case of Mental Abacus Arithmetic." *Cognitive Science* 42, no. 2 (2018): 554–75.

Brown, Phyllis R. "Hrotsvit's Sapientia as a Foreign Woman." In *Hrotsvit of Gandersheim: Contexts, Identities, Affinities, and Performances*, edited by Phyllis R. Brown, Linda A. McMillin, and Katharina M. Wilson, 160–76. Toronto: University of Toronto Press, 2004.

Bruce, Scott G. *Silence and Sign Language in Medieval Monasticism: The Cluniac Tradition c. 900–1200*. Cambridge: Cambridge University Press, 2009.

Bullinger, Ethelbert W. *Number in Scripture: Its Supernatural Design and Spiritual Significance*. London: Eyre and Spottiswoode, 1894.

Bury, Michael. "The Measure of the Virgin's Foot." In *Images of Medieval Sanctity:*

Essays in Honor of Gary Dickson, edited by Debra Higgs Strickland, 121–34. Leiden: Brill, 2007.

Bynum, Caroline Walker. *Wonderful Blood: Theology and Practice in Late Medieval Northern Germany and Beyond*. Philadelphia: University of Pennsylvania Press, 2007.

Carraher, Terezinha Nunes, David William Carraher, and Analúcia Dias Schliemann. "Mathematics in the Streets and in Schools." *British Journal of Developmental Psychology* 3, no. 1 (1985): 21–29.

Carruthers, Leo. "Allegory and Bible Interpretation: The Narrative Structure of a Middle English Sermon Cycle." *Literature and Theology* 4, no. 1 (1990): 1–14.

———. "The *Great Curse*: Excommunication, Canon Law and the Judicial System in Late Medieval Society, Through the Eyes of an English Preacher." *Caliban: French Journal of English Studies* 29 (2011): 45–60.

———. "'Know Thyself': Criticism, Reform and the Audience of *Jacob's Well*." In *Medieval Sermons and Society: Cloister, City, University*, edited by Jacqueline Hamesse, Beverly Mayne Kienzle, Debra L. Stoudt, and Anne T. Thayer, 219–40. Textes et études du Moyen Âge 9. Turnhout: Brepols, 1998.

———. "The Liturgical Setting of *Jacob's Well*." *English Language Notes* 24, no. 4 (1987): 11–24.

———. "Richard Lavynham and the Seven Deadly Sins in *Jacob's Well*." *Fifteenth-Century Studies* 18 (1991): 17–32.

———. "Where Did *Jacob's Well* Come From? The Provenance and Dialect of MS Salisbury Cathedral 103." *English Studies* 71, no. 4 (1990): 335–40.

Carruthers, Mary. *The Book of Memory: A Study of Memory in Medieval Culture*. Cambridge Studies in Medieval Literature 10. 2nd ed. Cambridge: Cambridge University Press, 2008.

———. "Thomas Bradwardine, 'De memoria artificiale adquirenda.'" *Journal of Medieval Latin* 2 (1992): 25–43.

Catto, Jeremy. "1349–1412: Culture and History." In Fanous and Gillespie, *Cambridge Companion to Medieval English Mysticism*, 113–32.

Celeyrette, Jean. "Mathematics and Theology: The Infinite in Nicholas of Cusa." *Revue de métaphysique et de morale* 70, no. 2 (2011/12): 151–65.

Charland, T. M., ed. *Artes Praedicand: Contribution à l'histoire de la rhétorique au moyen âge*. Ottawa: Institut d'Études Médiévales, 1936.

Christie, Anne. *Numerology, Plain and Simple: The Only Book You'll Ever Need*. Charlottesville, VA: Hampton Roads, 2015.

Clagett, Marshall. "The Impact of Archimedes on Medieval Science." *ISIS* 50, no. 4 (1959): 419–29.

Classen, Albrecht, ed. *Handbook of Medieval Culture: Fundamental Aspects and Conditions of the European Middle Ages*. 3 vols. Berlin: de Gruyter, 2015.

Connolly, Margaret. "Practical Reading for Body and Soul in Some Later Medieval Manuscript Miscellanies." *Journal of the Early Book Society* 10 (2007): 151–74.

———. "Preaching by Numbers: The 'Seven Gifts of the Holy Ghost' in Late Middle English Sermons and Works of Religious Instruction." In Driver and O'Mara, *Preaching the Word*, 83–100.

Contreni, John J. "Counting, Calendars, and Cosmology: Numeracy in the Early Middle Ages." In *Learning and Culture in Carolingian Europe: Letters, Numbers, Exegesis, and Manuscripts*, John J. Contreni, 43–83. Variorum Collected Studies Series 974. Farnham: Ashgate, 2011.

Cooper, Katherine. "'My Cruel Conscience with Sharpned Knife': Conscience as Vessel and Vivisector in *Jacob's Well* and a *Meditation of a Penitent Sinner*."

Exemplaria 24, nos. 1–2 (2012): 12–27.

Cooper-Rompato, Christine. "Decapitation, Martyrdom, and Late Medieval Execution Practices in *The Book of Margery Kempe*." In *Heads Will Roll: Decapitation in the Medieval and Early Modern Imagination*, edited by Larissa Tracy and Jeffrey Massey, 73–89. Leiden: Brill, 2012.

———. "Numeracy and Number in *The Book of Margery Kempe*." In *The Medieval Mystical Tradition in England: Papers Read at Charney Manor, July 2011, Exeter Symposium 8*, edited by E. A. Jones, 59–74. Woodbridge, UK: Boydell & Brewer, 2013.

———. "Traveling Tongues: Foreign-Language Phrase Lists in Wynkyn de Worde and William Wey." *Chaucer Review* 46, nos. 1–2 (2011): 223–36.

Costa, Nara Wanderleya Gonçalves. "From Work to Myths: A New Line on the Map of Ethnomathematics Research." *BOLEMA* 22, no. 32 (2009): 211–27.

Counet, J.-M. "Mathematics and the Divine in Nicholas of Cusa." In Koetsier and Bergmans, *Mathematics and the Divine*, 273–90.

Crump, Thomas. *The Anthropology of Numbers*. Cambridge: Cambridge University Press, 1990.

Darby, Peter. *Bede and the End of Time*. Studies in Early Medieval Britain and Ireland. Farnham: Taylor and Francis, 2016.

Davidson, Clifford. "Cain in the Mysteries: The Iconography of Violence." *Fifteenth Century Studies* 25 (2000): 204–27.

Davis, Isabel. "Men and Margery: Negotiating Medieval Patriarchy." In *A Companion to The Book of Margery Kempe*, edited by John H. Arnold and Katherine J. Lewis, 35–54. Cambridge: D. S. Brewer, 2004.

Davis, James. *Medieval Market Morality: Life, Law and Ethics in the English Marketplace, 1200–1500*. Cambridge: Cambridge University Press, 2011.

Davis, John. *Biblical Numerology: A Basic Study of the Use of Numbers in the Bible*. Grand Rapids, MI: Baker, 1968.

Delany, Sheila. "Sexual Economics, Chaucer's Wife of Bath, and *The Book of Margery Kempe*." *Minnesota Review* 5 (1975): 104–15.

Dickson, Leonard Eugene. *History of the Theory of Numbers*. Vol. 1, *Divisibility and Primality*. Dover Books of Mathematics. Mineola: Dover, 2005.

Dodds, Ben. "Managing Tithes in the Late Middle Ages." *Agricultural History Review* 53, no. 2 (2005): 135–40.

Driver, Martha W., and Veronica O'Mara, eds. *Preaching the Word in Manuscript and Print in Late Medieval England: Essays in Honour of Susan Powell*. Sermo 11. Turnhout: Brepols, 2013.

Eckhardt, Caroline D. *Essays in the Numerical Criticism of Medieval Literature*. Lewisburg: Bucknell University Press, 1980.

Edminster, Warren. *The Preaching Fox: Elements of Festive Subversion in the Plays of the Wakefield Master*. Studies in Medieval History and Culture. New York: Routledge, 2005.

Evans, Gillian R. "From Abacus to Algorism: Theory and Practice in Medieval Arithmetic." *British Journal for the History of Science* 10 (1977): 114–31.

———. "Introductions to Boethius's 'Arithmetica' of the Tenth to the Fourteenth Century." *History of Science* 16, no. 1 (1978): 22–41.

———. "Schools and Scholars: The Study of the Abacus in English Schools c. 980–c.1150." *English Historical Review* 94 (1979): 71–89.

Fanous, Samuel, and Vincent Gillespie, eds. *The Cambridge Companion to Medieval English Mysticism*. Cambridge Companions to Literature. Cambridge: Cambridge University Press, 2011.

Fideler, David. *Jesus Christ, Sun of God: Ancient Cosmology and Early Christian Symbolism*. Wheaton, IL: Quest, 1993.

Fienberg, Nona. "Thematics of Value in *The Book of Margery Kempe*." *Modern Philology* 87 (1989): 132–41.

Fitzgibbons, Moira. "*Jacob's Well* and Penitential Pedagogy." *Studies in the Age of Chaucer* 27 (2005): 213–37.

———. "Poverty, Dignity, and Lay Spirituality in *Pore Caitif* and *Jacob's Well*." *Medium Ævum* 77, no. 2 (2008): 222–40.

Flannery, Mary C., and Katie L. Walker. "'Vttirli Onknowe'? Modes of Inquiry and the Dynamics of Interiority in Vernacular Literature." In *The Culture of Inquisition in Medieval England*, edited by Mary C. Flannery and Katie L. Walker, 77–93. Cambridge: D. S. Brewer, 2013.

Fletcher, Alan John. *Late Medieval Popular Preaching in Britain and Ireland: Texts, Studies, and Interpretations*. Sermo 5. Turnhout: Brepols, 2009.

———. "'Magnus predicator et deuotus': A Profile of the Life, Work, and Influence of the Fifteenth-Century Oxford Preacher, John Felton." *Medieval Studies* 53 (1991): 125–75.

Folkerts, Menso. *The Development of Mathematics in Medieval Europe: The Arabs, Euclid, Regiomontanus*. Collected Studies CS811. Burlington, VT: Ashgate Variorum, 2006.

———. "Euclid in Medieval Europe." Questio de rerum natura 2. Winnipeg: Overdale Books, 1989. https://www.math.ubc.ca/~cass/euclid/folkerts/folkerts.html.

Foster, Edward, and David H. Carey. *Chaucer's Church: A Dictionary of Religious Terms in Chaucer*. New York: Taylor and Francis, 2020.

Francois, Karen, and Rik Pinxten. "Ethnomathematics: Development of a Concept and Its Shifted Meaning." *Volkskunde* 112, no. 1 (2011): 33–54.

French, Katherine L. *The People of the Parish: Community Life in a Late Medieval English Diocese*. Philadelphia: University of Pennsylvania Press, 2001.

Fulton, Rachel. "Praying by Numbers." *Studies in Medieval and Renaissance History*, 3rd ser., no. 4 (2007): 195–250.

Garii, Barbara, and Frederick Silverman. "Beyond the Classroom Walls: Helping Teachers Recognize Mathematics Outside of the School." *Relime* 12, no. 3 (2009): 333–54.

Gastle, Brian W. "Breaking the Stained Glass Ceiling: Mercantile Authority, Margaret Paston, and Margery Kempe." *Studies in the Literary Imagination* 36 (2003): 123–47.

Gay, John, and Michael Cole. *The New Mathematics and an Old Culture: A Study of Learning Among the Kpelle of Liberia*. Case Studies in Education and Culture. New York: Holt, Rinehart and Winston, 1967. Reprint, Washington, DC: Peace Corps Information Collection and Exchange, 1986.

Gillespie, Vincent. "1412–1534: Culture and History." In Fanous and Gillespie, *Cambridge Companion to Medieval English Mysticism*, 163–94.

Gittings, Claire. "Urban Funerals in Late Medieval and Reformation England." In *Death in Towns: Urban Responses to the Dying and the Dead, 100–1600*, edited by Steven Bassett, 170–83. Leicester: Leicester University Press, 1992.

Glick, Thomas F., Steven J. Livesey, and Faith Wallis, eds. *Medieval Science, Technology, and Medicine: An Encyclopedia*. London: Routledge, 2017.

Greer, John Michael. *Secrets of the Lost Symbol: The Unauthorized Guide to Secret Societies, Hidden Symbols, and Mysticism*. Woodbury, MN: Llewellyn, 2009.

Gregg, John Young. "The Exempla of 'Jacob's Well': A Study in the Transmission of Medieval Sermon Stories." *Traditio: Studies in Ancient and Medieval History, Thought, and Religion* 33 (1977): 359–80.

Grellard, Christophe, and Aurélien Robert. *Atomism in Late Medieval Philosophy and Theology.* Leiden: Brill, 2009.

Guillaumin, Jean-Yves. "Boethius's *De institutione arithemetica* and Its Influence on Posterity." In Kaylor and Phillips, *Companion to Boethius in the Middle Ages,* 135–61.

Gullberg, Jan. *Mathematics: From the Birth of Numbers.* New York: W. W. Norton, 1997.

Guvrilyuk, Paul L., and Sarah Coakley, eds. *The Spiritual Senses: Perceiving God in Western Christianity.* Cambridge: Cambridge University Press, 2011.

Harper, Elizabeth. "'A Tokene and a Book': Reading Images and Building Consensus in *Dives and Pauper.*" *Yearbook of Langland Studies* 28 (2014): 173–90.

Harvey, Margaret. *Lay Religious Life in Late Medieval Durham.* Woodbridge, UK: Boydell and Brewer, 2006.

Heinz, Werner. "History of Medieval Metrology." In Classen, *Handbook of Medieval Culture,* 2:1057–92.

Hellinga, Lotte. "Tradition and Renewal: Establishing the Chronology of Wynkyn de Worde's Early Work." In *Incunabula and Their Readers: Printing, Selling and Using Books in the Fifteenth Century,* edited by Kristian Jensen, 13–30 and 207–9. London: British Library, 2003.

Heng, Geraldine. "Feminine Knots and the Other *Sir Gawain and the Green Knight.*" *PMLA* 106, no. 3 (1991): 501–14.

Hicks, Michael. "The Rising Price of Piety in the Later Middle Ages." In *Monasteries and Society in the British Isles in the Later Middle Ages,* edited by Janet Burton and Karen Stöber, 93–109. Rochester, NY: Boydell, 2008.

Hill, Gabriel F. "Regendering the *Festial* in British Library MSS Harley 2247 and Royal 18.B.XXV." *Comitatus* 46 (2015): 117–40.

Hopper, Vincent Foster, *Medieval Number Symbolism: Its Sources, Meaning, and Influence on Thought and Expression.* Mineola, NY: Dover, 2000.

Horner, Patrick J. "Benedictines and Preaching the *Pastoralia* in Late Medieval England: A Preliminary Inquiry." In Muessig, *Medieval Monastic Preaching,* 279–92.

Høyrup, Jens. *In Measure, Number, and Weight: Studies in Mathematics and Culture.* Albany: State University of New York Press, 1994.

Hudson, Anne, and Helen Spencer. "Old Author, New Work: The Sermons of MS Longleat 4." *Medium Ævum* 53 (1984): 220–38.

Jensen, Robin M. *Living Water: Images, Symbols and Settings of Early Christian Baptism.* Supplements to Vigiliae Christianae: Texts and Studies of Early Christian Life and Language 105. Leiden: Brill, 2011.

Jiang, Nancy Haijing. "The Trade of Penance: Confession and Commerce in Late Medieval Literature." PhD diss., Northwestern University, forthcoming.

Johnson, Holly. "The Imaginative Landscape of an English Monk-Preacher: Robert Rypon and the Court of Memory." *Mediaeval Studies* 75 (2013): 177–204.

———. "Introduction." In Robert Rypon, *Selected Sermons,* edited and translated by Holly Johnson, vol. 1, 1–37. Dallas Medieval Texts and Translations 24, no. 1. Louvain: Peeters, 2019.

———. "Robert Rypon and the Creation of London, British Library, MS Harley 4894: A Master Preacher and His Sermon Collection." *Medieval Sermon Studies* 59 (2015): 38–56.

Jones, Michael John. "Origins of Medieval Exchequer Accounting." *Accounting History Review* 19, no. 3 (2019): 259–85.

Jordan, Juno. *Numerology: The Romance in Your Name*. Camarillo, CA: DeVorss, 2008.

Jussen, Bernhard, ed. *Ordering Medieval Society: Perspectives on Intellectual and Practical Modes of Shaping Social Relations*. Translated by Pamela Selwyn. Middle Ages Series. Philadelphia: University of Pennsylvania Press, 2001.

Kaplan, Robert. *The Nothing That Is: A Natural History of Zero*. New York: Oxford University Press, 2006.

Kaylor, Noel Harold, Jr., and Philip Edward Phillips, eds. *A Companion to Boethius in the Middle Ages*. Brill's Companions to the Christian Tradition 30. Leiden: Brill, 2012.

Keiser, George R. *Works of Science and Information*. Vol. 10 of *A Manual of the Writings in Middle English, 1050–1500*. New Haven: Connecticut Academy of Arts and Sciences, 1998.

Kerby-Fulton, Kathryn. "When Women Preached: An Introduction to Female Homiletic, Sacramental, and Liturgical Roles in the Later Middle Ages." In *Voices in Dialogue: Reading Women in the Middle Ages*, edited by Linda Olson and Kathryn Kerby-Fulton, 31–55. Notre Dame: University of Notre Dame Press, 2005.

Kermode, Jennifer. *Medieval Merchants: York, Beverley and Hull in the Later Middle Ages*. Cambridge Studies in Medieval Life and Thought, series 4. Cambridge: Cambridge University Press, 2009.

King, Pamela. "Playing *Pentecost* in York and Chester: Transformations and Texts." *Medieval English Theatre* 29 (2007): 60–74.

Kneidel, Greg. "*Ars Prædicandi*: Theories and Practice." In *The Oxford Handbook of the Early Modern Sermon*, edited by Peter McCullough, Hugh Adlington, and Emma Rhatigan, 3–20. Oxford: Oxford University Press, 2011.

Koetsier, Teun, and Luc Bergmans, eds. "Introduction." In Koetsier and Bergmans, *Mathematics and the Divine*, 3–43.

———, eds. *Mathematics and the Divine: A Historical Study*. Amsterdam: Elsevier, 2005.

Krug, Rebecca. *Margery Kempe and the Lonely Reader*. Ithaca: Cornell University Press, 2017.

Labbie, Erin Felicia. *Lacan's Medievalism*. Minneapolis: University of Minnesota Press, 2006.

Ladd, Roger A. "Margery Kempe and Her Mercantile Mysticism." *Fifteenth-Century Studies* 26 (2001): 121–41.

Lattin, Linda L. "Some Aspects of Medieval Number Symbolism in Langland's *Piers Plowman*, A-Text." "Three Studies in Middle English Literature." *Emporia State Research Studies* 14, no. 1 (1965): 5–13, 36–37.

Lawrence, C. H. *Medieval Monasticism: Forms of Religious Life in Western Europe in the Middle Ages*. 3rd ed. London: Routledge, 2013.

Lentes, Thomas. "Counting Piety in the Late Middle Ages." In Jussen, *Ordering Medieval Society*, 55–91.

Lucas, John Scott. *Astrology and Numerology in Medieval and Early Modern Catalonia: The Tractat de prenosticatión de la vida natural dels hòmens*. Leiden: Brill, 2003.

Mahoney, Michael S. "Mathematics." In *Science in the Middle Ages*, edited by David C. Lindberg, 145–78. Chicago: University of Chicago Press, 1978.

Mandziuk, Natalie M. "Drawn to Scale: The Medieval Monastic's Virtual Pilgrimage Through Sacred Measurement." In *Binding the Absent Body in Medieval and Modern Art: Abject, Virtual, and Alternate Bodies*, edited by Emily Kelley and Elizabeth Richards Rivenbark, 73–92. New York: Routledge, 2017.

Martin, C. A. "Middle English Manuals of Religious Instruction." In *So Meny People Longages and Tonges: Philological Essays in Scots and Mediaeval English Presented to Angus McIntosh*, edited by Michael Benskin and M. L. Samuels, 283–98. Edinburgh: Middle English Dialect Project, 1981.

Mattéi, J.-F. "Nicomachus of Gerasa and the Arithmetic Scale of the Divine." In Koetsier and Bergmans, *Mathematics and the Divine*, 123–32.

McCluskey, Stephen C. "Boethius's Astronomy and Cosmology." In Kaylor and Phillips, *Companion to Boethius in the Middle Ages*, 47–74.

Menninger, Karl. *Number Words and Number Symbols: A Cultural History of Numbers*. Translated by Paul Brenner. Boston: Massachusetts Institute of Technology Press, 1969.

Meyer, Heinz, and Rudolf Suntrup. *Lexikon der mittelalterlichen Zahlenbedeutungen*. Munich: Fink, 1987.

Minnis, Alastair J. "Religious Roles: Public and Private." In *Medieval Holy Women in the Christian Traditions c. 1100–c. 1500*, edited by Alastair J. Minnis and Rosalynn Voaden, 47–81. Turnhout: Brepols, 2010.

Morrée, Cécile de. "Singing Together Alone: Dynamics Between Individual and Community in Middle Dutch Religious Song Collections." *Journal of Medieval Religious Cultures* 45, no. 2 (2019): 85–112.

Morrison, Tessa. "Bede's *De Tabernaculo* and *De Templo*." *Journal of the Australian Early Medieval Association* 3 (2007): 243–57.

Morrissey, K., D. Hallett, R. Wynes, J. Kang, and M. Han. "Finger Counting Habits, Not Finger Movements, Predict Simple Arithmetic Problem Solving." *Psychological Research* 84, no. 1 (2020): 140–51.

Muessig, Carolyn, ed. *Medieval Monastic Preaching*. Brill's Studies in Intellectual History 90. Leiden: Brill, 1998.

———. *Preacher, Sermon and Audience in the Middle Ages*. Leiden: Brill, 2002.

Murphy, James J. *Rhetoric in the Middle Ages: A History of Rhetorical Theory from Saint Augustine to the Renaissance*. Berkeley: University of California Press, 1974.

Murray, Alexander. *Reason and Society in the Middle Ages*. Oxford: Oxford University Press, 1978.

Nishitama, Yutaka. "Counting with the Fingers." *International Journal of Pure and Applied Mathematics* 85, no. 5 (2013): 859–68.

Nunes, Terezinha, Analúcia Dias Schliemann, and David William Carraher. *Street Mathematics and School Mathematics*. Learning in Doing. Cambridge: Cambridge University Press, 1993.

O'Brien, Conor. *Bede's Temple: An Image and Its Interpretation*. Oxford Theology and Religion Monographs. Oxford: Oxford University Press, 2015.

O'Daly, Irene. "Talk to the Hand: Finger Counting and Hand Diagrams in the Middle Ages." medievalfragments blog, 14 March 2014. https://medievalfragments.wordpress.com/2014/03/14/talk-to-the-hand-finger-counting-and-hand-diagrams-in-the-middle-ages/.

Ore, Øystein. "I problemi di matematica nello Zibaldone da Canal." Translated by Bianca Strina. In *Zibaldone da Canal: Manoscritto Mercantile del sec. XIV*, edited by Alfredo Stussi, 69–76. Venice: Fonti per la Storia di Venezia, 1967.

———. *Number Theory and Its History*. New York: McGraw-Hill, 1948. Reprint, New York: Dover, 1988.

Orme, Nicholas. *Medieval Schools: From Roman Britain to Renaissance England*. New Haven: Yale University Press, 2006.

Owens, Kay. "Diversifying Our Perspectives on Mathematics About Space and Geometry: An Ecocultural Approach." *International Journal of Science and Mathematics Education* 12, no. 4 (2014): 941–74.

Owst, G. R. *Literature and Pulpit in Medieval England: A Neglected Chapter in the History of English Letters and of the English People*. 2nd rev. ed. Oxford: Blackwell, 1961.

———. *Preaching in Medieval England: An Introduction to Sermon Manuscripts of the Period, c. 1350–1450*. Cambridge Studies in Medieval Life and Thought. Cambridge: Cambridge University Press, 1926.

Pearsall, Derek. "G. R. Owst and the Politics of Sermon Studies." In Driver and O'Mara, *Preaching the Word*, 11–30.

Peck, Russell. "Number as Cosmic Language." In *Essays in the Numerical Criticism of Medieval Literature*, edited by Caroline D. Eckhardt, 15–64. Lewisburg: Bucknell University Press, 1980.

———. "Theme and Number in Chaucer's *Book of the Duchess*." In *Silent Poetry: Essays in Numerological Analysis*, edited by Alastair Fowler, 73–115. New York: Routledge and K. Paul, 1970.

Phillips, Susan E. *Transforming Talk: The Problem with Gossip in Late Medieval England*. University Park: Pennsylvania State University Press, 2007.

Pin, Antonio. "The Contribution of Luca Pacioli to the Development of Business Accounting." *Economic Notes, Monte dei Paschi di Siena* 22, no. 2 (1993): 161–77. In *Proceedings of the Conference Accounting and Economics: In Honour of the 500th Anniversary of Publication of Luca Pacioli's Summa de Arithmetica, Geometria, Proportioni et Proportionalita*, edited by Martin Shubik, 161–77. Siena: Monte dei Paschi di Siena, 1993.

Poleg, Eyal. "'A Ladder Set Up on Earth': The Bible in Medieval Sermons." In *The Practice of the Bible in the Middle Ages: Production, Reception, and Performance in Western Christianity*, edited by Susan Boynton and Diane J. Reilly, 205–27. New York: Columbia University Press, 2011.

Powell, Susan. "Untying the Knot: Reading *Sir Gawain and the Green Knight*." In *New Perspectives on Middle English Texts: A Festschrift for R. A. Waldron*, edited by Susan Powell and Jeremy J. Smith, 55–74. Rochester: D. S. Brewer, 2000.

Pranger, M. B. "Killing Time: An Essay on the Monastic Notion of Speed." In Muessig, *Medieval Monastic Preaching*, 319–34.

Preston, Jean F. "Playing with Numbers: Some Mixed Counting Methods Found in French Medieval Manuscripts at Princeton." In *Medieval Codicology, Iconography, Literature, and Translation: Studies for Keith Val Sinclair*, edited by Peter Rolfe Monks and D. D. R. Owen, 74–82. Leiden: Brill, 1994.

Pullan, J. M. *The History of the Abacus*. 2nd rev. ed. London: Hutchinson, 1970.

Rand, Kari Anne. "The Syon Pardon Sermon: Contexts and Texts." In Driver and O'Mara, *Preaching the Word*, 317–49.

Rashed, Roshdi, ed. *Al-Khwārizmī: The Beginnings of Algebra*. History of Science and Philosophy in Classical Islam. London: Saqi, 2009.

Reed, H. J., and Jean Lave. "Arithmetic as a Tool for Investigating Relations Between Culture and Cognition." *American Ethnologist* 6, no. 3 (1979): 568–82.

Reynolds, Mark A. "The Octagon in Leonardo's Drawings." *Nexus Network Journal* 10, no. 1 (2008): 51–76.

Reynolds, Roger E. "'At Sixes and Sevens'—and Eights and Nines: The Sacred Mathematics of Sacred Orders in the Early Middle Ages." *Speculum* 54 (1979): 669–84.

Ritz, Gisland. "Die christliche Gebetszählschnur: Ihre Geschichte, ihre Erscheinung, ihre Funktion." PhD diss., University of Munich, 1955.

Robertson, Elizabeth. "Julian of Norwich and the Digital." *Archive Journal* (September 2018). http://www.archivejournal.net/essays/julian-of-norwich-and-the-digital.

Rogerson, Margaret, ed. *The York Mystery Plays: Performance in the City*. Woodbridge: York Medieval Press, 2011.

Rust, Martha. "The *Arma Christi* and the Ethics of Reckoning." In *The Arma Christi in Medieval and Early Modern Material Culture: With a Critical Edition of "O Vernicle,"* edited by Lisa H. Cooper and Andrea Denny-Brown, 143–69. Farnham, UK: Ashgate; 2014.

Saltamacchia, Martina. "A Funeral Procession from Venice to Milan: Death Rituals for a Late-Medieval Wealthy Merchant." In *Dealing with the Dead: Mortality and Community in Medieval and Early Modern Europe*, edited by Thea Tomaini, 201–20. Leiden: Brill, 2018.

Saxe, Geoffrey B. "Developing Forms of Arithmetical Thought Among the Oksapmin of Papua New Guinea." *Developmental Psychology* 18 (1982): 583–94.

———. "The Mathematics of Child Street Vendors." *Child Development* 59, no. 5 (1988): 1415–25.

Saxe, Geoffrey B., with Indigo Esmonde. *Cultural Development of Mathematical Ideas: Papua New Guinea Studies*. Cambridge: Cambridge University Press, 2012.

Scheepsma, Wybren. *The Limburg Sermons: Preaching in the Medieval Low Countries at the Turn of the Fourteenth Century*. Translated by David F. Johnson. Brill's Series in Church History 34. Leiden: Brill, 2008.

Schiewer, Regina D. "*Sub Iudaica Infirmitate*—'Under the Jewish Weakness': Jews in Medieval German Sermons." In *The Jewish-Christian Encounter in Medieval Preaching*, edited by Jonathan Adams and Jussi Hanska, 59–91. New York: Routledge, 2015.

Schimmel, Annemarie. *The Mystery of Numbers*. New York: Oxford University Press, 1994.

Schirmer, Elizabeth. "Representing Reading in *Dives and Pauper*." In *Devotional Literature and Practice in Medieval England: Readers, Reading, and Reception*, edited by Kathryn Vulic, Susan Uselmann, and C. Annette Grisé, 85–117. Turnhout: Brepols, 2017.

Schliemann, Andalúcia D., Cláudia Araujo, Maria Angela Cassundé, Suzana Macedo, and Lenice Nicéas. "Use of Multiplicative Commutativity by School Children and Street Sellers." *Journal for Research in Mathematics Education* 29, no. 4 (1998): 422–35.

Sears, Elizabeth. *The Ages of Man: Medieval Interpretations of the Life Cycle*. Princeton: Princeton University Press, 1986.

Seife, Charles. *Zero: The Biography of a Dangerous Idea*. New York: Penguin, 2000.

Sellars, Maura, ed. *Numeracy in Authentic Contexts: Making Meaning Across the Curriculum*. Singapore: Springer, 2019.

Shippey, T. A. "Chaucer's Arithmetical Mentality and the *Book of the Duchess*." *Chaucer Review* 31, no. 2 (1996): 184–200.

Simpson, James. "Orthodoxy's Image Trouble: Images in and After Arundel's Constitutions." In *After Arundel: Religious Writing in Fifteenth-Century England*, edited by Vincent Gillespie and Kantik Ghosh, 91–114. Medieval Church Studies 21. Turnhout: Brepols, 2011.

Smith, Lesley J. *The Ten Commandments: Interpreting the Bible in the Medieval World*. Studies in the History of Christian Traditions 175. Leiden: Brill, 2014.

Somerset, Fiona. *Feeling Like Saints: Lollard Writings After Wyclif*. Ithaca: Cornell University Press, 2014.

Spencer, H. Leith. *English Preaching in the Late Middle Ages*. Oxford: Clarendon, 1993.

Steenbrugge, Charlotte. *Drama and Sermon in Late Medieval England: Performance, Authority, Devotion*. Kalamazoo, MI: Medieval Institute Publications, 2017.

Sticca, Sandro. "Sacred Drama and Comic Realism in the Plays of Hrotswitha of Gandersheim." In *Atti del IV Colloquio della Société Internationale pour l'Etude du Théâtre Médiéval*, edited by M. Chiabò, Federico Doglio, and Marina Maymone Siniscalchi, 141–62. Viterbo: Centro studi sui teatro medioevale e rinascimentale, 1984. Reprinted from *The Early Middle Ages*, edited by W. H. Snyder, Acta 6, 117–43. Binghamton: Center for Medieval and Renaissance Studies, 1979.

Stock, Brian. *The Implications of Literacy: Written Language and Models of Interpretation in the Eleventh and Twelfth Centuries*. Princeton: Princeton University Press, 1983.

Sturges, Robert S. *The Circulation of Power in Medieval Biblical Drama: Theaters of Authority*. New York: Palgrave MacMillan, 2015.

Sylla, E. D. "Swester Katrei and Gregory of Rimini: Angels, God, and Mathematics in the Fourteenth Century." In Koetsier and Bergmans, *Mathematics and the Divine*, 249–72.

Tavormina, M. Teresa. "Mathematical Conjectures in a Middle English Prose Treatise: Perfect Numbers in *Dives and Pauper*." *Traditio: Studies in Ancient and Medieval History, Thought, and Religion* 49 (1994): 271–86.

Thayer, Anne T. "Support for Preaching in Guido of Monte Rochen's *Manipulus Curatorum*." In *A Companion to Pastoral Care in the Late Middle Ages (1200–1500)*, edited by Ronald J. Stansbury, 123–44. Leiden: Brill, 2010.

Versluis, Arthur. "*Piers Plowman*, Numerical Composition, and the Prophecies." *Connotations* 1, no. 2 (1991): 103–39.

Voaden, Rosalynn. "Wolf in Sheep's Clothing: Margery Kempe as Underground Preacher." In *Romance and Rhetoric: Essays in Honour of Dhira B. Mahoney*, edited by Georgiana Donavin and Anita Obermeier, 109–21. Disputatio 19. Turnhout: Brepols, 2010.

Voigt, John. "Perfect Numbers: An Elementary Introduction." 1998. https://math.dartmouth.edu/~jvoight/notes/perfelem.pdf.

Wailes, Stephen L. "Hrotsvit's Plays." In *A Companion to Hrotsvit of Gandersheim (fl. 960): Contextual and Interpretive Approaches*, edited by Phyllis R. Brown and Stephen L. Wailes, 121–45. Companions to the Christian Tradition 34. Leiden: Brill, 2013.

Waldron, Ronald. "Susan Powell and the Growing Study of the Middle English Sermon." In Driver and O'Mara, *Preaching the Word*, xiii–xv.

Wallis, Faith. "'Number Mystique' in Early Medieval Computus Texts." In Koetsier and Bergmans, *Mathematics and the Divine*, 179–99.

Waters, Claire M. *Angels and Earthly Creatures: Preaching, Performance, and Gender in the Later Middle Ages.* Philadelphia: University of Pennsylvania Press, 2013.

Watson, Nicholas. "Conceptions of the Word: The Mother Tongue and the Incarnation of God." In *New Medieval Literatures*, edited by Wendy Scase, Rita Copeland, and David Lawton, 1:85–124. Oxford: Clarendon, 1997.

———. "The Making of *The Book of Margery Kempe*." In *Voices in Dialogue: Reading Women in the Middle Ages*, edited by Linda Olson and Kathryn Kerby-Fulton, 395–434. Notre Dame: University of Notre Dame Press, 2005.

———. "The Trinitarian Hermeneutic in Julian of Norwich's *Revelation of Love*." In *Julian of Norwich: A Book of Essays*, edited by Sandra J. McEntire, 61–90. Garland Medieval Casebook 21. New York: Garland, 1998.

Webb, Melanie. "Abraham, Samson, and 'Certain Holy Women': Suicide and Exemplarity in Augustine's *De ciuitate dei* 1.26." In *Sacred Scripture and Secular Struggles*, edited by David Vincent Meconi, S.J., 201–34. The Bible in Ancient Christianity 9. Leiden: Brill, 2015.

Wedell, Moritz. "Numbers." Translated by Erik Born. In Classen, *Handbook of Medieval Culture*, 2:1205–60.

Weisheipl, James A. "Curriculum of the Faculty of Arts at Oxford in the Early Fourteenth Century." *Mediæval Studies* 26 (1964): 143–85.

———. "Developments in the Arts Curriculum at Oxford in the Early Fourteenth Century." *Mediæval Studies* 28 (1966): 151–75.

Wenzel, Siegfried. *Latin Sermon Collections from Later Medieval England: Orthodox Preaching in the Age of Wyclif.* Cambridge Studies in Medieval Literature. Cambridge: Cambridge University Press, 2005.

———. *Medieval Artes Praedicandi: A Synthesis of Scholastic Sermon Structure.* Medieval Academy Books 114. Toronto: University of Toronto Press, 2015.

———. *Preaching in the Age of Chaucer: Selected Sermons in Translation.* Medieval Texts in Translation. Washington, DC: Catholic University of America Press, 2008.

———. "Preaching the Seven Deadly Sins." In *The Garden of Evil: The Vices and Culture in the Middle Ages*, edited by Richard Newhauser, 145–69. Papers in Mediaeval Studies 18. Toronto: Pontifical Institute of Mediaeval Studies, 2005.

Were, Graeme. "Objects of Learning: An Anthropological Approach to Mathematics Education." *Journal of Material Culture* 8, no. 1 (2003): 25–44.

White, Paul, Mike Mitchelmore, Sue Wilson, and Rhonda Faragher. "Critical Numeracy and Abstraction: Percentages." *Australian Primary Mathematics Classroom* 14, no. 1 (2009): 4–8.

Williams, Burma P., and Richard S. Williams. "Finger Numbers in the Greco-Roman World and the Early Middle Ages." *Isis* 86 (1995): 587–608.

Williams, David. *Deformed Discourse: The Function of the Monster in Mediaeval Thought and Literature.* Montreal: McGill–Queen's University Press, 1996.

Willmott, A. "An Edition of Selected Sermons from MS. Longleat 4." PhD diss., Bristol University, 1994.

Winston-Allen, Anne. *Stories of the Rose: The Making of the Rosary in the Middle Ages.* University Park: Pennsylvania State University Press, 1997.

Wise, M. Norton, ed. *The Values of Precision.* Princeton: Princeton University Press, 1997.

Wogan-Browne, Jocelyn, Nicholas Watson, Andrew Taylor, and Ruth Evans. *The*

Idea of the Vernacular: An Anthology of Middle English Literary Theory, 1280–1520. University Park: Pennsylvania State University Press, 1999.

Wood, Diana. *Medieval Economic Thought.* Cambridge: Cambridge University Press, 2002.

Wright, Charles D. "Vercelli Homilies XI–XIII and the Anglo-Saxon Benedictine Reform: Tailored Sources and Implied Audiences." In Muessig, *Preacher, Sermon, and Audience,* 203–27.

Yoshikawa, Naoë Kukita. *Margery Kempe's Meditations: The Context of Medieval Devotional Literatures, Liturgy and Iconography.* Cardiff: University of Wales Press, 2007.

Zaitsev, Evgeny A. "The Meaning of Early Medieval Geometry: From Euclid and Surveyors' Manuals to Christian Philosophy." *Isis* 90, no. 3 (1999): 522–53.

Zhang, Shaohua. "Euclid's Number-Theoretical Work." Ithaca: Cornell University, 2009; revised 2010. https://arxiv.org/abs/0902.2465.

INDEX

abacus, 4, 131–33
  See also counting board
abacus schools, 134, 136
Abel, 69–71, 153n25
Abraham, 20, 25, 107
abstinence, 84
accounting
  practices of, 4, 118, 161n10
  in sermons of Rypon, Robert, 9–10, 98, 110–14
accuracy, of calculation, 8, 24–25, 50–51, 64
Acker, Paul, 33–34
Adam
  and the ages of the church, 20
  hour that he ate the apple, 49
  hour that he was banished, 49
  letters of his name, 51, 108–9
  types of generation, 48
addition
  in the *Crafte of Nombrynge*, 134
  in *Dives and Pauper*, 44–45
  methods of, 129–30, 133
  in sermons, 4, 30–31, 50–51, 74–75, 112
  See also calculation
Aers, David, 118
ages of man, 5
ages of the world and church, 5, 10, 20, 21, 44, 49, 52
Alcuin of York, 57
algebra, 4
algorism, 22
allegorical numerology, 5, 18, 23, 139n32
Ambrose, Saint, 139n36
Ancrene Wisse, 11, 131, 162n12
Anselm, 108
Apocalypse, 19, 29, 44
Arabic numerals. *See* Hindu-Arabic numerals
Aristotle, 104, 109
arithmetic of salvation, 117
Arithmetica speculative, 42
"arithmetical mentality," 3–4, 9, 10, 98, 110
arithmetical operations. *See individual operations*
arithmetical treatises in Middle English, 133
arithmology, 137n9
Ars copiosa, 14
Ars praedicandi, 12
  See also Wenzel, Siegfried

Articles of the Faith, 12–13, 58, 64, 78, 91, 112
Arundel's Constitutions, 39, 144n5
Ash Wednesday, 65
Atchley, Clinton, 66, 152n7
Atkinson, Clarissa, 118
Augustine
  on Adam's name, 108;
  City of God, 59
  Commentary on Psalm 96, 108
  on the length of the world, 29
  on the number eleven, 59
  on the perfection of the number six, 24, 41
  on Samson, 100
  Tractates on John, 59–60
Ave Maria (Ave), 28, 73–75
Ayenbite of Inwit, 56

Barnum, Priscilla Heath, 39
Bartholomaeus Anglicus, 23
Bede
  De tabernaculo, 25
  Expositio Actuum Apostolorum, 151n80
  on finger counting, 25, 129, 141n70
  on Jesus's name, 105
  on the perfection of number six: 41, 142n83
  on the perfection of number 12, 151n80
  on the perfection of number 28, 41
  on the perfection of number 100, 25
Bergmans, Luc, 5, 141n64
Bernard of Clairvaux, 105
Bible Moralisée, Codex Vindobonesis 2554, 88
Bodleian Library, MS Bodley 806, 20, 36
Bodleian Library, MS Douce 53, 29, 143n91
Bodleian Library, MS Holkham misc. 40, 26–27, 32
  See also *Mirror, The*
Boethius
  De institutione arithmetica, 22, 25, 42, 53, 56: model for Cassiodorus, 23; number theory, 22–23, 133; on spherical numbers, 53; on (un)stable numbers, 55, 150n61; on superabundant numbers, 56–57, 58; on the perfection of the number ten, 25; on unity, 22, 60, 150n61; on prime numbers, 60
  in the quadrivium, 22
  See also number theory
Book of Margery Kempe
  Christ's wounds, calculation of, 76–78, 125

Book of Margery Kempe (continued)
  hybrid numeracy in, 10, 117, 119, 126–27
  infinity in, 79–81, 126
  quantitative reasoning in, 3, 124–26
  references to money and mercantilism, 4, 37, 118, 121–23, 125
  and time, counting of, 120–25
Book of the Duchess, The, 114
Boyer, Carol, 4
Bracciolini, Poggio, 11, 35, 52
Bradwardine, Thomas, 4, 42, 115–16
Brewer, Derek, 114
British Library MS Additional 40672, 19–20, 36, 54, 87–88
British Library, MS Additional 36791, 20–21, 30, 31
  See also *Speculum Sacerdotale*
British Library, MS Cotton Claudius A.ii, 30
  See also Mirk, John
British Library, MS Harley 2247, 29
British Library, MS Harley 2276, 29–30, 30–31
  See also *Filius Matri*
British Library, MS Harley 4012, 28–29
  See also Syon Pardon
British Library, MS Harley 4894, 7, 9, 94–114
  See also Rypon, Robert
British Library, MS Royal 18.B.xxiii, 30

Cain, 69–71, 153n25
calculation
  of area and volume, 135
  and arithmetical mentality, 3–4, 9, 10, 98, 110
  of Christ's wounds (see Christ: wounds of)
  definition of, 130
  as encouraged by pardons, 28–29
  by hand (see finger counting)
  (in)accuracy of, 8, 24–25, 50–51, 64
  in manuscripts (see *specific manuscript entries, listed by library*)
  mental calculation, 130–33
  methods and tools (see *individual tools, such as tally stick*)
  of the number of tears Mary shed, 31
  of profits, interest, discounts, 134
  regrouping, 133
  of tithes (see tithing)
  See also *acts of calculation such as addition and duplation*
Canterbury Tales, The, 2, 131
Carruthers, Leo, 64, 66, 152n2
Carruthers, Mary, 138n6
Cassiodorus, 22–23
Catherine of Siena, 2, 26

Charter of the Abbey of the Holy Ghost, The, 47
Chaucer, Geoffrey, 2, 114, 131
Christ (Jesus)
  anointing of, 68–69
  apostles, choice of, 50, 58, 60
  Ascension, 17, 64, 103
  betrayal by Judas, 68–69, 71–73
  birth of, 48
  casting out devils, 50, 103–4
  circumcision of, 21, 56, 76
  Coming of, 17, 20, 52
  entering Jerusalem, 15–16
  Epiphany, 30–31, 120, 122
  feeding of the multitude, 11, 19, 26–27, 31–32, 35–37, 48–49, 52
  geometry in the Eucharist, 85
  healing blind man, 58
  healing lepers, 50
  healing woman with hemorrhage, 20
  Incarnation of, 109–10
  infinity and, 35
  and Kempe, Margery, 118–26
  meaning of his name, 21, 97, 105–10
  and measure of love, 91–93
  miracle at Cana, 49, 60
  natures of, 108
  as number five, 109–10
  Passion and Crucifixion of, 31, 43, 48, 49, 58, 76, 94–95, 110, 124–26 (see also Christ: wounds of)
  Resurrection of, 82–83, 103, 107
  as shepherd, 51
  teaching at age of twelve, 58
  weeping of, 48
  at the well, 65–66
  in the wilderness, 17, 18, 29, 123
  wounds of, 21, 24–25, 29, 31, 48, 76–78, 83, 115–17, 121, 125–26
circle
  as aid for preaching, 13
  in Boethius, 22
  in Bede, 25
  circular numbers, 52–56, 149n53
  crown of the Wise Virgins, 56
  geometry of the Eucharist, 85
  in "Life of St. Edmund," 34
  in Nicholas of Cusa, 88
  representing infinity, 25, 88, 104
  squaring of, 135
Classen, Albrecht, 5
Cockcroft Report, 6
  See also numeracy
commerce. See mercantilism

Confessio Amantis, 131, 162–63n15
Connolly, Margaret, 6, 12
Cooper, Katherine, 93–94, 155n60
Corpus Christi College, MS 392, 15–16
counting (enumeration)
    accounting (*see* accounting; mercantilism)
    counting to infinity (*see* infinity)
    counting/tallying by devil or angel, 33, 77–78
    extreme counting, 76, 77, 81
    Lentes, Thomas and "Counting Piety," 5, 31, 76–77, 117, 132
    methods of counting (*see* abacus; counting board; finger counting; rosary)
    miscounting of Cain, 69–71, 153n25
    money (currency). (*see* mercantilism; *and individual authors and texts, especially* Book of Margery Kempe, The, *and* Rypon, Robert)
    Christ's steps on earth, number of, 76
    tears shed by Mary, number of, 76
    numerals for counting (*see* Hindu-Arabic numerals; Roman numerals)
    prayers, counting of, 117–18 (*see also* rosary)
    reckoning, 22, 131, 143n92 (*see also* calculation)
    tithing (*see* tithing)
    wounds of Christ, counting of, 76–77
    See also under number
counting board, 110, 111–13, 131–32, 106n57
Crafte of Nombrynge, The, 133
creation of the world, 18, 19, 24, 139n36
Creed, the, 28, 91
Crowther Report 6, 137n15
Crump, Thomas 6
cube, 25, 53, 55–56, 76, 88, 107, 130, 133
currency. *See* mercantilism

David (biblical figure), 20
Davidson, Clifford 60, 70
De Institutione arithmetica (De Arithmetica, On the Properties of Numbers). *See* Boethius; number theory
De modo componendi sermones, 15
De Proprietatibus Rerum, 23
Delany, Sheila 118
Delilah, 100
demon. *See* devil
devil
    Beast of the Apocalypse as, 19
    in *Book of Margery Kempe, The*, 80
    daughters of, 17
    Jesus casting out, 50, 103
    names of, 103–5
    tallying sins in writing, 16, 33, 78
    temptation by 17, 100
    Ten Commandments combatting, 30
Dialogue of Catherine of Siena 2, 26
Dives and Pauper, 8–9, 38–47, 62
divisio (division) of sermon, 13–17
dilatio (of sermon), 13
division (i.e. arithmetical act), 30, 32, 59–60, 61, 109, 133
doubling (duplation), 74–75, 102, 123–24, 133
Durham Priory 95, 96, 97, 111

Edmund, Saint, 33–34
Elements of Euclid 4, 23, 89
Elizabeth, Saint (biblical figure), 122
    See also Visitation, the
England, George, 70
Exchequer, 131, 163n21
enumeration. *See* counting
Epiphany, 30–31, 120, 122
Ethnomathematics, 130, 132–33
Etymologies of Isidore 23, 34–35, 141n60
    See also Isidore of Seville
Eucharist, 34–35
Euclid 4, 23, 89, 154n57
Exegetica de scripturis et scriptoribus sacris, 60

Facetiae of Bracciolini 11, 35, 52
factor (factoring)
    in Boethian number theory, 22, 24, 27, 56–57, 60
    in *Book of Margery Kempe, The*, 124
    in Hrotsvit of Gandersheim, 58
    in *Jacob's Well*, 72, 74–75
    in other sermons, 30, 41, 50–51, 103, 106–7
    in "York Play of Pentecost," 59–61
fasting, 20–21, 29–30, 48, 51, 57, 72, 78
feeding of the multitude. *See* Christ: feeding of the multitude
Felton, John, 34–35, 85
Festial of John Mirk, 30, 34
Fibonacci (Leonardo Pisano), 4, 130, 131, 136
Filius Matri, 29–30, 30–31
    See also British Library, MS Harley 2276
Finchale Priory 96, 97, 111
finger counting
    by Bede 25, 125, 129, 162n7
    in *De diversis artibus*, 130
    by monks, 129
    Murray on finger counting, 130
    by Romans, 129
Fitzgibbons, Moira, 64–66
Fletcher, Alan J., 17–18, 139n30
Flood, the (biblical event), 18
    See also Noah

Folkerts, Menso 4
fraction, 131, 134, 135–36
    See also ratio
Francesc Eiximenes, 12–13
Fulton, Rachel 6

gambling, 86
Gastle, Brian 118
geometry
    in abacus schools, 134
    in Archimedes, 154n57
    in Boethius, 22
    in Euclid, 4, 23, 89, 154n57
    in "Life of St. Edmund, The," 34
    in sermons, 9, 85, 87–94, 104
    See also individual shapes
Gerbert of Aurillac (Pope Sylvester II), 131
Gerhoch of Reichersberg, 107
Gifts of the Holy Spirit, 13, 64, 65, 100–101
Gillespie, Vincent, 39
Glossa Ordinaria, 36
God as geometer, 87, 88, 92
Golden Legend, The, 75
    See also individual saints
Gower, John, 131, 162n15
Grosseteste, Robert, 4, 35
Guide for Pilgrims unto the Holy Land, 134

Hadrian, Emperor, 57–58, 151n72
halving (mediation), 123–24
Hatfield House Cecil Papers 280, 16–17
Hell, 16, 32, 49–50, 54–55, 91, 143n92
Heng, Geraldine, 54
Hilton, Walter, 2
Hindu-Arabic numerals
    in abacus schools, 134
    in *Ancrene Wisse*, 33
    in arithmetical guides, 133
    in Fibonacci, 23
    in Rypon, Robert, 97, 110, 105–6
    system of, 131
Hrotsvit of Gandersheim, 57–58, 151n71
Hugh of St. Victor, 25, 60

indulgences, 96, 117–18
    See also pardons
infinity
    in Bede, 25
    in Boethius, 53–54
    in *Book of Margery Kempe, The*, 80–81, 126
    in *Dives and Pauper*, 42
    in Felton, John, 85
    in *Jacob's Well*, 78
    in Longleat 4, 52

    in Nicholas of Cusa, 88
    in Rypon, Robert, 104
    in *Sir Gawain and the Green Knight*, 54
Institutiones of Cassiodorus, 22–23
Isaac (biblical figure), 25, 107
Isidore of Seville, 23–24, 34–35, 85, 141n60, 149n53
Itineraries of William Wey, 134

Jacob's Well (Salisbury Cathedral Library 103)
    audience of, 64, 66
    enumeration in, 75–81
    geometry in, 87–94
    measure in, 81–87
    quantitative reasoning in, 7, 9, 67–95
    tithing in, 67–72
James the Mutilated, Saint, 75–76
Jefferson, Lisa, 134
Jerome, Saint, 48
Jesus. *See* Christ
Jettons, 111, 132
Jiang, Nancy Haijing, 161n10
John the Baptist, 101
Johnson, Holly, 2–3, 7, 95–96, 111, 155n5
Judas
    Christ wept for, 48
    Christ replacing Judas as apostle, 59–60, 151n80
    Judas as bad tither 67–69, 71–72
Julian of Norwich, 126, 162n25

Kempe, Margery. See *Book of Margery Kempe, The*
Kermode, Jennifer, 134
Killing of Abel, The (*Mactacio Abel*), 69–71
Koetsier, Teun, 5, 141n64

laborers in the vineyard, 20
Ladder of Love (Ladder of Charity), 66, 73–74, 87, 91–93
Lambeth Constitutions, 12
Langland, William, 60, 131, 162–63n15
Lazarus, 48
Lear, King, 17
Legenda Aurea, 75
    See also individual saints
Lentes, Thomas, 5, 31, 76, 117, 132
Leonardo Pisano (Fibonacci), 4, 130, 131, 136
Liber Abaci. See Fibonacci
"Life of Saint Edmund, The," 33–34
Lincoln Cathedral Library MS 133, 14, 19
loaves and fishes. *See* Christ: feeding of the multitude
Lollardy, 120, 123

Longleat 4 (Warminster, Longleat House MS 4): 7, 8–9, 38, 47–62
Lucas, John Scott, 18
Lydgate, John 2, 81–82, 84

Mactacio Abel (The Killing of Abel), 69–71
Magi, 30–31
Mandziuk, Natalie, 24–25
Mankind (drama), 82
Manuscripts. *See individual manuscripts listed by library or college*
Martin of Cordoba, 14
Marx, William G., 71, 143n92 143n93, 153n25
Mary (biblical figure), 20, 31, 49, 56, 122
Mary Magdalen (Magdalene), 20, 68–69, 100
Mathematics Counts (Cockcroft Report), 6
  See also numeracy
measurement
  ages of the world and church, 5, 10, 20, 21, 44, 49, 52
  in agriculture, 3
  in Bede, 24
  with the body, 130, 141n67 (*see also* Christ: wounds)
  in *Book of Margery Kempe, The*, 117–25
  definitions, 81–84
  in different parts of the world, 61
  God measuring world, 88
  in *Jacob's Well*, 67–94
  numeracy, aspect of, 6
  of Oksapmin, 130
  of pilgrimage routes, 134
  in "Song of Just Mesure, A," 81–82
  in "York Play of the Crucifixion," 82–83
  See also arithmetical operations; calculation; counting; weight; *and individual numbers*
mediation (halving), 123–24, 133
memory
  in Bradwardine, Thomas, 115–16
  memory grid, 138n6
  sermon division as aid to, 14–17, 37
  in Waleys, Thomas, 139n22
  See also Carruthers, Mary
Menninger, Karl, 129, 160n57, 163n21
mercantilism
  abacus schools, 134
  Alexander's stone, 84–85
  in *Book of Margery Kempe, The*, 118–19
  devil's accountant, 33
  in Fibonacci, *Liber Abacus*, 23, 30, 134
  greed, association with, 33
  numerate practices of merchants, 130–34
  merchants in *Jacob's Well*, 68
  relationship to calculation, 3–4

  in Rypon, Robert, 110–14
  in *Zibaldone da Canal*, 135–36
  See also accounting
mercy, 49, 50, 73, 80, 82–83, 90, 93
Merzback, Uta, 4
"Mesure is Tresour" 82
Meyer, Heinz, 5, 18
Mirk, John, 30, 34
Mirror, The, 26
Modus sermocinandi, 12–13
money. *See* mercantilism
Moses (biblical figure), 36, 115
multiplication
  in arithmetical treatises, 130
  in Bede, 142n83
  in Boethius, 133
  in *Book of Margery Kempe, The*, 77, 124–25
  of circular numbers, 52–56, 149n53
  cubing, 53
  factoring, examples, 24, 41, 50
  in *Jacob's Well*, 74, 75, 90–91
  in Lentes, Thomas, 117
  multiplication tables, 131
  in Noah plays, 83–84
  in *Orcherd (Orchard) of Syon, The*, 26
  in Rypon, Robert, 103, 106–7
  See also addition; calculation; duplation
Murray, Alexander, 3–4, 10, 130

New South Wales Department of Education, 6
Nicholas of Cusa, 88
Nicomachus of Gerasa, 22, 42, 140n51
Noah (biblical figure), 20, 25, 57, 83–84
Nota pro arte faciendi collaciones et sermones, 14
N-Town Woman Taken in Adultery, 143n92
number one
  Adam's name, meaning of, 51, 108–9
  Ave Maria, 73
  breaking commandments, 44, 72
  lost sheep, 51
  in *Orcherd of Syon, The*, 26
  as prime, 60
  representing wretched man, 109
  "Three in one," 76, 85, 88
  sermon division, 15
  unity, 22, 36, 60, 150n61 (*see also* number theory)
number two
  Bible, periods of, 48
  body and soul, 108, 109
  in *Book of Margery Kempe, The*, 120, 124
  cubed, 8, 56, 76, 109
  division between humans and God, representing, 109

number two (*continued*)
  division of Ten Virgins, 54
  Eucharist, division of, 85
  factoring (*see* factor)
  feeding of the multitude, 32, 36, 48, 55
  first even number, 23
  justice, parts of, 112
  Moses with horns, 115
  Precepts of the Gospel, 12
  senses, kinds of (*see* senses)
  sermon division (divisio), 14
  sin, dimensions of, in *Jacob's Well*, 86, 89–90
  squared, 109
  Ten Commandments, tablets of, 115
  Trinities, 87
  virtue, 90
number three
  in *Book of Margery Kempe, The*, 120–21, 122, 124, 126
  Christians come to Christ, 17
  Christ in wilderness, 17
  Coming of Christ, 17
  crowd following Christ, 19
  daughters of Lear, 17
  estates of humankind, 102
  Eucharist, division of, 85
  factoring (*see* factor)
  false prophets, 50
  false tithing, 71–72
  fasting, 21
  God, hope and vision of, 142n83
  Gospel, parts of, 58
  Greek form of counting, 106
  Israelites in desert, 19
  marriage, association with, 50, 73
  Marys, ointments, and spices, 20
  "most holy number," 23
  powers of the soul, 21, 31
  reasons to fear God, 16
  representing souls, 43
  sermon division (divisio), 14, 98
  sin and sinful people, 15, 49, 50, 108
  sin, dimensions of, in *Jacob's Well*, 85–86, 88–89
  and sins' remedy, 90–91
  Trinity, 23, 34, 50, 58, 76, 107–8, 109, 115, 121
  union of first odd and even numbers, 23
  virtues and virtuous people, 15, 57, 87
number four
  Adam's name, letters of, 51, 108–9
  ages of humankind, 21
  Apostles, as related to, 58
  in *Book of Margery Kempe, The*, 124
  cardinal virtues, 55
  component of number ten, 25–26
  division (divisio) in sermons, 14
  Doctors of the church, 36
  elements, number of, 21, 31, 42, 109
  factoring (*see* factor)
  fasting, length of, 21, 30, 51
  generation, types of, 48
  humors, 21, 30, 103
  in *Jacob's Well*, 86, 88, 89, 90–91
  as part of number five, 5, 108
  parts (corners) of the world, 29–30, 50, 61, 108
  representing humans divided from the Trinity, 109
  rules of nature, 99
  seasons of the year, 5, 103
  Scripture, senses of, 14
  as stable, square number, 55
  as twice two, 109
number five
  ages of the world and church, 20, 52
  in *Book of Margery Kempe, The*, 121
  Books of Moses, 36
  Christ, as incorruptible fifth being, 110
  Christ, reasons he ascended, 17
  Christ, represented by five, 108–9
  Christ, times he shed blood, 21
  Christ, times he wept, 48
  circularity of five, 52–54, 56
  elements of repentance, 48
  factoring (*see* factor)
  five loaves at the feeding of the multitude, 11, 26–27, 36, 48, 52
  Foolish and Wise Virgins, 54
  inward perfection, signs of, 99
  Jesus's name, 108–9
  sin, dimensions of, in *Jacob's Well*, 86, 98
  as unstable, round number, 55
  See also Christ: wounds; senses
number six
  Adam eating the apple, hour of, 49
  ages of the world, 20, 43–44, 49
  in *Book of Margery Kempe, The*, 120, 122
  conception of Christ, hour and day of, 49
  creation of the world in days, 18, 40–41
  Crucifixion of Christ, hour and day of, 49
  factoring (*see* factor)
  Jesus's name, letters of, 105
  office of the curate, parts of, 99
  perfection of, 6, 24, 40–43, 44, 49, 142n83, 145n16
  redemption, works of, 49
  sacraments, 49
  sin, dimensions of, in *Jacob's Well*, 86, 88, 89

sinner's journey from God, in days, 49
works of charity and mercy, 30, 49, 50, 83, 112
number seven
  ages of the world, 106
  in *Book of Margery Kempe, The*, 119, 120, 121–22, 124, 126
  clasps of John's book, 32
  dead bodies, properties of, 19
  deadly sins, 19, 43, 44, 65, 100, 101
  Gifts of the Holy Spirit, 65, 100, 101
  humility, steps of, 99
  loaves at the feeding of the multitude, 32, 36
  mercy, works of, 13, 73, 90
  petitions of the Pater Noster, 73
  rest, symbol of, 43–44, 106
  righteous brighter than the sun, 143n91
  sin, dimension of in *Jacob's Well*, 85, 86, 88
  virtues, 13, 99, 101
  vices, 13
number eight
  baptism, association with, 139n38
  Beatitudes, 13
  in *Book of Margery Kempe, The*, 77, 120, 124
  Circumcision of Christ, day of, 56, 76
  daughters of the devil and their husbands, 17
  as measurement of sin in *Jacob's Well*, 86, 89
  in number theory, 22, 56, 57, 107
  Resurrection of Christ and humankind, betokening, 106–7
number nine
  angels, orders of, 51
  banishment of Adam, hour of, 49
  counting in Greek, 105–6
  death of Christ, hour of, 49, 76
  heaven, ratio of angels to humans, 32
  as imperfect number, 45
  sin, dimensions of, 86
number ten
  factoring (*see* factor)
  fasting, 30
  in finger counting, 129
  inhabitants of heaven and hell, 32
  lepers, 50
  as perfect number, 25–27, 44–45, 50, 56, 60
  square and cube (powers of ten), 10, 25, 56, 42, 123
  tithing, 67–72
  Wise and Foolish Virgins, 54
  See also Ten Commandments
number eleven, 58–60, 86, 103–4
number twelve
  Apostles, number of, 50, 58–61, 151n80
  Articles of the Faith, 58, 78, 90–91
  in *Book of Margery Kempe, The*, 122, 124–25

Christ, age at which he first taught, 12, 58
  length of hemorrhage, 20, 57
  in Hrotsvit of Gandersheim, 58
  patriarchs of the Old Law, 58
  representing Scripture, 36
  sin, dimensions of, 86, 89
  as superabundant number, 56–58
number thirteen, 30
number fourteen, 12, 73, 89, 90, 121, 124
number fifteen, 48, 161n11
number sixteen, 77, 125
number seventeen, 101
number eighteen, 20, 85–86, 88
number twenty, 46, 70, 142n83
number twenty-four, 105–6
number twenty-five, 52–53, 120
number twenty-eight, 24, 41, 76
number thirty, 31, 50, 68–69, 71–73, 120, 142n83
number forty
  Adam's name, value of letter, 51
  Ascension, days after Resurrection, 103
  association with Jesus in the wilderness, fasting, and Lent, 21, 29–30, 57, 102–3
  in *Book of Margery Kempe, The*, 77, 120, 122–23, 125
  human life, length of, 103, 143n91;
  temple, dimensions of the 142n83
number forty-six, 51
number fifty, 51, 124
number sixty, 30, 50, 142n83
number one hundred, 25–26, 50, 56, 123–24, 125
number 496, 24, 42 (*see also* number theory: properties of numbers: perfect)
number 888, 106–7
numbers 1000 and 10,000, 26–27, 32, 36, 42, 101–2, 119, 123
number 8,128, 24, 42 (*see also* number theory: properties of numbers: perfect)
number theory
  authors and texts: Bartholomaeus Anglicus, 23; Boethius (*see* Boethius); Cassiodorus, 22–23; *De arithmetica* (*see* Boethius); *Etymologies* of Isidore 23, 34–35, 141n60 (*see also* Isidore of Seville); Nicomachus of Gerasa, 22, 42, 140n51; Trevisa, John, 23–24, 25, 53, 55, 150n59; in the quadrivium, 22–23
  properties of numbers: diminished (deficient), 22, 57, 60; evenly odd, oddly even, 22; factors (*see* factor); infinite (*see* infinity); perfect, 24, 42, 142n83, 151n80 (*see also* number six; number twenty-eight; number 496; number 8,128); prime number, 22, 29, 58–60, 101;

number theory (*continued*)
    number theoryround (circular) (*see* circle: circular numbers); stable, 55–56, 60–61, 76, 91, 104–5, 153n31; superabundant 22, 56–59; unity, 22, 36, 60, 150n61
    in sermons, overview of, 21–27
numeracy
    definition: Cockcroft Report ("Mathematics Counts"), 6; Crowther Report, 6, 137n15
    methods of counting and calculation, 129–36
    See also individual practices and skills such as addition, mercantilism, and individual texts and authors such as Jacob's Well *and* Robert, Rypon
numerals. *See* Hindu-Arabic numerals; Roman numerals
Numerology, 5, 18–21, 137n9
    See also individual numbers; individual texts and authors
Nuova Chronica, 134

O'Mara, Veronica, 7, 39
On Acquiring a Trained Memory, 115–16
On Genesis. *See* Bede
On the Property of Things 23–24, 25, 53, 55, 150n59
On the Tabernacle. *See* Bede
On the Temple. *See* Bede
Orchard (Orcherd) of Syon, 2, 26
Orme, Nicholas, 136
Owst, G. R., 96
Oxford Calculators, 4
    See also individual mathematicians

parables
    of the great supper, 49
    of the sower, 50
    of the unjust steward (Bailiff), 61–62
    of the laborers in the vineyard, 20
    of the wise and foolish virgins, 54
pardons, 28–29, 74–75, 117–18
    See also indulgences
Paternoster, 28, 73, 123
Paul, Suzanne, 7, 39
Pearl Poet 2, 114
    Sir Gawain and the Green Knight, 54
Peckham, John, 12
Pembroke College MS 285, 16
Pentecost, 58–60, 65, 120, 122
Pentienciam agite, 139n30
pericope, 13, 138n9
Peter (apostle), 58–60
Piers Plowman 60, 131, 162–63n15
    Pore Caitif, 47

postil, 145n25
Prick (Prik) of Conscience, The, 56
prime number, 22, 29, 58–60, 101
prism, 88–90, 154n57
Pythagoras, 22, 55, 138n36, 140n50

quadrangle, 150n59
quadratic equation, 23
quadrivium, 22–23

ratio, 32, 68, 133, 135–36
    See also fraction
Revelation, 44, 119
rhetoric of precision, 120
Ritz, Gisland, 132
Robert de Gretham, 26
Roman numerals, 21, 105, 131, 134
rosary 118, 132
    See also counting: prayers
Rypon, Robert, 99–114
    audience of sermons, 96–97
    sermon occasions: Blessed Mary Magdalene, First Sermon for, 100; Blessed Oswald, Second sermon for, 99, 101–2; Easter, First Sermon for, 102–3; Epiphany, First Sunday after, 98–99; Lent, Second Sunday in Lent, First Sermon for the, 100–101; Lent, Third Sunday in Lent (103), Fourth Sermon for the, 103–7; Lent, Sixth Sunday of Lent/Palm Sunday, Second Sermon for the, 107–8; Rogation Days, First Sermon for, 99

Saints. *See* individual names and under sermon occasions and topics
Salisbury Cathedral Library 103. *See Jacob's Well*
Samaritan woman, 65
Samson, 100
Sapientia, 57–58, 151n72
Satan. *See* devil
Saxe, Geoffrey, 132–33
Scale of Perfection, The, 2
Scheepsma, Wybren, 13
Sears, Elizabeth, 5
Secreta Secretorum, 25
senses
    bodily (exterior), 12–13, 17, 19, 26–27, 29, 36
    interior, 96, 112–13
    in Longleat 4, 48–49, 55, 65–66
    in Rypon, Robert, 98–100, 112–13
    of Scripture, 14
sermon structure, 12–18
    ancient form (sermo antiquus, homily), 13
    distinctio and dilatio, 13

division (divisio) and subdivision (subdivisio), 13–17
  modern form (sermo modernus, university, thematic, scholastic), 13
  numeracio, 14
  theme and pericope, 15, 138n9
  preaching wheel, 12–13
sermon occasions and topics
  "Alleluia," 17–18
  Ascension Day, 17
  Advent: First Sunday in Advent, 16; Second Sunday in Advent, 17
  All Souls, 31
  Circumcision of Christ, 56
  Common for a Virgin not a Martyr, 54
  Corpus Christi, 34–35, 85
  Easter, 20, 34–35, 85
  Epiphany: Sunday after Epiphany, 98–99; First Sunday after the Octave of Epiphany, 50, 58 ; Second Sunday after the Octave of Epiphany, 49
  Fasts of the Four Times, 20–21
  Lent: First Sunday in Lent, 17, 29–30, 51; Second Sunday in Lent, 100–101; Third Sunday in Lent, 103–7; Fourth Sunday in Lent, 26–27, 48
  "On the Dead" 143n91
  Palm Sunday, 15–16, 49, 107–10
  Quinquagesima, 50, 58
  Rogation Days, 96, 99
  Trinity: Second Sunday after Trinity, 48; Third Sunday after Trinity, 50–51; Fifth Sunday after Trinity, 48 ; Seventh Sunday after Trinity, 19, 31–32, 36, 49, 55; Eighth Sunday after Trinity, 50; Ninth Sunday after Trinity, 26, 85, 110–14; Tenth Sunday after Trinity, 48; Fifteenth Sunday after Trinity, 49; Twenty-Fourth Sunday after Trinity, 20, 57; Twenty-Fifth Sunday after Trinity 29, 36, 47, 48–49, 52, 143n91
  saints' days: St. Mary Magdalene, 100; St. Nicholas, 16; St. Oswald, 99, 101–2; Septuagesima, 19–20; Sexagesima, 30, 50; "Timor mortis conturbat me," 19
  unidentified occasion, 19–20, 20–21, 32
sermonist, 138n2
Shippey, Thomas, 114
Sidney Sussex College MS 74, 36
sin
  in *Ancrene Wisse*, 33
  in *Book of Margery Kempe, The*, 124
  in *Dives and Pauper*, 43–44
  in *Jacob's Well*, 63–65, 69, 71–72, 77–78, 85–89, 90, 92–94
  in Lambeth Constitutions, 12
  in other sermons, 15–17, 19, 20, 26, 36, 49–51, 57, 99
Sir Gawain and the Green Knight, 54
Solomon, King (biblical figure), 16
"Song of Just Mesure, A," 81–82
  See also Lydgate, John
South English Legendary, 33–34
speaking in tongues (xenoglossia), 120, 122
Speculum Sacerdotale, 20–21, 30, 31
Spencer, H. Leith, 66
square
  in arithmetical treatises, 133, 160n51
  in *Jacob's Well*, 75–76, 86, 88, 90–91
  in Rypon, Robert, 109
  square numbers 24, 55–56
  square of ten, 25–26
  squaring the circle, 135
  See also geometry
Stations of Rome, The, 117–18
St. John's College, MS G.22, 19, 36
Sticca, Sandro, 58
subtraction, 29, 129, 133
Suntrup, Rudolf, 5, 18
superabundance, 22, 56–59
Sylvester II (pope), 131
Syon Pardon, 28–29, 141n79

tally stick, 131, 162–63n15
Tavormina, M. Teresa, 5, 39, 42, 47
Taylor, William, 143n91
Ten Commandments, 12–13, 19–20, 30–31, 142n32
  in *Dives and Pauper*, 38, 40, 44–45, 50–51
  in *Jacob's Well*, 71–74, 76
  in Rypon, Robert, 101–4, 107, 112–13, 115
thema (theme), 12–15, 138n9, 138n17
  See also under sermon structure
Thomas of Todi, 14
tithing
  in *Dives and Pauper* 40, 45–46
  in *Jacob's Well* 63–64, 67–69, 73
  in medieval drama 69–72, 153n25
  in Rypon, Robert 97, 110, 114
Towneley Last Judgment, 83, 143n92, 153n25
Tractates on John, 59–60
  See also Augustine
transnumeration, 21
Trevisa, John, 23–24, 25, 53, 55, 150n59
triangle, 2, 25, 85, 86, 88, 89
Trinity College MS 241, 20, 21, 27, 26

unity, 22, 36, 60, 150n61
  See also number theory

Urban IV (pope), 74

Villani, Giovanni, 134
Virgin Mary, 20, 31, 49, 56, 122
Visitation, the, 47, 122

Wakefield Master, 69–71, 153n25
Waleys, Thomas, 15
Wallis, Faith, 5, 23
Warminster, Longleat House 4 (Longleat House), 7, 8–9, 38, 47–62
Watson, Nicholas 5–6, 77, 80–81, 126
Wedding at Cana, 49
Wedell, Moritz, 5, 129
weight
    as measurement, 64, 78, 84–85, 134
    in Scripture, 22, 38, 58, 85, 93, 151n71
Wenzel, Siegfried, 13–14, 85, 95–97, 99

Westminster Abbey Library MS 34/20, 32
Wey, William, 134
Wife of Bath, 2
Winston-Allen, Anne, 118
Wynkyn de Worde, 134

xenoglossia, 120, 122

York Play of Pentecost, 58–61
York Play of the Crucifixion, 82–83
Yoshikawa, Naoë Kukita, 120

zero
    in Hindu-Arabic numerals 131, 141n70
    in Julian of Norwich 162n25
    in Rypon, Robert, 97, 101–6, 110
Zibaldone da Canal, 135–37

www.ingramcontent.com/pod-product-compliance
Lightning Source LLC
Chambersburg PA
CBHW022057290426
44109CB00014B/1133